THE QUR'ANIC REVELATION: A REFORMED UNDERSTANDING

VOLUME 3

The Illusion of Eternal Religious Law

JOSEPH THE MONOTHEIST

First Edition: September 2024

ISBNs for this Title: 978-3-907677-06-3 (eBook), 978-3-907677-07-0 (Paperback), 978-3-907677-08-7 (Hardcover).

Published by: Joseph The Monotheist

For the latest updates and additional volumes, please visit:
www.josephthemonotheist.com

For Lucile

Contents

Expanded Table of Contents

Side Notes

Figures

Preface to Volume 3

This volume of the series is mainly concerned with explaining how the proposed interpretation of the Qur'anic revelation understands law. It elaborates on why the proposed interpretation of the Qur'anic revelation does not have a law component.

Islamic law is used as the vehicle to study the eternal applicability of the injunctions of the Qur'an and the *Hadith*. Aside from this objective to study Islamic law, the study of Islamic law provides the opportunity to realize the real-life manifestations of the sources of Traditional Islam in measurable terms (interpretations of). It will reveal the ramifications of adopting Traditional Islam as an interpretation of religion. The reader will come to realize that Islamic law is merely a consequence and reflection of Traditional Islam.

Islamic law constitutes a crucial component in any of the classical and dominant interpretations of Islam, a component that has shaped all interpretations of Islam. The study of Islamic law serves the purpose of allowing the reader to gain a better understanding of this component that has long shaped the various interpretations of Islam. It will allow the reader to understand how man has influenced and still influences the interpretations of Islam.

An interdisciplinary approach has been adopted. The book draws from numerous fields including the Qur'an, the *Sunna* (teachings of the Prophet), the *Hadith* (reports on the *Sunna*), Islamic law, philology, semantics, sociology, history, politics, philosophy of law, and philosophy of religion. This book does not merely talk in the abstract sense. Examples from Muslim history are presented throughout. Additionally, to understand the implications of accepting the legitimacy of religious law and the limitations of any attempt at religious law reform, an example from recent history is cited. The cited example has to do with what has been called "the Arab spring," where it aims to show how the different interpretations of Islamic law could be seen to have influenced the aftermath of the Arab spring.

This book is self-contained. It can be read as part of the series or independently. It does not require the reader to have previous knowledge in any of the topics discussed. The basics related to the Qur'an, the religion of Islam, and Islamic law, are explained both conceptually as well as historically. Various theological and legal terms and concepts are clarified.

Boxed notes and side notes at the end of sections provide additional background information on the discussed topics. Asterisks (*) within the text indicate that more details can be found in a specific boxed note at the end of the section. Note that not all boxed notes are referenced by in-text asterisks; some are included to provide supplementary information on the topics discussed.

In the first four chapters, I have included some of the subjects that have already been addressed in Volumes 1 and 2 in order to familiarize the reader with the necessary background to resume the discussion on the proposed interpretation—particularly useful for those who have not read the first two volumes.

A sequential reading is recommended, since arguments are presented in a sequential fashion steering the reader step by step through the various disciplines involved. Those who have recently read Volumes 1 and 2 will find the first four chapters to present necessary background material from these volumes in addition to some new topics relevant to the topic at hand.

As for the anticipated audience, this book is for people who are interested in learning about the Qur'an and its message. Among this group would be those searching for a reformed understanding of the Qur'an and how it applies today; those interested to learn about Islamic law—what it is and what it is not; and those interested in monotheistic religions in general, whether it is from a religious, social, or a scholarly perspective. This book will prove to be particularly useful to those seeking to understand the problems in the contemporary interpretations of Islam, and consequently how such problems affect the Muslim individual and societies in general.

It is my aim that this book serves as yet another step towards clarifying what I believe to be a more accurate representation of the Qur'anic revelation, that would help eliminate much of what has been falsely attributed to the Qur'an, its message, and to the last of the prophets.

Joseph the Monotheist
July 27, 2024

Preface to Volume 1

There are those who consider belief to be a choice, religion too. They choose to follow scripture not dogma. They believe that religion is not above reason. And they do not take for granted nor do they readily accept what others say about God. If you are among this group then do continue reading; otherwise, this book is probably not for you.

In this series, "The Qur'anic Revelation: A Reformed Understanding," I introduce the understanding of the Qur'anic revelation that my personal journey of discovery has brought me to realize. It is a journey that is still in progress. This is not the story of my journey but of what I have learned.

This series is for the curious. It is for those who want to learn about the Qur'an and what is so special about it. It is for those who want to learn about the message that the Qur'an brings that has attracted so many to it since the first verses of the Qur'an were revealed over fourteen centuries ago. In this book and the following volumes (the first three volumes have been published concurrently), I simply wrote the books I wish I had read earlier in life—books that surely would have allowed me to better understand the Qur'an and its message. The books of this series would have certainly helped me differentiate between scripture and religion, as well as understand how religion relates to life in a much clearer way.

I am extremely passionate about the Qur'an and the message it conveys. I believe that the Qur'anic message reaches out to all beings; it is a message that affects all followers of the revealed scriptures. I also believe that the numerous interpretations of Islam, which are considered to reflect interpretations of the Qur'anic revelation, are in fact unacceptable representations of the Qur'anic revelation. This is due to the fact that these interpretations resort to other sources besides the Qur'an to understand the Qur'an, and they take these other sources for granted. Even in some instances, such interpretations ignore what the Qur'an says altogether in favor of the other sources.

I by no means claim to have all the answers, nor do I claim to know the truth. In this series I choose to share my personal understanding of the Qur'anic revelation with those interested. It is presented from the perspective of a follower of the Qur'an who has actually taken the time to study the Qur'an; a follower of the Qur'an who believes that seeking to understand the Qur'an should not require the approval of specialized institutions or authorities. In more accurate terms though, I identify as a Monotheist who takes the Qur'an as scripture.

The series, "The Qur'anic Revelation: A Reformed Understanding," presents a perspective on what the Qur'an is saying—through a voice independent from the three major monotheistic religions, Judaism, Christianity, and Islam. It presents an interpretation of the Qur'an and explains how it would apply to people living in today's world. It is written taking into consideration those who have no previous knowledge about the Qur'an. It is the outcome of years of studying and contemplating the Arabic Qur'an.

I want to stress a key point: The proposed interpretation of the Qur'anic revelation is in no way a comprehensive interpretation of all topics addressed in the Qur'an. It is but the backbone of an attempt that aims to shed light on some of the most crucial issues this author finds pertinent to be included in a general overview about the Qur'an.

That being said, I find it important to point out that in the proposed interpretation of the Qur'anic revelation I have attempted to present what my rational side understands about the Qur'an. Though reading the proposed interpretation of the Qur'anic revelation relieves the reader from the challenges associated with studying the Qur'anic text first hand, it surely does not capture the spiritual experience and the feelings of satisfaction, serenity, and peace that the reading of (or listening to) the Arabic Qur'an evokes in one's being. Moreover, in no way am I suggesting that reading any interpretation of the Qur'an—including this one—could replace reading or studying the Qur'anic text itself. Reading an interpretation of the Qur'an merely provides a (subjective) general overview of the Qur'an. It gives the reader a specific outlook about the Qur'anic text, allowing for—when reading the actual text—a smoother understanding and comprehension of the text.

An interpretation of the Qur'anic revelation or a general understanding of the Qur'an's core teachings is generally what one aims to get out of reading the Qur'an. It is the interpretations of the Qur'an that have moved followers of the Qur'an across space-time; however, in most instances the interpretations have been different.

In spite the fact that the Arabic Qur'an and translations of the Qur'an were banned in numerous countries for several centuries, today, the Qur'an and its translations are available and accessible almost everywhere across the globe. Understanding the Qur'anic text in Arabic presents its own challenges, and though admitting to the importance of having translations of the Arabic Qur'an in other languages, it should be pointed out that reading translations of the Qur'an elevates the risk of misunderstanding the Qur'anic text. Aside from language differences and what is lost in translation, translations are subjective and merely convey the translator's understanding of the text under translation. Therefore, it is important to realize that translations of the Qur'an represent the translator's personal and subjective interpretation of the meaning of the words, independently and collectively. From here arises the importance of having clear and concise interpretations of the Qur'an. These too are subjective works that also reflect the views of their corresponding authors; however, they offer a holistic understanding of the text. It is through interpretations of the Qur'an that—what has been understood to be— the core teachings of the Qur'an have historically been conveyed to wider audiences independent of language, and this surely will continue to be the case.

This series attempts to unravel what can be described as the confusion surrounding the understanding of the Qur'an. It argues that this confusion experienced by Muslims and non-Muslims alike is a confusion arising from and depicted in the available interpretations of the Qur'anic revelation, the numerous interpretations of Islam. The only thing the present author takes for granted is that the Qur'an is the speech of God that was revealed to Prophet Muhammad, everything else is put in doubt. Alternatively, for those who do not recognize the Qur'an to be the speech of God, this series would represent a study of the Qur'an as an independent source of religious knowledge.

The first major argument that this series discusses is that the religion of Islam, or rather the numerous interpretations of Islam, are unacceptable representations of the Qur'anic revelation. This argument is the subject of the first three volumes of the series. Moreover, the first three volumes discuss topics you do not find in your typical books about the Qur'an or Islam, some of which will prove to be particularly useful to those seeking to understand the problems in the contemporary interpretations of Islam, and consequently how such problems affect the Muslim individual and societies in general.

I believe one of the main obstacles arising when people genuinely attempt to learn about and study the Qur'an is the myriad of disciplines involved and the vastness of the—to a great extent conflicting—material available on each of the topics. This, I believe, is mainly due to the fact that the religion of Islam, or rather the numerous interpretations of Islam, are usually bundled along with the Qur'an. They are presented as if the religion of Islam and the Qur'an were one and the same thing, while the Qur'an and the religion of Islam are definitely not one and the same thing.

This just leaves the common man in awe and wonder, not to mention perplexed, and most, simply give up on their endeavor to learn and understand. There are even more dire consequences. The more that things appear or are presented to be complex; that along with the less time people are willing to spend to understand, leaves us in the status quo. People, today, find the traditional narrative and dogma to be at odds with the lives that they lead. This leads more and more people to distance themselves from the whole thing. Even to drop it completely. Sadly, it is belief that they drop and not just religion. At the same time, others just inherit religion—unquestioned—as if it were something that could be inherited. And the stage is left unchallenged for the traditional interpretations to steer the masses to how they see matters from their traditional perspectives. Yet the curious and those who seek to understand simply do not give up. They keep on going no matter what obstacles they find or are thrown in their way.

Now, since we are not native Arabic speakers living in the space-time of the Qur'anic revelation; otherwise, we would have readily been able to understand what the Qur'an was saying. And to help alleviate the aforementioned challenges that one faces today when attempting to understand the Qur'an (there are many more challenges that have yet not been mentioned), I have tried to present my understanding of the Qur'anic revelation in a way that is comprehensible to both those who are familiar and those who are unfamiliar with the Qur'an and the religion of Islam.

In presenting the proposed interpretation of the Qur'anic revelation and in arguing why I find the religion of Islam to be an unacceptable representation of the Qur'anic revelation, I have dedicated a separate volume for each of the three core subjects that the proposed interpretation of the Qur'anic revelation differs with the religion of Islam about: inclusiveness, the sources of religious knowledge, and law. I have aspired for each of these volumes to be as comprehensive and independent from the other volumes as possible in regard to the subject matter discussed. This surely has been a contributing factor, among several others, to the fact that it has taken me more than ten years to produce these three volumes.

Initially, I set out to write about the relationship between law and the religion of Islam. Looking into the Qur'an for answers led me to an understanding of what the Qur'an meant by the word "Islam" and who it described as being a believer, an understanding that deviated from the traditional interpretations. Once an understanding of these terms was in place, the bigger picture became clearer. A picture that explained the essence of God's revelations—and the consequences this brings to the followers of the different revealed scriptures. Moreover, reconsidering the traditional classification of the injunctions of the Qur'an (*al-ahkam*; commands, rules, and directives) helped to provide the necessary backbone that made the task of looking into the relationship between law and religion a lot easier. This series talks about all that and much more, while approaching matters mainly from the perspective of argument.

In this first book of the series, I start at the very beginning. I start by going back to the Qur'an to find out what it meant by "Islam." I start by looking at the big picture, the role of religion and its scope. An attempt has been made to distinguish between what the Qur'an says and what the interpretations about the Qur'an and its message say: to distinguish between scripture and interpretation. Hence, in studying the Qur'an, an attempt is made to understand the Qur'an from within the Qur'an itself, independent from other sources. As the reader will come to realize, most of what is known about the Qur'anic revelation comes from the numerous interpretations of Islam, a great deal of which has no base in the Qur'an.

Aside from laying the groundwork for the major argument of this series, that the religion of Islam is an unacceptable representation of the Qur'anic revelation, this book also tackles the other major monotheistic scripture-based interpretations of religion: mainly bringing Judaism and Christianity into the discussion. It argues that these religions, as we know them today, (also) deviate from the essence of God's revelations.

An interdisciplinary approach has been adopted. The book draws from numerous fields including the Qur'an, the *Sunna* (teachings of Prophet Muhammad), the *Hadith* (reports on the *Sunna*), Islamic theology, Islamic law, the Arabic language, philology, semantics, sociology, history, politics, philosophy of law, and philosophy of religion. This book does not merely talk in the abstract sense. Examples from Muslim history are presented throughout. Moreover, a general understanding of some of the Qur'an's historical content pertaining to the time of the revelation is presented.

This book is self-contained. It does not require the reader to have previous knowledge in any of the topics discussed. The basics related to the Qur'an and the religion of Islam are explained, conceptual as well as historical. Various theological and legal terms and concepts are clarified.

Boxed notes and side notes at the end of sections provide additional background information on the discussed topics. Asterisks (*) within the text indicate that more details can be found in a specific boxed note at the end of the section. Note that not all boxed notes are referenced by in-text asterisks; some are included to provide supplementary information on the topics discussed.

The Qur'an was studied in the language it was revealed, the Arabic language. The transliteration of any referenced Arabic term appears in italics next to the English translation of the term, as best as possible.

A sequential reading is recommended, since arguments are presented in a sequential fashion steering the reader step by step through the maze of disciplines involved.

As for the anticipated audience, this book is for people who are interested in monotheistic religions in general, whether it is from a religious, social, or a scholarly perspective. It is also for those interested in learning about the Qur'an and its message in particular. Among this group would be those searching for a reformed understanding of the Qur'an and how it applies today, and those curious to learn how the Qur'anic message affects followers of the previous revealed scriptures.

It is my aim that this book serves as a first step towards clarifying what I believe to be a more accurate representation of the Qur'anic revelation, that would help eliminate much of what has been falsely attributed to the Qur'an, its message, and to the last of the prophets.

Joseph the Monotheist
April 9, 2024

1. Introduction

This book is the third in a series that presents an attempt to understand the Qur'anic revelation. It continues on the work presented in the first two volumes of this series to propose a new interpretation of the Qur'anic revelation that is claimed to constitute a more accurate representation of the revelation.

The reader might wonder, why do that—isn't that what the religion of Islam is all about? Isn't that what Muslim scholars have been doing for about fourteen centuries? And why a new interpretation—why not just add to or amend what is already there? To this reader, I repeat the same answer I responded with in Volume 1: The religion of Islam is a religion based on an interpretation of the Qur'anic revelation. However, that does not mean that the religion of Islam (the interpretation it is based on) constitutes an accurate or even acceptable representation of the Qur'anic revelation. The present author argues that the religion of Islam does not constitute an acceptable representation of the Qur'anic revelation, hence the need for a new interpretation.

To present the new interpretation of the Qur'anic revelation and why it is needed, we start by looking into the religion of Islam, or in more accurate terms we start by looking into the numerous interpretations of Islam, and we examine what makes them unacceptable representations of the Qur'anic revelation. In the process, the new interpretation of the Qur'anic revelation emerges, step by step along the way.

The first three volumes of this series argue that the religion of Islam, or rather the numerous interpretations of Islam, are unacceptable representations of the Qur'anic revelation. The proposed interpretation of the Qur'anic revelation challenges the standpoints of Traditional Islam on three key issues: inclusiveness, the sources of religious knowledge, and the composition of any acceptable Qur'anic-based interpretation of religion. Each of the first three volumes of this series is dedicated to one of these topics. Volume 1 addressed the inclusiveness aspect of the Qur'anic revelation. Volume 2 explained the stance of the proposed interpretation of the Qur'anic revelation in regard to the *Sunna* (teachings of Prophet Muhammad) and the *Hadith* (reports on the *Sunna*). And in this book the stance of the proposed interpretation of the Qur'anic revelation on law is addressed. This position will prove to be of special significance particularly in the context of modernity—and the modern state. Furthermore, Islamic law and its relationship to the religion of Islam is explored.

In general terms, in this volume of the series, we learn about the proposed interpretation of the Qur'anic revelation's stance on the composition of any acceptable interpretation of religion that is based on revealed scripture. The proposed interpretation of the Qur'anic revelation sees that any acceptable interpretation of religion that is based on revealed scripture should have no law component. It does not see religion to be the source of law, but rather, it sees religion to be a source of ethics. It rejects religious law altogether and calls for the implementation of secular law. In consequence, the proposed interpretation of the Qur'anic revelation would be redefining the role of religion and its domain of operation.

In this book's first four chapters, I will go over some of the subjects that have already been addressed in the first two volumes. This information is provided in order to familiarize those unacquainted with Volumes 1 and 2 with some relevant topics that serve as necessary background to the current discussion.

1.1 The numerous interpretations of Islam

In an attempt to understand the Qur'anic revelation, the numerous interpretations of Islam are analyzed in reference to the Qur'an to see whether or not they constitute acceptable representations of the Qur'anic revelation. Hence, at first, it is important to understand the numerous interpretations of Islam and to examine objectively how they stand when it comes to representing the Qur'anic revelation.

To begin with, let us start with defining some key terms. Historically, the term "Islam" has been used to signify a religion. A religion that is based on the revelation delivered by the last of the prophets, Prophet Muhammad ibn 'Abdulla. Islam is the term that has been used to represent the understanding of the revelation to Prophet Muhammad. However, there have emerged numerous such understandings: there are numerous interpretations of Islam.

1.1.1 That which is common: Traditional Islam

I will frequently refer to a specific interpretation of Islam—the core interpretation followed by the dominant varieties of Muslim religious groups (*firaq*, singular *firqa*)—an interpretation that I will call from now onwards "Traditional Islam." But does such an interpretation exist? The answer is, in theory it does! A need to better explain what I mean by Traditional Islam is in order.

Over the years, there have been numerous interpretations of Islam. The dominant and those known to us of the classical interpretations all share a common core. In order to be able to address all the interpretations of Islam collectively, I will refer to this basic core as "Traditional Islam." It is important to bear in mind that what I refer to as "Traditional Islam" only exists in theory, in this book, not in reality. A single interpretation of Islam simply does not exist.*1

Traditional Islam along with each of the numerous interpretations of religion that are based on Traditional Islam (another way to refer to the numerous interpretations of Islam), each on its own merits reflects an interpretation of the Qur'anic revelation. However, Traditional Islam does not consider the Qur'an the sole source of religious knowledge. Alongside the Qur'an, Traditional Islam considers the *Sunna* (teachings of Prophet Muhammad)—represented in the *Hadith* (reports on the *Sunna*)—to be a source of religious knowledge. Accordingly, in more accurate terms, Traditional Islam is an interpretation of religion that reflects an understanding of both the Qur'an and the *Hadith*.

Historically, Muslim scholars have categorized the sources of religious knowledge as the transmitted knowledge (*al-naql*; the Qur'an and the *Hadith*) and reason (*al-'aql*). To simplify our discussion and to avoid getting sidetracked, in any further discussion pertinent to the sources of religious knowledge, the discussion will be restricted to the transmitted knowledge, and the phrase "sources of religious knowledge," when used, will refer exclusively to the sources of transmitted knowledge, the Qur'an and the *Hadith*.

The fact that the numerous interpretations of Islam are all based on Traditional Islam is reflected in the composition of these interpretations: they all have the same composition as that of Traditional Islam. This composition will be thoroughly discussed in this book; however, for now, it suffices to know that it is a composition that reflects Traditional Islam's classification of the Qur'anic injunctions. Traditional Islam is based on four cornerstones or blocks. The four blocks of Traditional Islam are:

■ Belief (*al-'itiqad*): A Muslim believes in the five articles of faith. The five articles of faith are: the belief in the one and only God; the angels; the revealed scriptures sent prior to and including the Qur'an; all prophets/messengers of God, and not to make distinction between any of them—this includes believing that Prophet Muhammad was a messenger of God and the last of the prophets; and belief in the last day (resurrection and judgment).

■ Virtue (*al-khuluq*): A Muslim is obliged to develop and maintain good attitudes, temperament, and character traits, and is obliged to stay away from their opposites.

■ Acts of worship (man-God actions, *al-'ibadat*): A Muslim is required to perform enthusiastically, with steadfast, away from disdain and arrogance certain acts of worship to no other than God. These acts can be described as man-God actions, where God is at the receiving end. The particulars regarding the acts of worship—the how, where, and when to perform—are detailed in Islamic law (the component of Islamic law on acts of worship).

■ Law (worldly actions, *al-mu'amalat*): A Muslim is required to follow religious law in all man-world affairs as detailed by Islamic law (the component of Islamic law on worldly actions).

Technically speaking, to say that Traditional Islam represents the common core of all the interpretations of Islam is wrong. Simply because there exists no single and unique interpretation of Islamic law. No common denominator exists among the different interpretations of Islamic law, not even the penal code of the Qur'an is interpreted in the same way by the different schools of jurisprudence.

A more accurate statement would be that a common structure exists for all the interpretations of Islam: the four aforementioned blocks reflecting the themes of the Qur'anic injunctions. However, for the purposes of our analysis, I will assume for the sake of simplicity the existence of a uniform body of law—a fictitious existence from a reality perspective. This uniform body of law represents the general consensus of all schools of jurisprudence (and modern realizations of Islamic law). Having assumed the existence of this fictitious uniform Islamic law component, which accounts for the last two blocks in the structure (the actions blocks), we can go back and say that Traditional Islam represents the common core of all the interpretations of Islam.

From here onwards, when referring to Islamic law and a particular interpretation of Islamic law is implied, then the term represents the abovementioned hypothetical uniform interpretation of Islamic law that constitutes a component of Traditional Islam.

NOTE*1: Traditional Islam developed over a thousand years back from Muslim thought up until the mid-fourth century AH (second half of the tenth century CE). The Hijri year or era, AH (Anno Hegirae), is the era used in the Muslim calendar. The epoch of the Muslim calendar is the year 622 CE, marking the flight of Prophet Muhammad from his hometown, Mecca, to Medina fleeing religious persecution (*al-hijra*). Both Mecca and Medina are geographically located in what has historically been known as the Hijaz region (west Arabia). Today, the Hijaz region constitutes the west part of present-day Saudi Arabia. The Muslim calendar is a lunar calendar; years are lunar years consisting of 12 lunar months (defined by empirical observation of the new moon) with 354 or 355 days in a year.

NOTE: Throughout this book I use the term "God" to represent the Arabic term "Allah"—the Arabic term for God used by Arabic-speaking Muslims, Christians, and Jews.

1.1.2 That which is different amongst the numerous interpretations

Differences exist among the numerous interpretations of Islam. Each interpretation adds to Traditional Islam in a different way. Differences among the numerous interpretations of Islam could be attributed to either or both of the following:

- Theology: The study of the beliefs of the Islamic faith is the field of the schools of theology (*madhahib 'itiqadiyya*, singular *madhhab 'itiqadi*). Matters of belief are addressed by the science of discourse (*'ilm al-kalam*). Theological differences include numerous subjects such as the definition of a believer, disbeliever, and whether or not there is anything in between; whether or not the Qur'an is co-eternal with God (createdness versus uncreatedness of the Qur'an); the attributes of God; additions to the articles of faith; belief in predestination versus free will; events of Judgment Day and the hereafter—specifically, if anyone actually would see God, whether sinners remain in hell forever; and others.

- Islamic law: This is the field of the schools of law or jurisprudence (*madhahib fiqhiyya*, singular *madhhab fiqhi*).

Interpretations of Islamic law cover acts of worship and worldly matters. Worldly matters cover the whole spectrum of both private and public life. Topics range from the realm of the individual like marriage, divorce, adoption, and inheritance to the public realm of collectives of people such as the criminal justice system, taxation, and the economy. It even extends to matters of politics such as the selection of a ruler, international relations, and even to declaring war.*1

NOTE*1: There are numerous interpretations of Islamic law. In the classical sense, this translates to saying that there are numerous schools of jurisprudence. However, it is important to point out that modern realizations of Islamic law do not necessarily follow any of the classical schools of jurisprudence, but rather, they have their own independent approaches to arrive at their respective bodies of law.

1.2 Muslims and the interpretations of Islam

The distinct interpretations of Islam are at least as many as the possible combinations between the schools of theology and the schools of jurisprudence (the number grows considerably when further considering the modern realizations of Islamic law). The numerous interpretations of Islam, for the most part, do not take unique names; however, they are generally distinguished by the school of theology followed.

I do not want to get into the details of the various classifications of Muslim religious groups (*firaq*, singular *firqa*); therefore, I will use a generic classification and simply refer to followers of a particular school of theology as to constitute a religious group (*firqa*). As for the relationship between religious groups and Islamic law, a religious group does not necessarily have its own interpretation of Islamic law; in other words, several religious groups could follow the same interpretation of Islamic law. Moreover, subdivisions from a major religious group do not necessarily follow the same interpretation of Islamic law.*1

How could we describe the level of Muslims' knowledge about Islam—about the numerous interpretations of Islam or even about the particular interpretation followed? For most practicing Muslims in current times, Islam is a set of rituals and laws to abide by. The majority of Muslims seem to depend on indoctrination and mass media as sources of information when it comes to matters of religion. There are also those who receive (obligatory) Islamic religious education at school (a particular interpretation of), those living in Muslim-majority countries that have Islamic religious education as a basic requirement in the school curriculum. Most Muslims are unaware of the vast differences between the numerous interpretations of Islam. They are also unaware of the differences between the interpretations of Islamic law, where the majority regards Islamic law to be a single body of law that represents God's law. Most Muslims have general awareness of that part of Islamic law that relates to private life, and are unaware that Islamic law also details every aspect of public life from the economy to international relations. When it comes to knowledge about the Qur'an specifically, it is patchy and shallow knowledge—at a level that reflects the inability to distinguish between the sources of knowledge about religion.

This so-called knowledge about Islam is combined with resistance to change religious understandings. Resistance to change could be attributed to inertia. People are convinced, or rather convince themselves, that there is no reason to change since things have been going on the way they have for such a long time, and since the majority sees it to be the right way of doing things, hence, it must be the right way to do things: the "it is all good" attitude. On the other hand—when it comes to resistance to change, generally speaking—it could be argued, "the status quo is preserved precisely because of a lack of action or reflection, because prevailing habits, ideas and hierarchies are not called into question but accepted as inescapable or self-evident." (Zantvoort 2015, 358)

Living in the fifteenth century after the revelation of the first verses of the Qur'an, a time that can be described as the era of information, a question comes to mind: Is this the age of reason or is it the age of unreason? When it comes to matters of religion, I have come to conclude that the peoples of this era do not differ much from the peoples of previous eras. No matter what information is out there, sadly, the majority does not answer to reason.

NOTE*1: The aforementioned description of Muslim religious group composition is generally the case for the majority of the interpretations of Islam, those of the Sunnis. For the Shi'as on the other hand, the variation is more limited and well defined; in a sense, schools of jurisprudence vary with, and within, a specific Shi'a sect.

The primary factor behind the formation of distinct Shi'a sects was mainly political and can be attributed to historical events related to the succession of leadership (*imama*). This resulted in the division into sects. Further division within the sects themselves into subsects can also be attributed, in some cases, to this political factor, while in others, it was due to different theological and jurisprudential perspectives.

NOTE: Why don't Muslims identify by the different religious groups they actually follow? Most Muslims do not even realize that in reality they follow a specific interpretation of Islam. The majority follows what others in their (mostly) immediate environment tell them about religion (the state in modern times): they believe and do what they are told about Islam. Aside from there being two major branches, Sunni and Shi'a, where each branch pretty much considers followers of the other branch to be heretics, Muslims who are knowledgeable in matters of religion generally deny the reality of the actual existence of various subdivisions— created by the different schools—in fear of being seen as divided. The Qur'an called on all followers of the revealed scriptures, and its followers in particular, to not be divided. Nonetheless, I see it as mere fantasy to consider Muslims not to be divided in matters of religion.

NOTE: In this text, the term "state" is used interchangeably with "country" to denote a sovereign political entity. Throughout the document, these terms represent the same concept, and their usage is interchangeable.

Side note 1.1 The main branches based on Traditional Islam: Sunni & Shi'a

Most Muslims today follow either one of the two main interpretations of Islam, Sunni (the majority) and Shi'a. Each of these main branches includes several religious groups and subgroups (each adopting an interpretation of Islam that builds on and adds to that of the main branch—that of the consensus). Both branches have different compilations of *Hadith*, and for the most part both follow different interpretations of Islamic law.

Both Sunni and Shi'a Islam reflect theologies that developed gradually over the first four centuries AH. Shi'a Muslims believe in (divinely appointed) *imams*, spiritual and political successors to the Prophet—starting with 'Ali ibn Abi Talib—whereas Sunnis do not. There are further theological differences between these two branches, such as whether or not the Qur'an is considered co-eternal with God (createdness versus uncreatedness of the Qur'an); the divine attributes and how they relate to the nature of God; belief in predestination versus free will, and many others.

Who is 'Ali ibn Abi Talib? The Qur'an tells us that the Prophet was fatherless (*yateem*). The Qur'an also indicated that the Prophet did not have any male descendants. Meanwhile, the biography of the Prophet (*al-sira al-nabawiyya*) tells us that as a child, the Prophet—being fatherless (his father died before he was born)—after the death of his mother, had come under the care of his paternal grandfather, 'Abd al-Muttalib, who not long after also died. Then, the Prophet was under the care of a son of 'Abd al-Muttalib, his paternal uncle Abu Talib. The fourth to rule after the Prophet, 'Ali ibn Abi Talib, was a son of this uncle of the Prophet. Hence, 'Ali ibn Abi Talib was a first cousin of the

Prophet. 'Ali was also the son in law of the Prophet—he was married to the Prophet's daughter Fatima (d. 11 AH / 632 CE). 'Ali ibn Abi Talib was murdered in 40 AH / 661 CE.

From a historical perspective, Shi'ites started off as a political faction that supported the fourth to rule after the Prophet, 'Ali ibn Abi Talib, in his efforts to consolidate power (35–40 AH / 656–661 CE), which later developed into a religious movement. As far as differences go, Sunnis endorse the selection of the first three rulers (Abu Bakr al-Siddiq, 'Umar ibn al-Khattab, and 'Uthman ibn 'Affan) who ruled after the death of the Prophet (11–35 AH / 632–656 CE). Sunnis also acknowledge 'Ali ibn Abi Talib as the fourth to rule, whereas most contemporary Shi'ites do not approve of the selection before 'Ali.

Before the Umayyad era, 41–132 AH / 661–750 CE, out of the four companions of the Prophet to rule after the Prophet's death, Abu Bakr al-Siddiq, 'Umar ibn al-Khattab, 'Uthman ibn 'Affan, and 'Ali ibn Abi Talib, respectively (11–40 AH / 632–661 CE), the three after the first to rule were all murdered.

Side note 1.2 On the origins of the numerous interpretations of Islam

To understand the origins of the numerous interpretations of Islam and how these interpretations evolved, we go back in Muslim history and follow the events of the first four centuries AH.

■ Politics was behind the first schism between the followers of the Qur'an. It all started in 35 AH / 656 CE with the murder of 'Uthman ibn 'Affan, the third to rule after the Prophet. Some would argue that it even goes back to the death of the Prophet in 11 AH / 632 CE. However, after the death of the Prophet, followers of the Qur'an did not kill each other over differences concerning political leadership, and distinct political factions did not exist at that time. As for the so-called wars of apostasy (*hurub al-ridda*), which started right after the death of the Prophet (11–13 AH / 632–634 CE), it has been argued that these wars were about sovereignty and not apostasy as has traditionally been claimed (Shoufani 1973, 1995). Followers of the Qur'an fought each other after the murder of 'Uthman in the first civil war (35–40 AH / 656–661 CE)—a war that originated from dispute over political leadership: disagreement on who should rule after 'Uthman. It was not until the first civil war that we start to learn about the political factions of the Umayyads (supporters of Mu'awiya ibn Abi Sufyan), Shi'a (supporters of 'Ali ibn Abi Talib), Khawarej (opposed both Mu'awiya and 'Ali), and Murji'a (who were neutral and did not support either Mu'awiya or 'Ali). This schism led the early political factions to establish and develop independent interpretations of religion that aligned with their political viewpoints: religion (interpretations of) was used to justify the killing (or not killing) of others in the quest for power and denomination.

Within the Umayyad era, 41–132 AH / 661–750 CE, there were other interpretations that were also established, like that of the Mu'tazila (an early school of Islamic theology based on reason and rational thought), which—according to the traditional account—did not emerge out of a political faction. Around the late Umayyad era, one of the first comprehensive interpretations of

Islam relevant to Sunni Islam was formulated, that of Abu Hanifa (d. 150 AH / 767 CE). According to Amin (1964, 3: 320–322), some attribute Abu Hanifa to the Murji'a.

■ The first hundred years or so of the Abbasid era (132–656 AH / 750–1258 CE) witnessed the emergence and the later prevalence of the traditionalist view, a mostly literalist view heavily influenced by the *Hadith* that considered both the Qur'an and the *Hadith* to transcend space-time. This era is noted for the writing down of the *Hadith*, which probably commenced around the mid-second century AH. The endeavor to give the *Hadith* legitimacy—legislative value by the jurist al-Shafi'i—raised the interest in compiling the *Hadith*, at the same time the interest in forging *Hadith* escalated.

An inquisition in the early third century AH, led by three successive Abbasid Caliphs, to enforce the doctrine of the createdness of the Qur'an (rationalistic view asserting the Mu'tazila's position) drove the majority of Muslims to adopt its exact opposite (traditionalistic view asserting the position of the opponents of the Mu'tazila). Surely, assuming the Qur'an to be uncreated (to have a co-eternal with God status) reflected positively on the status of the *Hadith*. In the meantime, compilations of *Hadith* emerged like those of Ibn Hanbal, al-Bukhari and Muslim.

■ In the following hundred years (until around the mid-fourth century AH), theological schools emerged that tried to mediate between the traditionalist and rationalist views (the mediators: the Ash'ari and Maturidi schools of theology), and from then on this mediated position became the orthodox Sunni view (Goldziher 1981, 67–115). Furthermore, it was in this same period, the mid-third to the mid-fourth century AH, that the polarization into definite Sunni and Shi'a forms materialized (Watt 1985, 56–63).

1.3 The proposed interpretation of the Qur'anic revelation

Most people unfortunately do not differentiate between the Qur'an and the interpretations of Islam. The Qur'an directly addressed the beings in the space-time of the revelation, the space-time of Prophet Muhammad. Later generations interpreted how the Qur'anic revelation applied to them. That is how Traditional Islam came to be. Likewise, for anyone living outside the space-time of the revelation, one can only interpret (attempt to) what the Qur'an is saying and how the Qur'anic revelation applies in one's own space-time. When it comes to interpretation—being a matter of probability not certainty—no party can claim its interpretation to be the truth. There is no truth but the Qur'an, everything else is relative.

This book continues on the work presented in Volumes 1 and 2, which argues that Traditional Islam is an unacceptable representation of the Qur'anic revelation. In Volume 1 a new interpretation of the

Qur'anic revelation was proposed that claimed to constitute a more accurate representation of the revelation. The proposed interpretation of the Qur'anic revelation does not oppose the Qur'an; it opposes what men have said about the Qur'an. It is an interpretation that is based on reform in our understanding of the Qur'an.

This book, as well as the earlier two volumes of this series, do not delve into all the details of the proposed interpretation. They present the general backbone of the proposed interpretation: the fundamentals (its core matter). These books can be seen as to present the foundations of an interpretation of the Qur'anic revelation. The interpretation in question reflects this author's personal understanding of the Qur'anic revelation. They reflect an understanding resulting from adopting a holistic approach to study the Qur'an. It is an interpretation that is based on the Qur'an, and the Qur'an alone. The work is not an exegesis of the Qur'an, nor is it a translation of the Qur'an. It presents a subjective perspective—as any and all interpretations—of what can be understood from the Qur'an. The work focuses on the big picture, yet it goes into enough detail enabling one to differentiate between the proposed interpretation of the Qur'anic revelation and other interpretations—such as those reflected in Traditional Islam and all interpretations based on Traditional Islam.

It is the aim of the first three volumes of this series—in giving the reader a general view of the main ideas, concepts, and some of the historical content related to the Qur'an and *Hadith*—that a skeletal backbone of an understanding of the Qur'an is formulated, one that would facilitate any further study of the Qur'an. This skeletal backbone would help those who study the Qur'an organize Qur'anic content in a structured manner. It would aid in seeing subjects and issues presented in the Qur'an in their proper light.

1.4 The interpretation of the Qur'anic revelation as two distinct interpretations

It is my understanding that there are two aspects to the Qur'anic revelation: it has a message (the Qur'anic message), and at the same time, it is scripture (the Qur'an as scripture).

Traditional Islam considers itself to represent the Qur'anic revelation—it is a religion based on an interpretation of the Qur'anic revelation. However, there is more to this than meets the eye.

Traditional Islam constitutes an interpretation of the Qur'anic message. At the same time, Traditional Islam constitutes a Qur'anic-based interpretation of religion. Traditional Islam presents both interpretations bundled together and it does not distinguish between them. It is as if Traditional Islam considers both interpretations to be the same thing: the Qur'anic message to be Traditional Islam and vice versa. On the other hand, aside from disagreeing with Traditional Islam about the substance of each of the two interpretations, this author disagrees that both interpretations are one and the same thing. I understand the Qur'an itself to have differentiated between both aspects of the revelation. Thus, I differentiate between an interpretation of the Qur'anic message and the interpretation of religion that results from looking at the Qur'an as scripture.

In Volume 1 a new interpretation of the Qur'anic message was proposed that forwarded the framework for an interpretation of religion that is both Qur'an-congruent and Qur'anic-based, meaning it is in harmony with the teachings and principles of the Qur'an while also being firmly rooted in its scripture. In this book I continue to elaborate to some extent on the proposed interpretation of the Qur'anic message. I will also outline the composition of the interpretation of religion that arises as a result of the proposed interpretation of the Qur'anic message.

As a refresher to what was presented in Volume 1 about the two aspects of the Qur'anic revelation and the consequences thereof, it suffices to say, as stated above, that I understand the Qur'anic revelation as two distinct things or as having two distinct aspects. I understand the Qur'an itself to have differentiated between the two aspects of the revelation. The two distinct aspects of the Qur'anic revelation are: it has a message (the Qur'anic message), and at the same time, it is scripture (the Qur'an as scripture).

Let us take a look into what is meant by these two aspects:

■ The Qur'anic message

This aspect of the revelation relates to the Qur'an's address to all peoples, and in particular to all followers of God's revealed scriptures, including but not limited to the followers of the Qur'an. This is the aspect of the Qur'anic revelation that was the same for all messengers of God, the essence of which is what this work refers to as "Monotheism."

The Qur'anic message constituted a call to believe in the one and only God, to fulfill His code of ethics and worship, and no to be divided. In this work the usage of the term "Monotheism" (in capitalized form) is to represent belief in the five articles of faith and submission to God's code of ethics and worship, the Code— as conveyed to the prophets of God until the last of the prophets and revealed scriptures.

■ The Qur'an as scripture

This aspect of the revelation relates to the Qur'an's address to the followers of the Qur'an in particular separate from the followers of the other revealed scriptures. This is the aspect of the Qur'anic revelation that was unique to Prophet Muhammad—the particulars it contained—from which arises what could be called "the religion of the followers of the Qur'an."

From the perspective of the proposed interpretation of the Qur'anic revelation, this aspect of the revelation is important to understand for followers of the Qur'an outside the space-time of the revelation, particularly, so as to know the details related to religious practices, the acts of worship.

Understanding this distinction between the two aspects of the Qur'anic revelation, and particularly when understanding the Qur'anic message aspect of the revelation, we are able to:

■ Understand the inclusiveness that the Qur'an called for in regard to the followers of the different revealed scriptures

In Volume 1 it was proposed that in the Qur'anic context inclusiveness pertains to the choice of the path to God. It involves the encompassing of all those who follow the same path to God regardless of the revealed scripture they follow. Volume 1 argued that the Qur'anic message promotes unity among all followers of the revealed scriptures. Moreover, it was argued that according to the Qur'an, there were followers of the previous revealed scriptures who accepted the revelation yet maintained their religious identities.

■ Define the role and scope of religion

What religion are we talking about? It is the religion—or rather, the interpretation of religion—that arises as a result of the proposed interpretation of the Qur'anic message when looking at the Qur'an as scripture.

The claim that any acceptable Qur'anic-based interpretation of religion should not have a law component will be thoroughly addressed in Chapter 5. However, we can also look into this claim from the angle of the proposed interpretation of the Qur'anic message. But how could the proposed interpretation of the Qur'anic message affect how law is to be assessed in any acceptable Qur'anic-based interpretation of religion (or in any interpretation of religion based on any of the other revealed scriptures for that matter)?

The Qur'anic message calls people to fulfill God's code of ethics and worship, the Code. The objective of the Code was for justice to prevail in this life and the next. Hence, in order to be able to fulfill the Code we must keep in mind the objective of the Code: to uphold justice. The proposed interpretation of the Qur'anic message understands that the Qur'anic message would require a just implementation of the Code across space-time. This cannot happen if law was fixed with space-time: for law to be based on the punishments and social norms specified in the Qur'an (of a fixed space-time). Accordingly, the Qur'anic message would not see any Qur'anic-based interpretation of religion to be acceptable if it had a law component (it would be seen as unjust). Thus, as per the proposed interpretation of the Qur'anic message, an acceptable Qur'anic-based interpretation of religion would not have a law component.

1.5 The steps involved to arrive at the proposed interpretation of the Qur'anic revelation

From studying the Qur'an, the proposed interpretation of the Qur'anic revelation is formulated through four steps distributed across the first three volumes of this series: two steps in Volume 1 and one step in each of Volumes 2 and 3.

The four steps involved in formulating the proposed interpretation of the Qur'anic revelation are listed below. The parenthesized number identifies the volume of this series in which the step is covered:

(1) Re-examining the interpretation of key terms in the vocabulary of the Qur'an

This was addressed in Volume 1. It brings to light the inclusive quality of the Qur'anic message.

The major Qur'anic terms discussed in Volume 1 are:

▶ The term *al-islam* (the Islam)

It is proposed that the term *al-islam* as used in the Qur'an was not a name of a religion, but rather, it was the name the Qur'an gave to God's code of ethics and worship as revealed in all God's revelations. A code prescribed by God and no one else that set the standard for righteousness and piety. This term, *al-islam*, was the (same) term used to identify God's code that was revealed in the Qur'an, the Code.

▶ The term "*al-mu'minun* (the believers)—and its grammatical counterpart *al-mu'minin*" and the term "*al-ladhina amanu* (those who have believed)"

In connection with peoples in the time of the revelation, we find these terms in some instances to act as nouns, while in other instances to act in the adjectival sense. As nouns they were used to address or denote a particular group, the followers of the Qur'an at the time of the revelation. And in certain contexts, they were used in the adjectival sense to describe a particular group(s), those who believed in the five articles of faith and who did good irrespective of the scripture they followed.

Terms adopted in this series:

▶ Monotheists

I use the term Monotheist(s), in its capitalized form, to refer to followers of revealed scripture—regardless of the particular revealed scripture followed—who accept the five articles of faith and accept to submit to the Code.

▶ QMonotheists

I use the term QMonotheists (short for Qur'anic Monotheists) to refer to the historical group, the followers of the Qur'an in the time of its revelation.

(1) Proposing an alternative classification of the Qur'anic injunctions in light of the new interpretation of key vocabulary terms

This was addressed in Volume 1. It constitutes the first step to determine the composition of the interpretation of religion that arises as a result of the proposed interpretation of the Qur'anic message. The alternative classification of the Qur'anic injunctions is reproduced in Chapter 3.

(2) Recognizing the Qur'an as the sole source of religious knowledge and thereby rejecting the *Sunna* to represent an independent or complementary source of religious knowledge

This was addressed in Volume 2. It serves to determine the sources of religious knowledge for the proposed interpretation of the Qur'anic revelation.

(3) Exploring the applicability of the injunctions of the Qur'an

This is addressed in Chapters 5 through 9 of this book. It constitutes the second and final step to determine the composition of any acceptable Qur'anic-based interpretation of religion.

1.6 To challenge the standpoints of Traditional Islam on key issues

Now that the interpretation of Islam under study has been identified to be Traditional Islam, we can get to why I consider Traditional Islam not to be an acceptable representation of the Qur'anic revelation. The standpoints of Traditional Islam on key issues are the means I use to assess as to whether or not Traditional Islam can be considered an acceptable representation of the Qur'anic revelation.

Traditional Islam made claims regarding different issues. Traditional Islam regarded its claims to reflect the Qur'an's position on these issues. Traditional Islam considered the claims it made as its firm standpoints on these issues. Hence, Traditional Islam's claims became standpoints that the followers of Traditional Islam even take as absolute truths that ought not to be contested, forgetting they were merely claims to begin with.

It is my understanding that the standpoints of Traditional Islam on three crucial issues oppose the position of the Qur'an on the same issues. It is my understanding that the standpoints of Traditional Islam on three crucial issues oppose the position of the Qur'an on the same issues. If proven to be the case, as addressed in Volumes 1–3, Traditional Islam and interpretations that build on Traditional Islam should be dismissed as acceptable representations of the Qur'anic revelation.

16

In this work I challenge the standpoints of Traditional Islam on three key matters: inclusiveness, the sources of religious knowledge, and composition. Each of the first three volumes of this series is dedicated to one of these topics, respectively. In the following three subsections I present a rundown of the key points addressed in relation to each of these three matters.

1.6.1 Inclusiveness

The question to be asked: Was Traditional Islam correct in considering inclusiveness to be limited to the boundaries of religion? Volume 1 looked into the Qur'an for an answer to this question. It explored how the Qur'an understands inclusiveness and how it understands religion.

Volume 1 assessed the extent to which Traditional Islam's understanding of inclusiveness reflects that of the Qur'an. In studying key terms in the vocabulary of the Qur'an it was shown that Traditional Islam's standpoint regarding inclusiveness differed from that of the Qur'an. It was proposed that in the Qur'anic context inclusiveness pertains to the choice of the path to God. It involves the encompassing of all those who follow the same path to God regardless of the revealed scripture they follow.

1.6.2 The sources of religious knowledge

The question to be asked: Was Traditional Islam correct in what it considered to be the sources of religious knowledge? Traditional Islam considers itself to represent the understanding of the revelation to Prophet Muhammad. Alongside the Qur'an, Traditional Islam considers the *Sunna*—represented in the *Hadith*—to be a source of religious knowledge. Accordingly, Traditional Islam is an interpretation of religion that reflects an understanding of both the Qur'an and the *Hadith*. There are some interpretations based on Traditional Islam that even consider the revelation from God to Prophet Muhammad to have consisted of two components: the Qur'an and the *Sunna* (Hazm 1983, 1: 96–104). However, that is not the position of all the interpretations of Islam (Coulson 1978, 53–73; 1992, 81–103).

In Volume 2 the *Sunna* was examined for its eligibility to be considered a source of religious knowledge. It was argued that the Qur'an commanded to take divine instruction only from God, and that the Qur'an did not mention the revelation to the Prophet to have been in any form other than the Qur'an. Furthermore, it was shown—by applying the Qur'an's requirements for authenticating oral evidence to the *Hadith*—there is not a single *Hadith* that is certain in its attribution to the Prophet. Hence, the *Hadith* being not certain in its attribution to the Prophet cannot and should not be considered to represent the *Sunna* and should be rejected as a source of religious knowledge.

It is this author's viewpoint that the real *Sunna* is nothing but the Prophet's fulfilling of God's code of ethics and worship. Accordingly, the *Sunna* does not represent an independent or complementary source of religious knowledge.

1.6.3 The composition of any acceptable Qur'anic-based interpretation of religion

Traditional Islam is comprised of components on belief, virtue, worship, and law. These four components reflect Traditional Islam's classification of the Qur'anic injunctions (Q.I. classification). But what is the relationship between the composition of a Qur'anic-based interpretation of religion and the associated Q.I. classification? It is proposed that the choice of components that constitute an interpretation of religion (its composition) depends on two factors: the structure of the associated Q.I. classification, in addition to the injunction categories within the associated Q.I. classification that are considers to be eternally applicable.

In a Q.I. classification, injunctions are grouped into categories, formulating a particular structure. Moreover, the injunction categories are arranged in a hierarchy according to the understanding of the Qur'an's focus and emphasis. Traditional Islam forwards a Q.I. classification. Traditional Islam considers all the Qur'anic injunction categories in its Q.I. classification to be eternally applicable. The Questions to be asked: Was the structure of Traditional Islam's Q.I. classification representative of the Qur'an's focus and emphasis? Furthermore, was Traditional Islam correct in considering (claiming) all the Qur'anic injunction categories to be eternally applicable?

Volume 1 argued that the structure of Traditional Islam's Q.I. classification did not represent the Qur'an's focus and emphasis. A new Q.I. classification was proposed that is reproduced in Chapter 3 of this book. The structure of the proposed Q.I. classification reflects the focus and emphasis given in the Qur'an to God's code of ethics and worship. From the new Q.I. classification, it was proposed that only the injunction categories dealing with belief, ethics, and acts of worship could be considered to be of eternal applicability; thus, an acceptable Qur'anic-based interpretation of religion would be comprised solely of components on belief, ethics, and worship—it would not have a law component.

In this volume's Chapter 5, I present arguments that support the proposition that the Qur'anic injunctions that elaborated on regulating worldly affairs should not be considered applicable throughout space-time, but rather, that they were space-time specific. It will be argued that assuming them to be applicable across space-time would defy both reason and reality: it would not serve to uphold justice in any way.

1.7 Why study Islamic law?

To justify that the composition of any acceptable Qur'anic-based interpretation of religion should not include a law component, we need to examine the Qur'anic injunction category that deals with law for eternal applicability. We will do that in the context of examining Islamic law.

In Chapters 5 through 8, Islamic law will be studied and analyzed extensively. Besides the abovementioned objective to study Islamic law, the study of Islamic law provides the opportunity to realize the real-life manifestations of the sources of Traditional Islam in measurable terms (interpretations of). It will reveal the ramifications of adopting Traditional Islam as an interpretation of religion. The reader will come to realize that Islamic law is merely a consequence and reflection of Traditional Islam.

In studying Islamic law, it will become clear that injunctions of the Qur'an that elaborated on regulating worldly matters do not have eternal applicability. Recalling what is proposed regarding the composition of any Qur'anic-based interpretation of religion, that it reflects the Qur'anic injunction categories of eternal applicability of the associated Q.I classification; consequently, law would not constitute a component in an acceptable Qur'anic-based interpretation of religion.

The reader is called upon to distinguish between religious law reform and religious reform. Some problematic issues in Islamic law have drawn some to call for religious law reform, problematic by both the ethical and humane standards of modern times. However, religious reform through religious law reform is not the type of religious reform called for in this book. This work does not consider Traditional Islam to be an acceptable representation of the Qur'anic revelation; hence, it is a comprehensive religious reform that is being called for and that which is proposed. As for religious law reform, the proposed interpretation of the Qur'anic revelation sees that any acceptable interpretation of religion that is based on revealed scripture should have no law component. It does not consider religion to be the source of law; quite the contrary, it rejects religious law altogether and calls for the implementation of secular law. In consequence, the proposed interpretation of the Qur'anic revelation would be redefining the role of religion and its domain of operation. Religious reform beyond religious law reform is discussed in Chapter 9.

2. Background: The sources of religious knowledge

This chapter introduces what Traditional Islam regards to be the sources of religious knowledge of Islam, the Qur'an and the *Sunna*.

2.1 The Qur'an

We start with the holy book of Islam, the Qur'an—an Arabic word that (linguistically) means "that which is read or recited" or "that which brings together or consolidates." The Qur'an's text is exclusively in Arabic. Followers of the Qur'an consider the Qur'an divine revelation that relayed the speech of God verbatim. Besides its religious significance, from a language perspective, the Qur'an is recognized as the greatest literary masterpiece in the Arabic language.

The Qur'an is significantly shorter than the New Testament, let alone the Tanakh (the Hebrew Bible) (Ringgren and Sinai 2019, sec. 2, par. 1)—its length equals approximately 56% of the Greek New Testament (Sinai 2017, 11). The Qur'an consists of 114 chapters (by convention called *suwar*, singular *sura*)—the Qur'an does not give names to its chapters. Several verses (by convention called *ayat*, singular *aya*—linguistically means "sign" or "indication") constitute a chapter. The length of a verse varies as well as the number of verses in each chapter. Generally, verse length within the same chapter is much more uniform than across the Qur'an as a whole (with increase in verse length as the Qur'an was revealed) (Sinai 2018, 10). The way the chapters are ordered in the (written form of the) Qur'an is mostly by length. After a single short chapter, *al-fatiha* (the opening), comes the longest chapter, which is subsequently followed by chapters that (roughly) decrease in length until ending with Chapter 114. The first 18 chapters comprise around half the text. The first half of the chapters amounts to roughly 90% of the text.

The Qur'an was revealed gradually. It is believed to have been revealed over a twenty-three-year period, the years 610–632 CE. Some verses, even complete chapters were revealed before the flight of the Prophet from his hometown, Mecca, to Medina fleeing religious persecution (Mecca era); while others after the migration (Medina era). The ratio of Mecca to Medina text is 1.6 to 1. The distinction between these two eras is important, since in general, besides the differences in style, the topics covered in the Meccan verses differ from the topics covered by the verses of the Medina era.

The particular print of the Qur'an that this work references is the *mus-haf* of Medina print (*mus-haf al-Madina al-Nabawiyya*), the transmission reported by Hafs as taken from the reading of 'Asim—printed by King Fahd Complex for Printing of the Holy Qur'an, Medina, KSA, 1406 AH / 1986 CE. I will refer to this print from now onwards as "the *mus-haf* of Medina print." The print falls in 604 pages of Arabic text. There are 15 lines of text per page with eight words on average per line. When citing verses of the Qur'an, the categorization of Meccan and Medinan chapters, and any other matters related to a particular print of the Qur'an, it is the *mus-haf* of Medina print that is being referenced. In this work citations from the Qur'an take the form "Q. chapter#:verse#."

NOTE: The Qur'an is not ordered by subject, nor does the order of its chapters reflect any chronological order of revelation. Any ordered list claiming to depict the chronological order for the revelation of the chapters of the Qur'an merely represents the viewpoint of the individual who compiled such a list.

If a Qur'anic chapter is labeled Meccan or Medinan, that does not necessarily mean that all verses within the chapter were considered to be from that particular era. Moreover, there is disagreement when it comes to the classification of some Qur'anic chapters as to whether they belonged to the Mecca or Medina eras. The late Moroccan Arab philosopher Mohammed Abed al-Jabri (d. 2010 CE), in his introduction to the Qur'an (*Madkhal ila al-Qur'an al-Karim: al-Ta'rif bi-l-Qur'an*), writes that the scholar al-Suyuti (d. 911 AH / 1505 CE) found there was disagreement in regard to 30 of the Qur'an's chapters as to whether they were Meccan or Medinan. Al-Jabri also stated, that according to some scholars—out of the Qur'an's 114 chapters—there was agreement that 20 chapters were from the Medina era, while there was debate over 12 other chapters as to whether or not they belonged to the Medina era. These scholars went on to say, that anything besides those 32 chapters was regarded by agreement to be from the Mecca era (al-Jabri 2006, 235–238). I find it interesting to note that al-Jabri, in his own three-volume exegesis of the Qur'an, in which he interpreted the Qur'an's chapters according to what he assumed to be their chronological order of revelation, identified 90 of the Qur'an's chapters to be of the Mecca era and 24 to be of the Medina era (al-Jabri 2008–9, 3: 36). The referenced *mus-haf* of Medina print recognizes 28 of the Qur'an's chapters to be from the Medina era.

Side note 2.1 On citing verses of the Qur'an

The most cited source in this work is the Qur'an. The reader is encouraged to refer to the verses cited. When it comes to citing verses of the Qur'an, I would like to draw the reader's attention to the following points:

■ What is cited is the idea intended

When citing from the Qur'an, I have tried to cite the idea intended. Sometimes it is adequate to cite a single verse, when the verse is self-contained and citing it independently does not deform the meaning it was originally intended to convey in the context in which it appeared; however, in other times, reading a single verse in isolation would take that particular verse out of context and would distort the original intended meaning of that verse. Therefore, in such situations several verses are cited so as not to distort the intended meaning.

■ Non-comprehensive listing of verses

When verses of the Qur'an are cited, it is to be noted that this is not a comprehensive list of all verses on the topic. The cited verses are merely examples, unless explicitly stated otherwise.

Side note 2.2 The translations of the Qur'an: The Qur'an in languages other than Arabic

The Qur'an has been translated into most major African, Asian, and European languages (Wikipedia 2003c, par. 1). The earliest surviving complete translation is from the tenth century CE, it was the first Persian translation of the whole Qur'an along with the translation of the Arabic commentary of the Persian Muslim scholar al-Tabari (d. 310 AH / 923 CE), the translation of *Tafsir* al-Tabari (Wikipedia 2006, sec. 1.2; Yahaghi 2002).

In regard to European languages, Robert of Ketton (d. 1160 CE) produced the first complete medieval Latin translation in 1143 CE (slightly over five hundred years after the revelation), in the era of the Crusades, the work was titled "Lex Mahumet pseudoprophete (English: Law of Muhammad the pseudo-prophet/false prophet)." Ketton's translation enjoyed a considerable circulation in manuscript. In 1543 CE, exactly four centuries later, it was published in printed form in Basel. It was edited by Theodor Bibliander (Buchmann) of Zurich (d. 1564 CE) and included a Praefatio (Latin term commonly translated as "preface" or "foreword") penned by Martin Luther (d. 1546 CE) and a Praemonitio (Latin for "warning" or "caution"—though translated as "preface" in most sources) by Philip Melanchthon (d. 1560 CE)—both pieces of the front matter would fall under being Protestant polemics (Greifenhagen 2017; Smith 1923). A. J. Arberry (d. 1969 CE) described this medieval Latin version that was the standard translation for Europeans until the eighteenth century: "It abounds in inaccuracies and misunderstandings, and was inspired by hostile intention; nevertheless it served as the foundation of the earliest translations into modern European idioms." (Arberry 1996, 1: 7)

On the Catholic side, Di Cesare et al. (2013) recount that shortly after the Basel publication, in the year 1559 CE, this edition was listed among the texts considered officially prohibited by the Roman Catholic Church in its Index Librorum Prohibitorum (Index of Prohibited Books, 1559–1966 CE). In later years, other editions were also listed in the Indices as well as the prohibition of the publication of all Muslim religious texts (the last implementation of the prohibition banned "all books belonging to the rites of the Mahometan sect and books for their instruction").

The prohibition lasted until 1917 CE. The list had official sanction in all Catholic countries (87–88).

In spite of the Catholic prohibition, and during close to four centuries following the first edition of the index (mid-sixteenth century until early twentieth century CE), over 200 different editions of translations of the Qur'an in European languages were published (Di Cesare et al. 2013, 87–88). I would like to draw attention to two of these editions:

■ The first, a translation in Latin, "Alcorani textus universus" (1698 CE) by Ludovico Maracci

Ludovico (also known as Louis or Luigi) Maracci's 1698 CE Latin translation directly from Arabic is considered to have furnished the template for subsequent translations in other European languages. According to Shah (2020), one notable achievement in the field of translations was Ludovico Marracci's (d. 1700 CE) comprehensive Latin rendition of the Qur'an. Originally intended to expose "Islam as a heresy," Marracci's work, "Alcorani textus universus" (1698 CE), presented a complete bilingual Arabic-Latin text of the Qur'an, accompanied by an extensive commentary and a rebuttal of the Qur'an that Marracci had previously published in 1691 CE. Acquiring a copy of the Qur'an was challenging due to its inclusion in the list of prohibited books (Index Librorum Prohibitorum) and a decree by the Holy Congregation of Roman Censors, which banned its publication in any form. Consequently, Marracci had to seek permission to obtain a copy (3).

■ The second of the prominent European translations is George Sale's 1734 CE English translation, "The Koran, commonly called the Alcoran of Mohammed"

Sale's translation of the Qur'an is considered the first rendering of the Qur'an into English directly from Arabic, although indebted to Marracci's Latin version of 1698 CE (Thomas and Chesworth 2019, 325–337). Sale's translation was one of the earliest English translations of the Qur'an, and for quite some time had significant influence, at least in Europe, on shaping the perception about the Qur'an. On the influence of Sale's translation, A. J. Arberry comments: "Sale's translation was not supplanted for some 150 years. Its influence was thus enormous; this was the Koran for all English readers almost to the end of the nineteenth century; many even now living have never looked into any other version" (Arberry 1996, 1: 11). Arberry adds, "It was on the basis of Sale's version that Thomas Carlyle commented [who is considered to have been in his times remarkable for the liberality of his attitude towards Islam]: 'It is as toilsome reading as I ever undertook, a wearisome, confused jumble, crude, incondite. Nothing but a sense of duty could carry any European through the Koran'" (Arberry 1996, 1: 12). Arberry described Sale's work on this version of the Qur'an: "Though Sale approached his labour better qualified and better supplied than his predecessor [referring to Alexander Ross, who in 1649 CE produced the first English translation of the Qur'an, more than one thousand years after its revelation; Ross based his translation on Du Ryer's 1647 CE French version], he was not troubled by motives of scholarly impartiality. He states his position clearly enough in the first pages of his justly celebrated version." (Arberry 1996, 1: 10)

A good free online source for the Qur'an (Arabic text of—the transmission reported by Hafs as taken from the reading of 'Asim) with interpretations of the meaning of its verses provided in several languages is quran.com and its legacy page legacy.quran.com. This website mainly covers word for word translations. From the English translations listed at this website, I find the translations of Pickthall (d. 1936 CE), Abdullah Yusuf Ali (also known as Yusuf Ali) (d. 1953 CE), and M. A. S. Abdel Haleem to represent scrupulous attempts at the literal rendering of the Qur'an's meaning in English. Other prominent English translations I find worthy of mention are those of Muhammad Asad (d. 1992 CE) and A. J. Arberry (d. 1969 CE); the former recognized for its rationalistic approach while the latter is famous for its lyrical richness and is widely used in academic circles—regarded as the scholarly standard for English translations. I usually consult all five of these translations concurrently, though for those new to the Qur'an I would recommend Arberry together with Asad's translation. In this work, when citing a translation of the Qur'an, I have selected the translation of Pickthall as a reference, since out of the five aforementioned translations it seems to be the easiest to access online and the most widespread.

I am personally of the view that the Qur'an cannot be translated in the standard sense of the word translation. From a technical perspective, aside from the differences between languages and the intricacies involved in translation, for one to properly translate, one first needs to understand exactly what is being said. In the case of the Qur'an, and reflecting on my personal experience, one can only interpret what the Qur'an is saying. Thus, in the case of the Qur'an, translations reflect the translator's personal and subjective interpretation of the meaning of the words, independently and collectively. This comment is not to be understood as to discourage the translation of the Qur'an into different languages or to discourage non-Arabic speakers from reading translations of the Qur'an. On the contrary. I undoubtedly recognize the importance and necessity of having translations of the Qur'an available in different languages. This comment is merely to point out that such translations reflect the translators' subjective interpretations of the Qur'an rendered in different languages; in as much as Arabic exegeses of the Qur'an (*tafasir*; a critical explanation, commentary or interpretation of a text), which count in the hundreds if not the thousands, reflect interpretations by their corresponding authors written in the Arabic language. As I see it, the translation of the Qur'an into other languages represents a subjective rendering of its meaning in other languages.

I would like to quote the words of Muhammad Marmaduke Pickthall regarding his view on the translation of the Qur'an. Pickthall was the author of one of the most popular translations of the Qur'an, the first English translation of the Qur'an by an Englishman who was a Muslim. Pickthall wrote in the forward to his translation of the Qur'an: "The Koran cannot be translated. That is the belief of old-fashioned Sheykhs and the view of the present writer. The Book is here rendered almost literally and every effort has been made to choose befitting language. But the result is not the Glorious Koran, that inimitable symphony, the very sounds of which move men to tears and ecstasy. It is only an attempt to present the meaning of the Koran—

and peradventure something of the charm—in English. It can never take the place of the Koran in Arabic, nor is it meant to do so" (Pickthall 1930, vii). And on why he did not translate the Arabic word Allah in his translation of the Qur'an, in the translator's note he wrote: "I have retained the word Allah throughout, because there is no corresponding word in English. The word Allah (the stress is on the last syllable) has neither feminine nor plural, and has never been applied to anything other than the unimaginable Supreme Being. I use the word 'God' only where the corresponding word ilah [diety] is found in the Arabic" (Pickthall 1930, 20). He titled his work that he finally published in 1930 CE, "The meaning of the glorious Koran : an explanatory translation."

I also find appropriate to quote the words of A. J. Arberry (d. 1969 CE)—as found in the preface to his translation of the Qur'an (the preface of Volume 1; it is to be noted that Volume 2 of the two-volume translation also had a preface)—which reflect, as well, his view on translating the Qur'an. Arberry stated: "In choosing to call the present work *The Koran Interpreted* I have conceded the relevancy of the orthodox Muslim view, of which Pickthall, for one, was so conscious, that the Koran is untranslatable. ... Briefly, the rhetoric and rhythm of the Arabic of the Koran are so characteristic, so powerful, so highly emotive, that any version whatsoever is bound in the nature of things to be but a poor copy of the glittering splendour of the original. Never was it more true than in this instance that *traduttore traditore* ["Translator, traitor," that is to say: "To translate is to betray"]." (Arberry 1996, 1: 24–25)

2.1.1 History

Muslim traditions agree that it was scribes who initially recorded the Qur'anic revelations in writing; the Prophet would recite the Qur'anic revelations as they were revealed and scribes would write them down (al-Jabri 2006, 213–217). There are two traditional sources that report on the collection of the Qur'anic revelations and their compilation (the authoritative writing down of the complete text of the Qur'an): the Shi'a traditional sources and the Sunni traditional sources.

To begin with, it is important to know that it was the year 11 AH / 632 CE when Prophet Muhammad died (al-Tabari 1967, 3: 199–203 1/1815), and with the death of the Prophet the Qur'anic revelation was brought to an end. The Shi'a traditional sources maintain that the text of Qur'an was compiled into a single codex (*mus-haf*) in the time of Prophet Muhammad (al-Jabri 2006, 219–222). The Sunni traditional sources (al-Zurqani 1995, 1: 204–209), on the other hand, maintain that a complete written collection of the Qur'anic revelations was not produced until after the Prophet's death.

The Sunni account—its most popular sources—reported (al-Jabri 2006, 217–219; al-Zurqani 1995, 1: 204–209), that shortly after the death of the Prophet, 'Umar ibn al-Khattab advised 'Abdulla ibn 'Uthman (nicknamed Abu Bakr al-Siddiq), the first to rule after the Prophet, that the Qur'an should be collected since a great number of those who had memorized the Qur'an, mostly bits and pieces of it (various chapters or verses), yet some possibly most if not all of it, were being killed on the battlefield. The objective was to have the whole Qur'an in written form and in one place. Abu Bakr agreed, and the scattered written pieces of the Qur'an were collected and copied out on sheets of parchment (this was done for each of the Qur'an's chapters), thereby fixing the text and length of the (written) chapters in agreement with the oral recitations of the companions of the Prophet (*sahaba*). After the two-year rule of Abu Bakr 11–13 AH / 632–634 CE, 'Umar ibn al-Khattab was the next to rule. 'Umar ruled for around ten years—until he was murdered in 23 AH / 644 CE. And nothing changed to the state of the Qur'anic corpus during the rule of 'Umar.

The Sunni traditional sources go on to state that the Qur'an was compiled into a single *mus-haf* (codex) and took its final form, with the order of the chapters as the *mus-haf* we have today, during the rule of 'Uthman ibn 'Affan ('Ashur 1984, 1: 84–92), the third to rule after the Prophet, whose rule lasted almost twelve years—until he was murdered in 35 AH / 656 CE.

Muslim traditions hold that 'Uthman ordered copies of the Qur'an to be made and to be distributed to various cities (al-Jabri 2006, 217–222). It is believed four to eight copies, most likely not less than six, were made (Altikulac, Eren, and Ihsanoglu 2007, 37; Altikulac and Eren 2009, 34–35), and 'Uthman ordered all other Qur'anic fragments and compilations in circulation to be destroyed: 'Uthman standardized the written text of the Qur'an.

The present state of the Qur'anic text is accepted by Muslims to be the same as that in the time of 'Uthman. Though appearing in different calligraphy styles (*khatt*), nowadays, most copies of the Qur'an are even printed in agreement (in general) to the orthography (basically the *rasm*; consonantal skeleton) of the *mus-haf* of 'Uthman (the most agreed upon representation of its orthography) (Altikulac, Eren, and Ihsanoglu 2007, 91–93; Altikulac and Eren 2009, 133–136).

Besides being transmitted in written form, the Qur'an was also orally transmitted (*qira'at*). Brockett (1988) is of the view that this dual form of transmission of the Qur'an provided the means for its static transmission, and he describes the parallel interplay between these two forms of transmission as: "There must have been a parallel written transmission limiting variation in the oral transmission to the graphic form, side by side with a parallel oral transmission preserving the written transmission from corruption. ... The transmission of the Qur'an has always been oral, just as it has always been written." (44–45)

Side note 2.3 The terms *Qur'an* and *mus-haf*

Although the terms *Qur'an* and *mus-haf* are generally used interchangeably to describe the holy book of Islam. The Qur'anic term *Qur'an* specifically refers to the revealed speech of God, through the angel Gabriel (*Jibril*), to the last of the prophets, Prophet Muhammad ibn 'Abdulla. The non-Qur'anic term *mus-haf*, which linguistically means "codex," denotes the written form of this revelation. From here onwards, the term *Qur'an* exclusively will be used to refer to the holy book of Islam unless a particular print of the Qur'anic text is referenced, then the term *mus-haf* will be used.

Side note 2.4 The *mus-haf* of 'Uthman

In the *mus-haf* of 'Uthman—the standardized *mus-haf(s)* considered to have been made by the order of 'Uthman (ruled 24–35 AH / 644–656 CE)—the text of the Qur'an had a particular *rasm* or consonantal skeleton. The spelling was different in some aspects from the conventional Arabic orthography that was only developed years later (Altikulac, Eren, and Ihsanoglu 2007, 35–57; Altikulac and Eren 2009, 31–60). Furthermore, the script was only in the form of *rasm* or a consonantal skeleton. That is to say, the script did not have vowel diacritics and consonant points (*'alamat tashkil wa i'jam*) (Altikulac, Eren, and Ihsanoglu 2007, 9). It is important to emphasize that 'Uthman's standardization pertained only to the *rasm* of the script, its consonantal skeleton short of any auxiliary signs (Ringgren and Sinai 2019, sec. 3, par. 2).

Modern-day scholars with expertise in the codicology and palaeography of early Qur'an manuscripts would agree that a *mus-haf* in the time of 'Uthman would be (expected to be) written on parchment; would not have verse (*aya*) markings nor partition markings as those of later prints; furthermore, the *mus-haf* would not have any decorative chapter separators (Altikulac, Eren, and Ihsanoglu 2007, 9, 11; islamic-awareness.org 2008).

Side note 2.5 The various readings of the Qur'an (*al-qira'at*): the variant readings of the standard *rasm*

The various readings of the Qur'an (*qira'at* plural, *qira'ah* singular) represent forms of the oral transmission of the Qur'an. A *qira'ah* refers to how the text of the Qur'an is recited, punctuated, and vocalized (Gacek 2001, 113). It was the *rasm* (consonantal skeleton) of the *mus-haf* of 'Uthman that allowed for the variant readings of the Qur'an. That is, the variant readings emerged from the standard *rasm* (Sinai 2017, 30–34). Qur'anic words that can be read in multiple ways—constitute the basis of the seven canonical readings—make up less than 1% of the total words of the Qur'an (Khatib and Khan 2019). On the variant readings, Campanini (2007, 18) comments: "In spite of [the existence of seven readings all equally legal and canonical], the text is fixed definitively, although there are some possible phonetic variations, some differences in techniques of recitation that lead to slight modifications in the textual style of writing. None of these modifications, it is generally agreed, have any significance for the dogmatic and doctrinal teaching of the [Qur'an]."

The first to limit the number of acceptable readings that were in accordance with the *mus-haf* of 'Uthman to seven was Ibn Mujahid (d. 324 AH / 936 CE). These seven readings represented readings that were prevalent in different localities: Mecca, Medina, Damascus, Basra, and three from Kufa—they were all considered authentic and of equal authority. Other early Muslim scholars recognized three additional authentic readings. All ten readings had two transmissions each (reported independently, *riwaya*)—with slight differences between the two transmissions of each reading. Besides the ten readings mentioned, there were another four readings that were not considered authentic (Bell and Watt 1970, 49; Kuwait Ministry of Awqaf and Islamic Affairs 1995, 33: 44–46) (variants that deviated from the standard *rasm*; sometimes substituting one expression for another or even having additional words or phrases).

The Qur'anic text that we find in print today is in accordance with the authentic readings—with some readings being more predominant than others. Only four (authentic) transmissions are found currently in print: The transmission of Hafs (the transmission reported by Hafs as taken from the reading of 'Asim) that is popular everywhere except most of Africa (excluding Egypt)—most digital representations of the Qur'an use this transmission. The transmission of Warsh that is popular in West and North-West Africa. The transmission of al-Duri in Sudan, Nigeria and Central Africa. And the transmission of Qalun in Libya and most of Tunisia.

Sadeghi and Goudarzi (2012, 2) summarize the early history of the standard text of the Qur'an as follows: "[The traditional account] held that the Prophet Muhammad (d. AD 632) disseminated the Qur'an gradually. Some of his Companions compiled copies of the scripture. These codices had differences. Motivated by the differences and seeking uniformity among Muslims, the Caliph 'Uthman (d. AD 656), himself a Companion, established a standard version. He—or, more precisely, a committee of Companions appointed by him—did so by sending master copies of the Qur'an to different cities—codices that themselves differed slightly in a small number of spots—and people in turn made copies of them. In subsequent decades and centuries, this standard text was read differently by different readers. For example, they often vowelled and pointed the consonants differently, but many of these readings—including those of the famous "Seven Readers"—adhered to the undotted consonantal skeletal form of the original master codices."

Side note 2.6 On textual criticism and a critical edition of the Qur'an

Textual criticism is concerned with the identification of textual variants in manuscripts and printed books. "Scribes can make alterations when copying manuscripts by hand. Given a manuscript copy, several or many copies, but not the original document, the textual critic might seek to reconstruct the original text (urtext, archetype or autograph) as closely as possible. ... The objective of the textual critic's work is a better understanding of the creation and historical transmission of texts. This understanding may lead to the production of a 'critical edition' containing a scholarly curated text." (Wikipedia 2002b)

As of today, no critical edition of the Qur'an exists (Donner 2015, 25–33; Wikipedia 2010). Moreover, the current printed texts of the Qur'an are based on the oral tradition and not on the collation and analysis of extant manuscripts (Neuwirth 2009 00:14:06–00:14:40; Small 2011, 3–13).

2.1.2 The book

The communications from God have traditionally been called "the revealed scriptures." In order not to get distracted from this book's main theme, this work has assumed the same; furthermore, the terms "revealed scripture" and "scripture" are used interchangeably.

Traditional Islam recognizes the revealed scriptures named in the Qur'an to be:

▶ *suhuf ibrahim*, the scripts of Prophet Abraham (*ibrahim*);

▶ *al-tawra* (the Torah, originally means "instruction") revealed to Prophet Moses (*musa*);*1

▶ *al-zabur* (singular of *al-zubur*, the writings) revealed to Prophet David (*daoud*);

▶ *al-injil* (the Gospel, originally means "good news") revealed to Prophet Jesus Christ son of Mary (*al-masih isa ibn Maryam*; the Messiah Jesus son of Mary);

▶ The Qur'an revealed to Prophet Muhammad.

The followers of the Qur'an recognize the author of the Qur'an exclusively as God. To the followers of the Qur'an, the Qur'an, literally, represent the verbatim speech of God (Q. 2:75 in 2:75–82, 9:6, 42:51–53), divinely revealed (Q. 2:97, 16:102 in 16:98–105, 26:192–195 in 26:192–227), divinely guarded (Q. 15:6–9), and inimitable (Q. 2:23–24, 10:37–39, 11:13–14, 17:88, 52:33–34) (some understand the inimitability of the Qur'an to be in its content, its style, or in the synthesis of both) (Abu-Zayd 2003).

30

The Qur'an that we possess today represents the compilation of the divine revelations to one of God's prophets, Prophet Muhammad of the Gentiles, rendered as reported by this messenger of God himself—verbatim, not in meaning—in his language, the Arabic language. The Qur'an is accepted to have been revealed over the period 610–632 CE, and that it was compiled into a single book, if not during this time period, then immediately after. To the followers of the Qur'an, it is only the Arabic Qur'an—not any translation of the text in any other language—that is recognized as sacred and used in religious worship.*2

The Qur'an in this differs from what we today possess of the other revealed scriptures, which in turn each represents the accumulated works (books/gospels) of more than one person (mostly anonymous; not necessarily a messenger of God; not necessarily contemporaries to a messenger of God).

The different works comprising each revealed scripture—in which each work represents its author's understanding of a particular revelation (in meaning)—were mostly authored over different time-periods, and originally (even in the earliest manuscripts) were not necessarily in the same language as conveyed by the messenger(s) of God. Furthermore, in some cases, a single work could itself be a compilation from different sources (oral and written transmissions) that originally were not all necessarily in the same language.

To many followers of these scriptures, translations of the text in languages other than the language in which the text was first set down (originally compiled in) are recognized as sacred and are used in religious worship (Wikipedia 2003d).*3

NOTE*1: The Qur'an did not explicitly refer to what was revealed to Prophet Moses as *al-tawra* (Q. 2:51–56, 2:87, 6:91, 6:154, 11:110, 17:2, 21:48). Nevertheless, the Qur'an did state that *al-tawra* was a revelation (Q. 3:64–68, 3:93–95, 5:44–45), along with the other revelations from God (Q. 3:3–4, 5:65–69). Furthermore, the Qur'an asserted the revered position of *al-tawra* in the times of both Prophets Jesus Christ and Muhammad (Q. 5:43–50, 5:65–69, 5:109–110, 7:157 in 7:155–159, 9:111).

NOTE*2: The Qur'an represents a communication from God to His creation. It was a communication that was in God's own words; a communication that was delivered in seventh century CE Arabia, in the Arabic language, by a native non-Israelite Arabic-speaking prophet.

NOTE*3: In regard to translations of scripture, one should bear in mind that in some cases there are layers of translation involved (Wikipedia 2003a). That is to say, a translation of scripture (or part of) is not a direct translation from the original revelation as conveyed by a messenger of God (in the language of the messenger). Naturally, with more layers involved, there is an increased risk of the misrepresentation of the original revelation: authenticity and accuracy are jeopardized by translation and re-translation.

2.1.3 Its content

The Qur'an covers the following main topics:
- God
- The creations of God
- The creation of beings and things
- The last day
- The afterlife
- Stories of previous prophets/messengers
- Stories of previous peoples and communities
- The story of Prophet Muhammad in Mecca and Medina
- An offer made by God
- The injunctions of the Qur'an

From the topics covered in the Qur'an, the first three volumes of this series mainly address only some of the Qur'an's historical content about Prophet Muhammad and his time in Mecca and Medina (Volume 1); that, in addition to the injunctions of the Qur'an (as discussed in this book).

Followers of the Qur'an believe and accept all verses of the Qur'an to be the revealed speech (*kalam*) of God, through the angel Gabriel (*Jibril*), to the last of the prophets, Prophet Muhammad ibn 'Abdulla (Q. 2:97 in 2:97–99, 16:102 in 16:98–105, 26:192–195 in 26:192–227, 42:51–53). The Qur'an's attribution to the Prophet is definitive. All verses of the Qur'an—and as a consequence all Qur'anic injunctions—are certain (definitive) in their attribution (*qat'iyyat al-thubut*). This is due to the writing down of the text of the Qur'an from early on.

Traditional Islam considers the injunctions of the Qur'an to be of two categories when it comes to clarity of meaning. The first category includes injunctions that are definitive in meaning (*qat'iyyat al-dalala*), which have only one meaning. The second category includes injunctions that are speculative in meaning (*zanniyyat al-dalala*), where their wording has more than one possible meaning, allowing for more than one interpretation, and presuming one over the other is considered to be mere speculation.

NOTE: In this book I do not discuss the Qur'an's addressing the issue of the existence and the oneness of God. A multitude of the Mecca era chapters and several verses of both the Mecca and the Medina eras addressed this topic. I believe this to be a vast research topic and a very important subject in and of itself that goes beyond the scope of this book. I believe it to deserve its own chapters and even volumes.

The Qur'an was intended for the common man. The Qur'an eloquently presented arguments about the existence and the oneness of God in a manner simple enough for the common man to comprehend and reflect upon. The Qur'an repeatedly asserted that those who think, both about themselves and in God's creations, reach to believe in God and the oneness of God.

Having said that, and aside from the Qur'an's indicating that God repeatedly sent messengers and scriptures that basically all conveyed God's existence and oneness to humanity, we find statements about this topic that stand out in and by themselves. My favorite Qur'anic statement in connection with this matter is one in which God, since in the Qur'an God is the one speaking, directly testifies that He is Allah (God), the one and only God (Q. 3:18).

We find statements in the Qur'an that describe God (the nature of?). God described Himself in the Qur'an as that there was nothing like Him (Q. 42:11) and there is none equal with Him (Q. 112:4). We also find in the Qur'an God to describe Himself with divine attributes. Take Q. 59:22–24 for instance, in which we find a number of the divine attributes when God stated that He is, the All-knowing, the All-merciful, the All-compassionate; the King, the Holy, the Giver of peace, the Granter of security, the Guardian over all, the All-mighty, the All-compeller, the All-sublime; the Creator, the Maker, the Shaper—To Him belong the Names Most Beautiful.

In Chapter 5 I touch upon the divine attributes and the historical ramifications that their interpretation—specifically, how they relate to the nature of God—had on the religion of Islam.

Side note 2.7 Prophet versus Messenger

My interpretation of the Qur'anic terms (equivalents for) "prophet" and "messenger" (of God), when used in the Qur'an to refer to or describe a man, is that these terms represented the same individual but from different perspectives. The term "prophet" was used to depict that the individual received a communication from God. The term "messenger" was used to depict that the individual delivered a communication from God. Thus, every prophet was a messenger, and every (human) messenger was a prophet.

2.1.4 Its style

In the Qur'an, God speaks directly throughout—as the first person. This applies to all chapters except the first chapter, *al-fatiha* (the opening), which is in a form of a prayer to God (the creation speaks to its creator). The first chapter of the Qur'an is recited daily in the daily-prayers of the followers of the Qur'an.

In the Qur'an, one finds verses where God directly addressed the Prophet, the followers of the Qur'an, the peoples of previous scriptures, the disbelievers, the associators, and all beings. There were also leaps in space-time where God speaks about believers, disbelievers, associators, angels, prophets, and others of His creation in times prior to the revelation and also on the last day. All this was expressed with aid of literary tools: metaphors, analogies, allegories, parables, etc.

The Arabic language is a literary language that combines a rich poetic heritage, literary refinement, and extremely sensitive readership (Gu 2014). The literary form of the Qur'an is considered an unmatched unique expression of the Arabic language. Linguistically, the literary form of the Qur'an can neither be described as that of prose nor poetry. The best it can be described is that it has its unique literary form, with its unique magic of sound, rhythm, and imagery.

The language of the Qur'an is regarded to be unparalleled in its beauty, precision, and perfection. Throughout Muslim history, the Qur'an has been considered a linguistic miracle. The Qur'an's linguistic excellence is believed to reflect the divine nature of the scripture. It is of a caliber that cannot be—and has proven not possible to be—replicated by human beings.

This unique style cannot be appreciated by the non-Arabic speaker when reading translations of the Arabic text (the representation of interpretation(s) of the meanings of the Arabic text in other languages), which lack the powerful beauty of the Arabic Qur'an. Nor can it be appreciated by an Arabic-speaking individual who does not have a good command of the Arabic of the Qur'an (or by those to whom the Arabic of the Qur'an does not come naturally)—to whom the art of composition would be separated from content. The ability to appreciate the language of the Qur'an is like the ability to appreciate any form of art. For example, when looking at a great painting, to the non-trained eye or for someone who cannot feel art, any portrait is pretty much a portrait, and a masterpiece would pass un-noticed even if it were Leonardo da Vinci's Mona Lisa.

Side note 2.8 On symbolism and allegory in the Qur'an

It is important to realize the presence of symbolism and allegory in the Qur'an and not to always take things literally—as many have done throughout Muslim history and many still do today. I, for one, surely acknowledge the presence of symbolism and allegory in the Qur'an; however, I will not discuss my views on this matter in this short side note.

I find Muhammad Asad's (d. 1992 CE) exploration of symbolism and allegory in the Qur'an to be significant. Interpretations supporting symbolism and allegory often cite Q. 3:7 to bolster their arguments. From the time of the rational Mu'tazila interpretations (an early school of Islamic theology based on reason and rational thought that was prominent particularly from the 8th to the 10th century CE) and the early Sufi (mystical) interpretations, Q. 3:7 has been a cornerstone. According to these groups and numerous others, this verse suggests that parts of the Qur'anic text allow for more than one meaning and interpretation. I present Asad's perspective on Q. 3:7 as an illustrative example of this idea.

Below is Muhammad Asad's translation of Q. 3:7 (Asad 2008, 80)—reflecting his personal interpretation of this verse, which may not necessarily align with the views of the aforementioned groups:

> He it is who has bestowed upon thee from on high this divine writ, containing messages that are clear in and by themselves [*ayat muhkamat*] – and these are the essence of the divine writ – as well as others that are allegorical [*ayat mutashabihat*]. Now those whose hearts are given to swerving from the truth go after that part of the divine writ which has been expressed in allegory, seeking out (what is bound to create) confusion, and seeking (to arrive at) its final meaning (in an arbitrary manner); but none save God knows its final meaning. Hence, those who are deeply rooted in knowledge say: "We believe in it; the whole (of the divine writ) is from our Sustainer[;"] – albeit none takes this to heart save those who are endowed with insight.

In Muhammad Asad's translation of the Qur'an, titled "The message of the Qur'an," first published in 1980 CE, Asad dedicated an appendix exclusively to address the symbolism and allegory in the Qur'an. In Appendix I (Asad 2008, 1129–1132), Asad gives an example of the Qur'an's allegorical depictions: its depiction of the afterlife and heaven and hell. But how can we perceive an existence in Paradise, an existence articulated in the Qur'an to be in infinite space and for infinite time (Q. 3:133, 5:119), when we are limited by the fact that all our thinking and imagining is connected with the concepts of finite space and finite time? In other words, how can we imagine a state of existence independent of space and time? The following is an excerpt from what Asad said on this (Asad 2008, 1131–1132):

> [W]e know that every Qur'anic statement is directed to man's reason and must, therefore, be comprehensible either in its literal sense (as in the case of the *ayat*

muhkamat) or allegorically (as in the *ayat mutashabihat*); and since, owing to the constitution of the human mind, neither infinity nor eternity are comprehensible to us, it follows that the reference to the infinite "vastness" of paradise cannot relate to anything but the intensity of sensation which it will offer to the blest.

By obvious analogy, the principle of a "comparison through allegory" applied in the Qur'an to all references to paradise – i.e., a state of unimaginable happiness in afterlife – must be extended to all descriptions of otherworldly suffering – i.e., hell – in respect of its utter dissimilarity from all earthly experiences as well as its unmeasurable intensity. In both cases the descriptive method of the Qur'an is the same. We are told, as it were: "Imagine the most joyous sensations, bodily as well as emotional, accessible to man: indescribable beauty, love physical and spiritual, consciousness of fulfilment, perfect peace and harmony; and imagine these sensations intensified beyond anything imaginable in this world – and at the same time entirely different from anything imaginable: and you have an inkling, however vague, of what is meant by 'paradise'." And, on the other hand: "Imagine the greatest suffering, bodily as well as spiritual, which man may experience: burning by fire, utter loneliness and bitter desolation, the torment of unceasing frustration, a condition of neither living nor dying; and imagine this pain, this darkness and this despair intensified beyond anything imaginable in this world – and at the same time entirely different from anything imaginable: and you will know, however vaguely, what is meant by 'hell'."

It should be emphasized that, in Asad's translation of the Qur'an—with his rationalistic approach to interpretation—it was not only transcendental matters that Asad gave allegorical or metaphorical interpretations for. He also applied his rationalistic approach to Qur'anic narratives that included myths or miracles (matters of supernatural nature), giving them allegorical or metaphorical interpretations, even those involving prophets, with the exception of the virgin birth of Jesus Christ. Asad in his approach did not reject the said miracles; however, he sought to explain them in a rational way to free them from their mythic context. Asad's interpretation reflects his belief that the Qur'an places these narratives within the context of the Prophet's society, where such legends had widespread acceptance. He sees these sacred narratives as serving the function of presenting inspiring models rather than as literal historical events (Chande 2004, 82–83).

I would also like to draw attention to a particular trend in interpretation adopted by some modern Muslim thinkers regarding Qur'anic verses they perceive as not to be clear in and of themselves—they consider them to be allegorical (seen as *ayat mutashabihat* and not *ayat muhkamat*). The basic approach these thinkers undertake is to forward new interpretations of these verses (reinterpret) in light of today's world. That is to say, they assume the verses to carry new meanings that are revealed as time goes by. And in some cases, these modern Muslim thinkers even give new meanings to the Qur'anic vocabulary (beyond the meanings understood from the Qur'an and how the terms were used in the Qur'an). They do this rather than to understand the issues presented within the contexts in which they are found. And they choose to reinterpret rather than to reflect on whether the presented issues

36

could or would even apply in today's world. Historically, a similar interpretation approach is found in the mystical interpretations of the Qur'an: the mystics assumed the verses to carry layers of meaning.

I find the interpretation approach of these modern Muslim thinkers to be a consequence of assuming everything in the Qur'an to have eternal applicability. Which, in essence, is not that far from the interpretation approach of Traditional Islam that also considers everything in the Qur'an to be eternal, yet Traditional Islam takes the same Qur'anic statements—in most cases—literally and claims them to be applicable today in the same manner (as it interpreted them to have been applicable in the space-time of the revelation). The aforementioned interpretation approach of the modern Muslim thinkers assumes the Qur'an to be eternal through reinterpretation: by taking statements out of context or by reinterpreting certain Qur'anic terms out of their Qur'anic context. I totally disagree with this interpretation approach as I disagree with that of Traditional Islam.

As a result of the myriad of different interpretations, we find some modern Muslim thinkers to have argued for the need to contain and sift through the interpretation chaos that has accumulated throughout Muslim history, including the numerous new interpretations that are coming out that have no purpose other than to serve and advocate a myriad of—mostly conflicting and self-serving—ideologies. One such modern thinker was the late Dr. Nasr Hamid Abu Zayd (d. 2010 CE), who proposed standards for what he considered to be acceptable interpretations (Zayd 1990, 264–266).

2.1.5 The principle of abrogation

The principle of abrogation (*naskh*) is a well-established principle in the Qur'anic sciences and Islamic law. Abrogation has been used by Muslim exegetes and jurists as a solution for seemingly contradictory material within or between the Qur'an and the *Hadith* to suspend and substitute one with another (earlier by later in chronology)—not applicable to belief injunctions. Those in support of abrogation claim that all instances of abrogation occurred before the death of the Prophet.

Muslim exegetes and jurists have disagreed on and disputed the number of Qur'anic verses and *Hadiths* recognized as abrogated. On abrogation in the Qur'an, Powers (1982) states that by the fourth century AH (tenth century CE), Muslim scholars had identified over 235 instances of abrogation in the Qur'an, and that this number later doubled. Today, King Fahd Complex for Printing of the Holy Qur'an (KFGQPC 2016) puts the number of (alleged) abrogated Qur'anic verses at 45, only two of which the complex considers there was consensus on having been abrogated, which are Q. 58:12 and Q. 73:1–3—according to the scholars the complex referenced. On the other hand, al-Shanqiti (19--?) is of the view that there were but nine instances of abrogation in the Qur'an, with only a single instance in which there was consensus on abrogation, Q. 58:12—according to the scholars he referenced. The discrepancy in the number of abrogated verses can be attributed to how each party interpreted the verses in question, and what they meant by "abrogation."

Historically, not all Muslims accepted the principle of abrogation. The most recent notable figure being the reformer Muhammad 'Abduh (d. 1905 CE) (Powers 1982). Those against abrogation held the view that all disputed verses were in fact specification (*takhsis*) and qualification (*taqyid*) of one text by another (Kamali 2003, 202–227)—they interpreted disputed verses with a more rationalistic viewpoint. For instance, the Mu'tazila (an early school of Islamic theology based on reason and rational thought) believed there existed no contradictions in the Qur'an; therefore, there was no abrogation within the Qur'an itself (Q. 4:82, 18:1–2). The abrogation that was accepted by the Mu'tazila was inter-scripture (between the revealed scriptures, where certain injunctions in later scripture abrogated those in earlier scriptures, Q. 3:50 in 3:45–51, 7:157 in 7:155–159), not intra-scripture (within the Qur'an), and surely not abrogating the Qur'an by the *Hadith*.

From here onwards, when referring to the definitive injunctions of the Qur'an (as per the hypothetical uniform interpretation of Islamic law), besides being definitive in attribution and meaning, they will also be assumed to be non-abrogated unless explicitly stated otherwise. The same applies to the definitive injunctions of the *Hadith*.

Side note 2.9 A thought on abrogation

Anyone who has ever written or attempted to write a book knows how ideas evolve; how paragraphs or entire chapters are often revised, deleted, or completely re-written; the continuous need to edit and proof-read; the numerous versions; the amount of individual or collective effort involved even in the current era of the computer and word-processor software. Anyone who has attempted such an endeavor would know that it is plainly impossible for a man to have gradually relayed a book like the Qur'an over several years and for it not to have any contradictions unless divine intervention was involved (according to the orthodox view, the Qur'an was dictated by the Prophet and it was written down by scribes over a twenty-three year period). In my viewpoint, this is one of the miracles of the Qur'an.

For any written material, the need for abrogation within the completed work would acknowledge the existence of contradictions within the text. Thus, abrogation represents a means to remedy contradictions found within a text. In the case of the Qur'an, the need for abrogation would imply an author other than God, a human author who is likely to err and who is neither omniscient nor omnipotent, especially since the authoring extended over a long period of time. However, the Qur'an itself stated that there were no contradictions within it. Q. 4:82 stated (in meaning): "Do they not reflect upon (contemplate) the Qur'an? If it had been from any source other than God, they would have found contradictions (differences) within it." Thus, for a text authored by God, there must be no contradictions within it. Accordingly, the mere idea of abrogation within the Qur'an is an insult to the holy book.

Side note 2.10 Abrogation: Its incentives & consequences

Most Muslim exegetes and jurists rather than to reconcile what seemed to be contradictory in the verses of the Qur'an adopted the principle of abrogation. The following could explain the incentives/causes behind adopting the principle of abrogation:

- To forward (or support) a particular general viewpoint of what the Qur'an was saying (politically motivated?), such as who to fight, when to fight, who was the enemy, who is a believer, who is a disbeliever, etc.

- To favor one legal viewpoint over another

- To support the *Hadith*: to find an explanation for contradicting *Hadiths*

- To support exegeses that depended on the *Hadith*

- The effect of Jewish culture and converts

Amin (1964, 1: 353–354) suggested that it was a Jewish influence that initiated the idea of abrogation in the Qur'an, as abrogation had already been explored for the Torah.

Accepting the principle of abrogation (intra-scripture) has consequences. It leads to:

- Accept attribution of authorship to other than God

According to the Qur'an, accepting that the Qur'an contains contradictions necessities accepting that the Qur'an was not from God and that there was some other party behind its authorship (Q. 4:82).

- Accept change in the divine will

It could be argued that if intra-scripture abrogation and the attribution of authorship of the Qur'an to God were both to be accepted, then this would mean acceptance of change in the divine will (or even to accept change due to new knowledge). Whereas, in rejecting intra-scripture abrogation, what seemingly appears as contradictions in the verses would be attributed to differences in interpretation of the divine speech rather than to abrogation and change in the divine will.

■ Discern that Traditional Islam contradicts itself

The principle of abrogation is in itself in contradiction with Traditional Islam's claim of the eternal applicability of all injunctions of the various injunction categories of the Qur'an. How can injunctions assumed to be of eternal applicability be abrogated? Since as a result of abrogation, some Qur'anic injunctions would be rendered inapplicable.

■ Discern that Islamic law contradicts itself

For those who accept that the *Hadith* can abrogate the Qur'an, abrogation reduces the authority of the Qur'an as the source of law.

■ Increase differences amongst Muslims

Schools of jurisprudence differed on which verses were abrogated and by what. In effect, acceptance of the principle of abrogation led to expand the differences between the interpretations of Islamic law adopted by the schools of jurisprudence.

■ Increase the complexity level required to understand the Qur'an and causes confusion for the readers of the Qur'an

The principle of abrogation assumes that (some of the) later injunctions abrogated earlier injunctions on the same subject. The reader of the Qur'an would not readily be able to tell which verses were abrogated and for what reason. To understand the applicability of the injunctions of the Qur'an, a reader of the Qur'an would be required to have knowledge of what is known as "the occasions or circumstances of revelation (*asbab al-nuzul*)," which are vastly disagreed upon (not to even mention the unreliability of these sources). Supporters of the principle of abrogation claim that such knowledge is required in order to know the chronological order for the revelation of the chapters and verses of the Qur'an. Accordingly, the understanding of the applicability of the injunctions of the Qur'an would lie beyond the knowledge of the regular reader of the Qur'an and would require the expertise of the scholar—scholarly expertise depending on the particular school of jurisprudence followed.

2.2 The *Sunna*

The usage of the term *Sunna* adopted in this work follows Traditional Islam's understanding of the *Sunna* to be the deeds, sayings, and silent approvals of Prophet Muhammad. According to Traditional Islam, the *Hadith* is the reports (narratives) that recorded the *Sunna*: the the reports on the deeds, sayings, and silent approvals of the Prophet. This usage of the term *Hadith* refers to all reports collectively. *Hadith* is also used to refer to a single report. The particular usage will be clear from context. In English, the word *Hadiths* is often used as the plural word for a group of these reports although the plural in Arabic is *ahadith*.

Numerous Muslim references use the terms *Sunna* and *Hadith* synonymously; however, for the most part, I have tried to differentiate between the two terms. Nevertheless, there are times when I do use the term *Hadith* synonymously with *Sunna*. There are also times when I refer to Traditional Islam's understanding of the *Hadith* or to the understanding of the *Hadith* of any of the interpretations based on Traditional Islam as to represent the *Sunna*. I would like to point out, that in such instances, what is being referenced is the portion of the *Hadith* that is accepted by the party in question to represent the *Sunna*.*1

NOTE*1: The clarification about what of the *Hadith* is recognized to represent the *Sunna* is necessary since Traditional Islam does not accept all the *Hadith* to be certain in its attribution to the Prophet. The different interpretations of Islam differ in what portion of the *Hadith*—beyond that considered certain in its attribution to the Prophet—each recognizes to be of reliable authenticity. For each party, it is only *Hadith* of reliable authenticity (accepted, recognized) that is considered to represent the *Sunna*. As a consequence, the schools of jurisprudence differed in what portions of the *Hadith* each regarded to be authoritative in matters of creed, religious practice, and law.

2.2.1 The compilation of the *Hadith*

There are mixed reports as to whether or not the Prophet prohibited writing down the *Sunna* (Lewis et al. 1986, 24; Shuhba 1983, 51–57), nevertheless, compilations of *Hadith* emerged long after 11 AH / 632 CE, the year the Prophet died. Efforts to compile the *Hadith* most probably started in the second half of the second century AH (Amin 1964, 2: 107), during what is known as the era of recording (*asr al-tadwin*).

2.2.1.a The parts of the *Hadith*

A *Hadith* has two parts. When compiling the *Hadith* both parts were recorded. The two parts of a *Hadith* are:

(1) The *sanad* also known as *isnad* (the chain of narrators)

The *sanad* is the chain of narrators going right back to the source. The *sanad* for a *Hadith* is a sequential listing of the names of the narrators who reported the *Hadith* (the people involved in transmitting it), from the last, all the way to the first to report from the Prophet.

The *sanad* precedes the actual text of the *Hadith* (*matn*) and generally takes the form:

> It has been related to us (*haddathana*)—or we have been informed (*akhbarana*) (the usage of the plural pronouns "us, we" is equivalent to the singular pronouns "me, I")—by narrator-stage5 on the authority of narrator-stage4 on the authority of narrator-stage3 on the authority of narrator-stage2 on the authority of narrator-stage1 that the Prophet said …

In this work we will be examining the *sanad* from the perspective of stages of narration or stages for short. If we were to think of the *sanad* in terms of stages of narration—with a single narrator per stage—then the *sanad* would reflect multiple stages of narration (ordered in sequence from last stage to first stage). For the numbering of the stages of narration, as far as our analysis is concerned, the numbering commences from the end closest to the Prophet (easier for standardization purposes). The first to report from the Prophet would be in the first stage of *sanad* and so on.

(2) The *matn* (text of the *Hadith*)

The *matn* is the text of the *Hadith*. For all the *Hadith*, the text of the *Hadith* was reported in meaning. Some have argued that there exists a single *Hadith* where the text of the *Hadith* was reported in its exact wording (verbatim). More on this shortly.

2.2.1.b The transmission of the *Hadith*

The *Hadith* was transmitted orally until it was compiled. Unlike the Qur'an, which was transmitted in both oral and written forms side by side, transmission of the *Hadith* by narrators was oral in (at least) the interval comprising the first three eras (*'usur*, singular *'asr*), starting with the companions of the Prophet. Typically, the report by a narrator within an era spanned the entire era. Thus, usually a stage of *sanad* spanned an entire era. This will be assumed unless stated otherwise. The primary eras of oral transmission were:

(1) The *sahaba* era (the first stage of *sanad*): The era of the companions of the Prophet.

(2) The *tabi'in* era (the second stage of *sanad*): The era of the successors of the Prophet's companions.

(3) The *tabi'in al-tabi'in* era (the third stage of *sanad*): The era of the successors of the successors. It was in this era that the writing down of the *Hadith* commenced.

2.2.1.c The oral reporting of the *Hadith*: one-from-one reporting

The way the *Hadith* reached those who finally wrote it down, or rather, the way (mechanism or means) that was used to record the *Sunna*, was through oral reporting (*al-riwaya*). In particular, it was in the form of one from one, from one, until we reach the Prophet, 1–1 reporting (*riwayat wahid 'an wahid*).

A report (*khabar*) reported in this manner is called a *khabar al-ahad*. *Khabar al-ahad* literally means "the report of the singles." Each and every *Hadith* was reported either by a single or by multiple *khabar al-ahads*, as depicted in Figure 1.

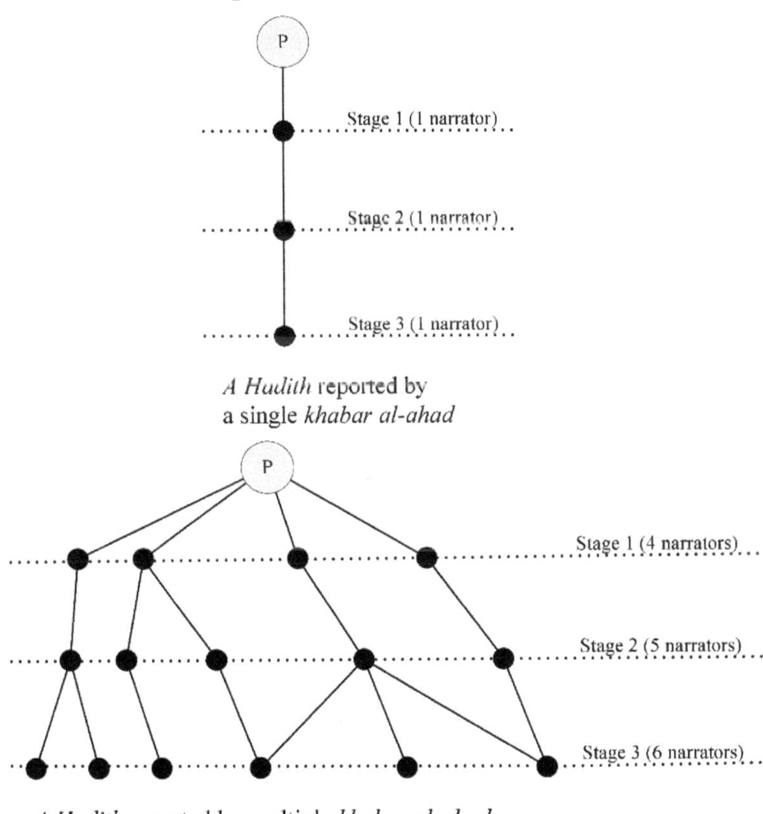

A Hadith reported by
a single *khabar al-ahad*

A Hadith reported by multiple *khabar al-ahads*
(8 *khabar al-ahad* reports counting from the bottom up)

Figure 1: The reporting of a *Hadith* (1–1 reporting)

2.2.1.d The compilations of *Hadith*

The earliest compilations of *Hadith* are works of the second and third centuries AH (eighth and ninth centuries CE). Compilations of *Hadith* and other books of religious significance became prevalent in the early Abbasid era (the first century or so of the Abbasid rule; the Abbasid era spanned the years 132–656 AH / 750–1258 CE). This can largely be attributed to paper having become affordable and commonplace in Muslim lands. The writing down of the *Hadith* could be viewed as the turning point after which the *Hadith* did not depend solely on oral transmission.*1

There are six compilations of *Hadith* that are recognized by Sunni Muslims and four alternative compilations that are recognized by Shi'a Muslims, with each branch having its own reliable narrators.

The two compilations considered most authentic to Sunni Muslims are those of al-Bukhari and Muslim. We find early Muslim scholars to have recorded the count of unique *Hadiths* in each of these compilations (the count of non-repeated *matns*, the text of the *Hadith*). It is reported that al-Bukhari (d. 256 AH / 870 CE) listed without repetition 2761 *Hadiths* in his *sahih* (sound) compilation of *Hadith* (Shaker 1983, 23—footnote 1). Muslim (d. 261 AH / 875 CE), a student of al-Bukhari, is reported to have listed, without repetition, 4000 *Hadiths* in his *sahih* compilation of *Hadith* (Shaker 1983, 23)— that is a 45% increase when compared to al-Bukhari's compilation, though not including all *Hadiths* of al-Bukhari.

NOTE*1: Muslims learned papermaking and established paper mills in Samarqand 133 AH / 751 CE, Baghdad 178 AH / 794 CE, and other cities across the Abbasid territories (Hunke 1993, 45–47). (Baghdad was the capital of the Abbasids. It was built 145 AH / 762 CE.)

The use of paper within Muslim lands in the mid-eighth century CE had a revolutionary effect on knowledge, government administration and other aspects of civilization. This was roughly a millennium after the invention of paper in China and around half a millennium before the establishment of paper mills in Christian Europe. Muslims were the first to establish paper mills in Europe, in the Iberian Peninsula, almost a century before they were established in other parts of Europe (Bloom 2001, 87–89). It is worth noting that Chinese paper was mostly made of bast fibers, while paper made by Muslims, and later by European Christians, was primarily made of waste material like rags (Bloom 2001, 8–10, 42–45).

2.2.1.e The jurists and the compilations of *Hadith*

The Arabic word *faqih* (plural *fuqaha'*) is commonly translated into English as "jurist." Historically, the jurists may have focused on, and in other times often specialized in, specific aspects of legal scholarship, such as teaching, issuing legal opinions, or engaging in theoretical analysis of legal principles. These roles are interconnected and contributed to the development and application of Islamic law. It should be noted that while some jurists may have also served as judges, this function does not align with the traditional roles of a jurist.

A *faqih* (jurist) is expected be more cautious and stringent than a collector of *Hadith* (*muhaddith*) in his approach to the *Hadith*. When it comes to *Hadith* that is of legal value, more caution is required because a jurist is concerned with the legal application of *Hadith*, whereas a collector of *Hadith* is more concerned with the collecting of *Hadith*.

Jurists varied in the extent to which they depended on the *Hadith*. The Arab Muslim historiographer and historian Ibn Khaldun (d. 808 AH / 1406 CE), in his "The Muqaddima" (often translated as "Introduction" or "Prolegomenon"), which is the first volume of his work on world history, known as the "Book of Lessons, Record of Beginnings and Events in the history of the Arabs and Foreigners and Berbers and their Powerful Contemporaries," noted the number of *Hadiths* commonly associated with three prominent Sunni jurists who were attributed to have established independent schools of jurisprudence. Ibn Khaldun stated that Abu Hanifa (d. 150 AH / 767 CE) reported (transmitted) only 17 to 50 *Hadiths* (Ibn Khaldun 1858, 2: 404); Malik ibn Anas (d. 179H / 798 CE) accepted as sound only the *Hadiths* that he listed in his Muwatta' which were at most three hundred or so (Ibn Khaldun 1858, 2: 404; 1980, 2: 460–461; 2000, 1: 561); while Ahmad ibn Hanbal (d. 241H / 855 CE) listed around thirty thousand *Hadiths* in his Musnad (Ibn Khaldun 1858, 2: 404; 1980, 2: 460–461).*1

It can be understood from Ibn Khaldun's statement that the majority of the *Hadith*, as compiled in the later books of *Hadith* (as in those of Ahmad ibn Hanbal, his student al-Bukhari, and Muslim, the student of al-Bukhari), was not recognized for jurisprudence purposes by the early prominent jurists Abu Hanifa and Malik ibn Anas, and their respective schools of jurisprudence.*2

NOTE*1: In some extant manuscripts of Ibn Khaldun's "The Muqaddima," the number of *Hadiths* listed to have been included in the Musnad of Ahmad ibn Hanbal go up to as many as forty and fifty thousand *Hadiths*, though (mostly) corrected in the margins to thirty thousand (Ibn Khaldun 1980, 461—footnote; 2000, 1: 561).

NOTE*2: Abu Hanifa assumed only very few *Hadiths* could be proven to be authentic (D.W. Brown 1999, 114), even though far less forged *Hadiths* must have been in circulation in Abu Hanifa's time than in the time of later Muslim scholars. Some early Muslim scholars, such as al-Tabari (d. 310 AH / 923 CE), who established his own (now obsolete) school of Jurisprudence, did not regard Ibn Hanbal a jurist at all but merely a collector of *Hadith* (Ibn al-Athir 1987, 7: 8–9).

2.2.2 The classification of the *Hadith*

The Muslim scholars involved in studying the *Hadith* were faced with the problem of *Hadith* authenticity: What of the *Hadith* was authentic and what was not—how to know? There were numerous other contentious matters such as: Should the *Hadith* be considered a source of religious knowledge? If that was the case, then does that make the *Hadith* a source of religious law?*1

We find the *Hadith* to be classified in more than one way. The classifications reflect the interest of the parties behind the classifications from the *Hadith*. There were two major parties involved in the classification of the *Hadith*; therefore, we find two major classifications. First, the legal scholars' classification. This classification represents an attempt to sort the *Hadith* from the viewpoint of what of the *Hadith* is reliable as a source of law (this group devised a measure for certainty of attribution to the Prophet). Second, the classification of the *Hadith* collectors, the traditionists (*muhaddithun*). This classification represents a way to organize the collected *Hadith* according to transmission quality—with reference to the variables involved in the transmission (this group devised measures for individual transmission quality). Nonetheless, in a manner of speaking, both classifications complement each other.

When looking at both classifications together, we understand the following in regard to the *Hadith*:

■ The legal scholars' classification: a classification based on transmission mechanism

Traditional Islam considers widespread consecutive transmission as the standard to determine the authenticity of *Hadith* (the certainty of attribution to the Prophet). If a *Hadith* is *mutawatir* (widespread consecutive transmission), then the *Hadith* is considered certain in its attribution to the Prophet. Traditional Islam argues that it would be virtually impossible for a large number of narrators, at each stage of the transmission, to have agreed on a fabrication.

■ The traditionists' classification: a classification based on individual transmission quality

Except for a handful of *Hadiths*, all *Hadith* is not *mutawatir*: some said *mutawatir* didn't exist, others said there was one, while there were those who said the count did not exceed seven (Amin 1969, 218). Thus, the *Hadiths* that were not transmitted in a widespread consecutive manner were further classified according to the quality of the transmission (with reference to set measures for individual transmission quality).

In the following two subsections, we examine the aforementioned classifications in further detail.

> NOTE*1: On *Hadith* authenticity, questions arise like: Can the authenticity of *Hadith* be determined or measured? How to measure the authenticity of *Hadith*? What degree of authenticity is acceptable for matters of creed, religious practice, and law?

2.2.2.a The legal scholars' classification of the *Hadith*: The measure of certainty of attribution to the Prophet

Muslim jurists established a classification of the *Hadith* according to how it was transmitted. They considered the transmission mechanism of the *Hadith* as the measure to determine the authenticity of *Hadith*. Widespread consecutive transmission was the standard used to establish certainty of attribution to the Prophet.

In quantitative terms, they classified the *Hadith* according to the number of narrators involved in the transmission of a *Hadith*. For each *Hadith*, the method counted the narrators who narrated the *Hadith* in each of the stages of oral transmission. The classification looks into the number of narrators only within the first three eras of oral transmission, since afterwards (for the following eras)—it can be inferred, with the commencement of the writing down of the *Hadith*—access to compilations of *Hadith* had become possible.

The classification of the *Hadith* according to its transmission mechanism, or as it is also known, the classification per number of narrators, represents the accepted standard set by Traditional Islam to differentiate *Hadith* according to certainty in attribution to the Prophet.

The Hanafi Sunni school of Jurisprudence classified the *Hadith* according to the number of narrators into three groups (al-Bardisi 198-?, 198–200):

■ *Mutawatir* (widespread and consecutive transmission)

A *mutawatir Hadith* is a *Hadith* that was narrated by a large number of narrators at each of the first three stages of *sanad*. Narrators are so many at each stage that, it had been argued, it was virtually impossible for such a large number of people to have agreed on a fabrication.

A *mutawatir Hadith* is considered to be certain in its attribution to the Prophet (*qat'iy al-thubut*). Seldom is there *mutawatir Hadith* that reports a saying by the Prophet (Khallaf 1968?, 41–42). *Mutawatir Hadith* that reports a saying by the Prophet can be further classified as reporting the text of the *Hadith* in meaning or in its exact wording (verbatim). Some agreed there was but a single *mutawatir Hadith* that reported a saying by the Prophet in its exact wording, "Whoever intentionally attributes a lie against me, should prepare his seat in the Fire." (al-Barri 1974, 49; al-Dimashqi 1961, 172–173; al-Kattani 19--?, 19–20)

There are conditions that are required to be met by a *Hadith*—reported by multiple *khabar al-ahads*—in order to be classified as *matuwatir*:

▶ The individual transmissions (each of the *khabar al-ahads* reporting the *Hadith*) should be continuous until reaching the Prophet;

▶ Many narrators in each stage of the transmission;

▶ The narrators of the first stage in the chain of narrators reported on what they had seen or heard (directly) from the Prophet. They were sure of what they had observed. It was based on sensory perception (*al-idrak al-hissi*) and not based on a deduction they made (inference).

■ *Mash-hur* (famous)

For a *mash-hur Hadith*, the number of narrators at the first (*sahaba*) stage of *sanad* is less than the number of narrators at the first stage of *sanad* for *mutawatir*, while the number of narrators is as many as *mutawatir* for subsequent stages of *sanad*.

A *mash-hur Hadith* is speculative and uncertain in its attribution to the Prophet, however, to a lesser degree than *ahad*. It is reported that there are only few *Hadith*s of this type.

■ *Ahad* (single or isolated)

For an *ahad Hadith*, the number of narrators at each stage of *sanad* is less than the number of narrators at each stage of *sanad* for *mutawatir*.

Attributing an *ahad Hadith* to the Prophet is speculative and uncertain (*zanni al-thubut*). Most *Hadith* is of this type.

Side note 2.11 Classifying the *Hadith* based on the number of narrators into two groups

The outlined three-group classification per number of narrators is followed by *Fiqh* (jurisprudence) scholars of the Hanafi Sunni school of jurisprudence. It is the classification per number of narrators referenced in this work. The Hanafi school of jurisprudence has the most followers compared to other schools of jurisprudence. It is predominant in countries that were once part of the Ottoman Empire. It is estimated that the adherents of the Hanafi Sunni school of jurisprudence constitute more than one-third of the world's Muslims (Ziadeh 1995, 2: 459).

When classifying the *Hadith* based on the number of narrators, instead of classifying the *Hadith* into three groups as the Hanafi scholars, Shi'a scholars and scholars of the other Sunni schools of jurisprudence classify the *Hadith* into two groups. In spite of the different count of groups, the *mutawatir* (widespread and consecutive transmission) remains to be the only group that is considered certain in its attribution to the Prophet (*qat'iy al-thubut*).

According to Shuhba (1983), the two-group classification per number of narrators is as follows:

■ *Mutawatir* (widespread and consecutive transmission), as previously explained, and

■ *Not-mutawatir*, also called *ahad* (single or isolated), which is considered speculative and uncertain in its attribution to the Prophet (*zanni al-thubut*). However, for Sunni schools (besides Hanafi), the *ahad* in this case is further classified into three subgroups:

▶ *Mash-hur* (famous): Each stage has at least three narrators. However, the number of narrators in each stage does not reach the number of narrators as in *mutawatir*.

▶ *Aziz* (rare): At least one of the stages has two narrators. Other stages have two or more narrators.

▶ *Gharib* (strange): At least one of the stages has one narrator. Other stages have one or more narrators (189–203).

2.2.2.b The traditionists' classification of the *Hadith*: The measures of individual transmission quality

Aside from the classification of the *Hadith* according to transmission mechanism that was devised by the legal scholars (the field of legal methodology, *usul al-Fiqh*), the traditionists (*muhaddithun*)—also called the *Hadith* collectors—devised a classification that categorized the individual transmissions, the *khabar al-ahad*, according to quality, or more accurately, it was according to transmission quality.

NOTICE: The reporting of *Hadith* by narrators was solely in one form, and that is in the form one from one, from one, until we reach the Prophet, 1–1 reporting (*riwayat wahid 'an wahid*). A report (*khabar*) reported in this manner is called a *khabar al-ahad*. *Khabar al-ahad* literally means "the report of the singles." Each and every *Hadith* was reported either by a single (the majority) or by multiple *khabar al-ahads*.

Thus far in our discussion, all *khabar al-ahad* involved in the reporting of *Hadith* have been assumed to be sound (*sahih*) in their *sanad*. Note that "sound" does not mean "certain," as the jurist and *Hadith* scholar al-Nawawi (d. 676 AH / 1277 CE) put it (Hallaq 1999, 85). For the *sanad* to be considered sound (*sahih*) the following is required:

(1) The *sanad* is continuous until reaching the Prophet (*musnad*)

It is unbroken (*muttasil*) without the omission of any narrator in between until reaching the Prophet.

(2) Each of the narrators included in the *sanad* is considered to be trustworthy in righteousness (*'adl*)

(3) Each of the narrators included in the *sanad* is considered to be trustworthy in accurateness (*dhabitt*; the narrator has reliable ability to preserve the narration)

The narrators are able to recall the narration from memory as they heard it; alternatively, they had written the narration as they heard it and had preserved the written document unchanged.

In addition to the basic three requirements above, we also have two additional requirements that need to be met for the *sanad* to be considered sound (*sahih*):

(4) The *sanad* must not have flaws (*mu'allal*)

A *sanad* that has passed the three requirements above would not have any apparent flaw; however, it still could have concealed flaws. Thus, this fourth requirement is to make sure the *sanad* does not have a concealed flaw. An example of having a concealed flaw in the *sanad* is the case when two consecutive narrators in the *sanad*, although cotemporaries, never actually met or shared the *khabar al-ahad*.

(5) The *sanad* must not be aberrant (*shadh*)

This requirement would be checked (only) in cases that have multiple *khabar al-ahads* reporting on the same issue; otherwise, if there was only one *khabar al-ahad* reporting the *Hadith*, then by definition there is no aberrance.

A *sanad* is anomalous (*shadh*) if it is reported by a trustworthy person who contradicts the *sanad* of others better known for trustworthiness.

An example of a *khabar al-ahad* that is anomalous in its *sanad* would be the case where we have a *Hadith* that is reported by multiple *khabar al-ahads*, each having a five-stage *sanad*. All *khabar al-ahads* except one share the same narrators in the first four stages of the *sanad*. The remaining *khabar al-ahad*, the anomalous one, is reported by a trustworthy person (fifth stage in the *sanad*), yet less in the degree of trustworthiness than the others (of the same fifth stage in the *sanad*), who reports this *khabar al-ahad* with a *sanad* that differs from all the other *sanads* in the first four stages.

It is my understanding, originally, Muslim scholars attempted to evaluate the reliability of the *sanad* of *khabar al-ahad*. And classified *khabar al-ahad* based on the *sanad* into *sahih* (sound) and *da'if* (weak). Thereafter, a third category was added to the classification, the *hasan* (fair), the *sanad* had one or more narrators of questionable trustworthiness. As a result, for the *sanad*, and its corresponding *khabar al-ahad*, the *da'if* (weak) became to be the *sanad* that did not qualify as either *sahih* or *hasan*, where the trustworthiness of one or more of its narrators was subject to serious criticism.*1

Therefore, the designation of the *sanad* as *sahih* (sound), *da`if* (weak), and *hasan* (fair) was used to classify *khabar al-ahad*. Accordingly, based on its *sanad*, the *khabar al-ahad* was classified as *sahih* (sound), *da`if* (weak), and *hasan* (fair).*2

Subsequently, this three-type categorization was used to classify the *khabar al-ahad* based on both its *sanad* and *matn*. That is, the classification of *khabar al-ahad* into *sahih* (sound), *da`if* (weak), and *hasan* (fair) was no longer utilized to merely classify individual transmissions based on transmission quality (represented by the *sanad*), but it was used—and regarded—to classify individual transmissions based on individual transmission quality (represented by both the *sanad* and *matn*). As a result, the classification of *khabar al-ahad* into *sahih* (sound), *da`if* (weak), and *hasan* (fair) came to be regarded as to depict *khabar al-ahad* quality.

Muslim scholars have claimed to use the last two requirements above, #4 and #5, although I must add, rarely, in the evaluation of the *matn*: the careful scrutiny of the text of the *khabar al-ahad*. I say rarely because this was not done in the case when having only one *khabar al-ahad* reporting on an issue, which is the situation for the majority of the *Hadith*. In the case of having a single *khabar al-ahad* reporting on an issue, if the *sanad* was considered sound, then the *khabar al-ahad* itself, by default, would be considered sound.

The evaluation of the *matn* was done only in cases when having more than one *khabar al-ahad* reporting on the same issue. This is because the procedure used to verify the *matn* was based on comparing it with the *matn* of other *khabar al-ahads* that were reported by (more) trustworthy narrators. The objective was to make sure there were no textual conflicts among these reports. Textual conflicts arise when certain reports on the same matter vary in words and meaning. The evaluation criterion used, though, was still the trustworthiness of the narrators (the people involved in transmitting the *matn*). It is to be noted that each of the *khabar al-ahads* involved would have already passed the first five requirements for the soundness of its *sanad*.

In such cases, in order to classify the *khabar al-ahad* as *sahih*, its *matn* would also be verified for not having concealed flaws and aberrance. Therefore, two additional requirements would need to be verified:

(4') Not to have a concealed flaw in the *matn*

An example of a concealed flaw in the *matn* would be when we have multiple *khabar al-ahads* sharing the same *matn*. And in one particular *khabar al-ahad* of this group, we find words added to the (common) *matn* that affect its meaning. And when compared to the other *khabars* of the group, it is deduced that these words were added and they were not part of the original report.

(5') Not to have an anomaly in *matn*

A *khabar* is anomalous if it is reported by a trustworthy person who contradicts the narration of a person better known for trustworthiness who reported on the same issue (or it could be to contradict the narration of several others of equal trustworthiness).

One point I would like to emphasize: To classify the *sanad* of a *khabar al-ahad* as sound, or to classify the *khabar al-ahad* itself as sound, does not make the *khabar al-ahad* certain in its attribution to the Prophet. When it comes to certainty of attribution of a *khabar al-ahad*, such quality measures for the transmission of *khabar al-ahad* or the quality measures for the *khabar al-ahad* themselves could increase the level of uncertainty of attribution, but surely, they cannot affirm a *khabar al-ahad* to be certain in its attribution to the Prophet. Even by Traditional Islam's standards, an *ahad Hadith* (includes those of the *ahad* classified as sound) is speculative and uncertain in its attribution to the Prophet (*zanni al-thubut*).

NOTE*1: In the traditionists' classification of the *Hadith*, the measure of the trustworthiness of the narrators included in the *sanad* would affect the degree of reliability given to the *sanad*, with verdicts such as *sahih* (sound), *hasan* (fair), and *da`if* (weak). The method devised to evaluate the trustworthiness of the narrators was based on the critique of the narrators (assessing trustworthiness)—the science of impugnment and validation (*'ilm al-jarh wa al-ta'dil*) or what is called biographical evaluation (*'ilm al-rijal*)—where, in order to establish credibility, the individual narrators were examined for deficiencies in righteousness and accurateness.

Muslim scholars compiled biographies of the narrators of *Hadith*. Though the terminology varied—some having up to six levels of praise and six levels of criticism, individual biographies concluded by describing the standing of each narrator. Narrators of *Hadith* were generally placed into one of four categories:

trustworthy, weak, unreliable, or fabricators. According to Khan (2010), "[b]earing in mind the variations which existed in the views of investigators concerning narrators (whose number runs into around a million), we can divide their classification into four main categories: (1) those whose [trustworthiness] is unanimous, (2) those whose weakness is non-controversial, (3) those concerning whom there exists controversy among scholars, and (4) those who have been unanimously declared as liars and fabricators." (24)

The problem with this method is that it is subjective. For some scholars, a particular narrator would be regarded as trustworthy, whereas for other scholars the same narrator would be found a liar or something in between (Amin 1969, 215–217).

NOTE*2: According to Ibn Taymiyya (d. 728 AH / 1328 CE), it was al-Tirmidhi (d. 279 AH / 892 CE) who was the first to use the *hasan* as a distinct category in the classification of the *Hadith* (Taymiyah 2004, 18: 23–27).

2.2.3 The traditional view on *Hadith* authoritativeness

Traditional Islam acknowledges that only *mutawatir Hadith* is certain in its attribution to the Prophet; nevertheless, according to Traditional Islam, *Hadith* authoritativeness in matters of religious practice and law does not require absolute *Hadith* authenticity (some interpretations based on Traditional Islam even extend that to include matters of creed).

For the majority of the *Hadith*, the probable type, the schools of jurisprudence differed regarding the degree of probable knowledge attained from it; in consequence, they differed in the degree of authoritativeness associated with this type and its sub-types.

There are so many *ahad Hadith*s that detail various issues. There are some *ahad Hadith*s that contradict logic, some contradict each other, and some yet even contradict the Qur'an (al-Ghazali 2003, 168–174, 179–182). A Muslim is left in awe in what to follow and what not to follow.

In recent times, pertaining to legislation, some Muslim religious institutions clearly made public their stand towards the *Hadith*. On this, al-Ghazali (2003) reported that a *fatwa* (religious legal opinion, edict or ruling) by al-Azhar University of Cairo, Egypt, in 1990 CE, stated to the effect:*2

Only a source that is definitive in both attribution and meaning has the power to independently affirm prohibition (*tahrim*) or obligation (*wujub*). For the *Sunna*, this is only attainable through *mutawatir Hadith*. Given that *mutawatir Hadith* is almost unknown, as scholars have not agreed on it; therefore, the *Sunna* cannot independently affirm prohibition or obligation unless it is practice-*Sunna* (*al-sunna al-fi'liyya*; reports on the deeds of the Prophet) or it is associated with a verse from the Qur'an (176–179).

NOTE*1: Historically, we find some, like the Mu'tazila, an early school of Islamic theology based on reason and rational thought, to have argued that probable knowledge was not authoritative, since according to the Qur'an, speculation can by no means take the place of truth (Q. 10:36 in 10:34–43, 53:28 in 53:26–30). Furthermore, in relation to religious matters, to follow probable knowledge goes against the Qur'anic directive commanding only to follow that which is based on knowledge (Q. 6:148 in 6:148–150, 17:36 in 17:22–39), i.e. scripture from God.

NOTE*2: The Egyptian mosque-university al-Azhar in Cairo dates back to when the city of Cairo itself was founded over ten centuries ago (361 AH / 972 CE). The Egyptian mosque-university al-Azhar follows the Ash'ari school of theology. Historically, those who have headed al-Azhar (Grand Imam of al-Azhar; *shaykh* of al-Azhar), since the time the post was formally established in 1679 CE, were followers of the Hanafi, Maliki, and (almost half the times) the Shafi'i schools of jurisprudence.

NOTE: When it comes to clarity of meaning, the injunctions of the *Hadith*, as those of the Qur'an, were considered by Traditional Islam to be of two categories: definitive in meaning (*qat'iyyat al-dalala*), which only have one meaning; and speculative in meaning (*zanniyyat al-dalala*), in which the wording has more than one possible meaning.

Side note 2.12 The *Hadith* and the four major Sunni schools of jurisprudence

The four major Sunni schools of jurisprudence ordered in chronological order of establishment are: Hanafi, Maliki, Shafi'i, and Hanbali. These schools were named after their eponymous founders. The schools were named after the scholars, Abu Hanifa (d. 150 AH / 767 CE), Malik ibn Anas (d. 179H / 798 CE), Muḥammad ibn Idris al-Shafi'i (d. 204 AH / 820 CE), and Ahmad ibn Hanbal (d. 241H / 855 CE), respectively. It should be noted that each of the schools developed from the effort of numerous scholars, starting with the students of the eponymous founder.

The four schools vary in the degree of relying on the *Hadith* as a source of law. Though all four Sunni schools of jurisprudence consider the *Sunna* to be a source of religious knowledge, the later the chronological order of a school, the more the school relied on the *Hadith* as a source of law.

As for what *Hadith* each of the four schools recognized to be reliable: The Hanafis acknowledged only the *mutawatir* and *mash-hur Hadiths* (Khallaf 1971, 71–94); the Malikis, additionally, approved, to the most part, *Hadith* that was affirmed by the actions of the people of Medina (the Maliki school of jurisprudence placed additional restrictions on accepting the non-*mutawatir Hadith*, the prime of which were: not to contradict the actions of the people of Medina; not to contradict analogical reasoning; not to contradict the Qur'an); the Shafi'is and Hanbalis recognized more *Hadiths* than the Hanafis and Malikis, yet they differed in what each considered its accepted authenticity threshold. The Hanbali school recognizing the most *ahad*.

The increased interest in the *Hadith* and its compilation in the late second century AH and onwards can be attributed to the jurist Muḥammad ibn Idris al-Shafi'i (d. 204 AH / 820 CE), whose surname, al-Shafi'i, as aforementioned, served as the eponym of the Shafi'i school of jurisprudence. Al-Shafi'i considered the *Sunna*—represented in the *Hadith*—to be divine revelation (*wahy ilahi*), not verbatim but in meaning (*bil-ma'na*; giving the sense or gist of what was said), and he established the *Sunna* to be a source of law (Coulson 1978, 53–61; 1992, 81–90; Lowry 2007, 165–187; Musa 2007).

Side note 2.13 The forging of *Hadith*

Amin (1969) pointed out that the statement that is attributed to the Prophet, "Whoever intentionally attributes a lie against me, should prepare his seat in the Fire," most probably was in response to a forging of *Hadith* incident. He suggested that this would indicate that forging of *Hadith* was already underway while the Prophet was still alive.

Amin was of the viewpoint that not compiling the *Hadith* early on by the early generations, in addition to the reliance solely on oral transmission to transmit the *Hadith*, resulted in the forging of more and more *Hadiths* that were falsely attributed to the Prophet. According to Amin, reasons to forge *Hadith* included:

■ Political, tribal, and regional biases: *Hadiths* were forged by followers of various competing political factions as a means to strengthen the position of those whom they supported, or as a means to degrade their opponents. This can be viewed as an approach that was used to religiously legitimize the right of one party to rule over the others. Then there were those *Hadiths* that were forged with the objective of expressing the preferences of the Prophet on various subjects, like alleging his preference of certain Arab tribes—following in the footsteps of Arabic poetry in glorifying tribal affiliations; his preference of Arabs over other peoples; his preference of certain cities, regions, lands, etc.

■ Theological and legal schools' differences: Differences in theological and legal viewpoints (*ikhtilafat fiqhiyya wa kalamiyya*) amongst the scholars of the different schools contributed to the forging of *Hadith*. The forging of *Hadith* represented a way to strengthen positions in disputed matters. A forged *Hadith* would include so much detail, even to the extent of claiming the Prophet to support certain religious groups over others (prophesying on behalf of the Prophet since no groups existed at the time of the Prophet). Legal works became full of numerous *Hadiths*. This affected even the works of followers of earlier jurists like Abu Hanifa, who himself was renowned for recognizing but very few *Hadiths*.

■ Desire for status and wealth: Some would forge *Hadiths* in accordance with the interests of rulers and princes (regardless of the topic), in an effort to please them. This was done as a means to gain reward in return.

■ No harm done attitude: In some circles, it was considered not harmful to forge *Hadiths* as long as it did not permit a prohibition or prohibit a permissible. Examples are found in *Hadiths* on inspiriting and disheartening (*al-targhib wa al-tarhib*); *Hadiths* on virtues of verses and chapters of the Qur'an; *Hadiths* on virtues of individuals, some of whom were not even alive at the time of the Prophet.

■ Closed mindedness: The resistance of people to readily accept or recognize religious instruction unless it came from the Qur'an or the *Hadith* also encouraged the forging of *Hadith* (210–215).

3. The classification of the Qur'anic injunctions: Traditional and proposed

In a classification of the Qur'anic injunctions (Q.I. classification), injunctions are grouped into categories, formulating a particular structure. Moreover, the injunction categories are arranged in a hierarchy according to the understanding of the Qur'an's focus and emphasis.

I propose that there is a direct relationship between the composition of a Qur'anic-based interpretation of religion and the associated Q.I. classification. It is proposed that the choice of components that constitute a Qur'anic-based interpretation of religion (its composition) depends on two factors: the structure of the associated Q.I. classification, in addition to the injunction categories within the associated Q.I. classification that are considers to be eternally applicable. Hence, the composition of any Qur'anic-based interpretation of religion reflects the injunction categories of eternal applicability of the associated Q.I. classification.

Traditional Islam forwards a Q.I. classification. Traditional Islam considers all the Qur'anic injunction categories in its Q.I. classification to be eternally applicable. Traditional Islam is comprised of components on belief, virtue, worship, and law. These four components reflect Traditional Islam's Q.I. classification.

The proposed interpretation of the Qur'anic revelation comes with its own Q.I. classification. In Volume 1 I introduced the proposed Q.I. classification. It is a Q.I. classification where the Qur'anic Action-Type II category of injunctions does not have eternal applicability. As a result, the interpretation of religion associated with the proposed Q.I. classification would not have a law component. In this book's Chapter 5, I present arguments that support the claim that the Qur'anic Action-Type II category of injunctions of the proposed Q. I. classification does not have eternal applicability.

Volume 1 of this series presented both the traditional and the proposed Q.I. classifications. Both Q.I. classifications are reproduced herein for reference.

3.1 The traditional Q.I. classification

According to Traditional Islam, the injunctions (*al-ahkam*) within the verses of the Qur'an address three domains: belief (*al-'itiqad*), virtue (*al-khuluq*), and actions (*al-ahkam al-'amaliyya*) (al-Bardisi 198-?,

58

183). Traditional Islam considers all injunctions of the Qur'an within these three domains to be eternally applicable across space-time.

Traditional Islam's Q.I. classification is as follows:

■ **Belief: the belief injunctions** (*al-ahkam al-'itiqadiyya*)

Belief injunctions direct on what to believe. Belief injunctions cover the five articles of faith:

▶ Belief in the one and only God;

▶ Belief in the angels;

▶ Belief in the revealed scriptures (sent prior to and including the Qur'an);

▶ Belief in all prophets/messengers of God, and not to make distinction between any of them—this includes believing that Prophet Muhammad was a messenger of God and the last of the prophets;

▶ Belief in the last day (resurrection and judgment).

■ **Virtue: the virtue injunctions** (*al-ahkam al-khuluqiyya*)

Virtue injunctions direct on what kind of person a Muslim should be (moral character). A Muslim is obliged to develop and maintain good attitudes, temperaments, and character traits and to stay away from their opposites. Examples of virtues include honesty, compassion, integrity, fairness, self-control, fidelity, forgiveness, respectfulness, humility, and kindness.

■ **Action: the action injunctions** (*al-ahkam al-'amaliyya*)

Action injunctions direct the actions of Muslims—details of which appear mostly in verses of the Medina era. They constitute the area of study of Islamic law. The best way to picture the action injunctions is according to the realm in which they operate (direct action in).

Action injunctions can be categorized based on their plane of operation into two types:

▶ **Action-Type I**

Action injunctions of type I cover the man-God plane. They instruct on actions to be performed that are related to the relationship between man and God, the acts of worship (*al-'ibadat*). These acts can be described as man-God actions where God is at the receiving end. Action injunctions of type

I do not involve any other party besides the Muslim individual.

▶ Action-Type II

Action injunctions of type II cover the man-world plane. They instruct on actions to be performed that regulate and are related to organizing man-world relationships and affairs (*al-mu'amalat*). It is important to note that this type of action injunctions includes Qur'anic injunctions of both law and ethics (excluding virtues).

As is the case of categorizing the action injunctions of the Qur'an (*al-ahkam al-'amaliyya*) into two types, man-God and man-world, based on the realm in which they operate (direct action in), the action injunctions of the *Hadith* are also categorized into the same two types. This two-type categorization is further extended to the domain of operation of the laws extracted directly and indirectly from the Qur'an and the *Hadith*.

Side note 3.1 Al-Nuwayhi: Toward a Revolution in Religious Thought

In recent times, we find those who rejected Traditional Islam's claim that all Qur'anic injunctions have eternal applicability across space-time, yet they called for religious law reform rather than the outright rejection of religious law.

In the seventies of the twentieth century CE, Muhammad al-Nuwayhi (d. 1980 CE) published a series of articles on seeking progress in thinking within the Arab world. Some of his articles were later compiled into a book, *Nahwa Thawra fi al-Fikr al-Dini* (Toward a Revolution in Religious Thought)—the book title follows the title of its sixth and last article. In the book's sixth and final article, which was originally published in 1970 CE, al-Nuwayhi makes the point for a need to change people's understanding of Islam and its role in society, where he considers traditional religious thought as the milestone that needs to be overcome for any progress to be achieved in the Arab world.

Al-Nuwayhi (2010) held the view that injunctions of both the Qur'an and the *Hadith* that did not deal with belief (*al-'itiqad*), virtue (*al-khuluq*), and acts of worship (*al-'ibadat*), but rather dealt with man-world affairs (*al-mu'amalat*) were not obligatory to Muslims across time, even if they had been obligatory at the time of the Prophet. Al-Nuwayhi stated that he believed this view to have also been held by Muhammad 'Abduh (d. 1905 CE) and his students of al-Manar school, 'Abd al-Muta'al al-Sa'idi (d. 1966 CE), besides numerous others who did not dare to declare their views (148–149).

3.2 How the proposed Q.I. classification differs from the traditional Q.I. classification

The proposed Q.I. classification is a classification that I believe better reflects and is more consistent with the reinterpreted key terms of the Qur'anic vocabulary that were introduced in Volume 1. In essence, I see the proposed Q.I. classification to appropriately reflect the focus and emphasis given in the Qur'an to God's code of ethics and worship.

NOTICE: The reinterpretation of the term "Islam" to represent God's code of ethics and worship is essentially what led me to the proposed Q.I. classification.

Both the traditional and proposed Q.I. classifications include the same injunctions; it is just the classification structure that varies from one classification to another: how injunctions are grouped and organized.

In the proposed Q.I. classification, the injunction categories are rearranged in a hierarchy that reflects the proposed interpretation of the Qur'anic revelation's understanding of the Qur'an and its message. To ease in the comparison with the traditional Q.I. classification, the proposed Q.I. classification uses the same injunction category names as those of the traditional Q.I. classification.

Before presenting the proposed Q.I. classification, the following points explain how the proposed Q.I. classification differs from the traditional Q.I. classification:

<u>Change in structure and the shifting of injunction groups</u>

■ The proposed Q.I. classification classifies the Qur'anic injunctions into three main categories: Belief, The Code (Ethics, Worship), and Action (Type I, Type II). The first category covers the belief injunctions. The second category includes the injunctions relevant to the Code. The third category of injunctions, Action, is where we find the injunctions that were primarily different in each of the revealed scriptures.

This third category of injunctions includes the injunctions that expound and detail the Code. The injunctions of the Code are injunctions that bestow legitimacy (*shar'iyyat*), the judgment of

God on subjects. They generally do not include the fine details (the how, when, and where). Such details can be found in the third category of injunctions, the category "Action."

■ In the proposed Q.I. classification the ethics injunctions that the traditional Q.I. classification considered to belong to the actions category no longer appear in the actions category. Instead, all ethics injunctions are filed under a category of their own, the "ethics" category that appears as a subcategory under the new parent category "the Code."

■ The new category "the Code" in the proposed Q.I. classification includes two subcategories: ethics and worship. The subcategory "Ethics" includes besides the ethics injunctions that used to be under the Action-Type II category of the traditional Q.I. classification, the injunctions appearing under the category "Virtue" of the traditional Q.I. classification. The subcategory "Worship" outlines God's commands on worship. This subcategory simply names the different types of worship; however, it does not get into the details of each type. The fine details concerning worship remain to be filed under the Action-Type I category.

Injunction groups that remain to be the same

■ In the proposed Q.I. classification the categories of "Belief" and "Action-Type I" are the same as those appearing in the traditional Q.I. classification.

■ Except for the ethics injunctions, all groups of injunctions appearing originally under the Action-Type II category of the traditional Q.I. classification remain to be classified under the Action-Type II category of the proposed Q.I. classification.

Applicability of the (new) Action-Type II category

■ In Chapter 5 the applicability of the Qur'anic injunctions is explored. It will be argued that as per the proposed Q.I. classification, the applicability of the Qur'anic Action-Type II injunctions is non-eternal but rather space-time specific.

■ The most important aspect about the proposed Q.I. classification is that it distinguishes between the injunctions of ethics (the moral code) that it considers eternally applicable and its Action-Type II category of injunctions that it considers not to be eternally applicable. The Action-Type II category includes, among other types of injunctions, the injunctions relevant to the application mechanism of the moral code in the time of the revelation.

■ The proposed Q.I. classification is based on the understanding that the injunctions of the Qur'an were injunctions conveyed to the peoples in the space-time of the revelation. Thus, when it comes to the applicability of the Qur'anic injunctions, the proposed Q.I. classification claims the eternal applicability of all Qur'anic injunctions except those appearing under the (new) Action-Type II category. The injunctions of the Action-Type II category were customized (optimized), so to speak, for the space-time of the revelation.

■ I understand the Action-Type II injunctions to have addressed, specifically, the followers of the Qur'an in the time of its revelation, the QMonotheists. Thus, the applicability of these injunctions would be tied to the space-time of this particular historical group. The further away we go in either space or time from the space-time of this historical group the less applicable these injunctions become. This is mainly because the Action-Type II injunctions were linked to the norms of this historical group. And norms are affected by both space and time.*1

NOTE*1: In this work the term "social norms" or sometimes "norms" for short is used to refer to the customary rules that govern behavior in a group or society: they are the unplanned, unexpected result of interaction between individuals. Factors that influence the social norms of a group or society in a particular space-time include its moral codes, legal rules, values, customs, traditions, and ways of thinking.

3.3 The proposed Q.I. classification

The proposed Q.I. classification takes the following structure:

■ **Belief: the belief injunctions** (*al-ahkam al-'itiqadiyya*)

Injunctions of this category direct on what to believe and constitute the belief system. They are centered around (and stem from) the belief in the one and only God and not to associate with God. The five articles of faith lie within this category.

■ The Code (*al-islam*)

The Qur'an commanded to take God as the source of instruction on the Code (Q. 39:11 in 39:1–18, 98:5 in 98:1–8). The Qur'an declared that the sole source of instruction in the Code, *al-islam*, was God (Q. 3:79–85, 10:104–105, 12:39–40, 109:1–6).

The Qur'an tells us that God's code is the only acceptable code on Judgment day (Q. 3:85 in 3:79–85). On Judgment Day, God will judge the beings according to the Code (the Qur'an called Judgment Day *yawm al-din*, "the day of the Code," Q. 1:4 in 1:1–7). Thus, in the earthly life, it would not be of use to abide by any other code. Furthermore, it should not be acceptable for others to change/amend the Code and claim it to be God's code, since unauthorized amendments would result in a distorted code, whereas judgment would be according to God's code, the official code.

The Code is composed of injunctions in the fields of both ethics and worship. Hence, the Code has two components: one on morality, the other on worship. Injunctions of the Code are injunctions that determine legitimacy (*shar'iyyat*) (state as legitimate or illegitimate): they declare the judgment of God on subjects.*1

Let us explore the injunctions pertaining to each of the two components of the Code:

▶ On morality (the ethics injunctions)

This category of injunctions addresses righteousness in both conduct and character. It is the component of the Code that applies in the man-world dimension. Injunctions in this category provide a moral code in the descriptive sense of morality. They constitute the ethical system of God; they identify Qur'anic morality. The term "morality" as used in this work will not be distinguished from "ethics."

The ethical system of God (the moral code) encompasses what the Qur'an considered the approved versus the disapproved in both conduct and character.

An ethical system is comprised of ethics not laws. Ethics are sometimes confused with law; it is important to distinguish between the two. Ethics provide guiding principles for the creation of laws. Ethics provide guiding principles that are applicable across space-time. Ethics do not specify punishments for their violation. On the other hand, laws carry with them punishments for violations. One can think of punishments as a means to enforce the ethics, or rather some of them, keeping in mind that punishments change over space-time.

Injunctions of this category provide instruction in the following areas:

◘ On conduct: The obliged actions

a. Direct address: Injunctions of this group identify the approved versus disapproved actions. We find injunctions of this group to have been used when the Qur'an called to uphold agreements and treaties; not to kill; not to steal; not to cheat; not to give false testimony; instruction on sexual relations and marital sexual intercourse (the when and how); etc.

b. Indirect address: Actions relating to the referenced matters are considered actions that are approved or disapproved. Injunctions of this group identify the prohibited foods, prohibited women (to marry), the sacred places (where man and beast are safe), the sacred months (the months when fighting was prohibited unless attacked), the prohibited practices (such as *al-riba*: a lending practice with unreasonably high rates of interest), etc.

◘ On character: The virtues

Injunctions of this group compel one to do and say good through providing instruction on what one should be. They address the traits of human character.

► On worship

Injunctions of this category involve acts that reflect reverence and adoration for God. They instruct to perform enthusiastically, with steadfast away from disdain and arrogance certain acts of worship to no other than God. They do not include the fine details (the how, when, and where).

These acts of worship can be described as man-God actions where God is at the receiving end.

Acts of worship are of two sorts:

◘ External acts (expression of reverence and adoration for God, the rites)

These acts echo faith in body and wealth. These acts cover performing daily prayers (*salat*); reading scripture (or listening to scripture being read); voluntary and obligatory giving (*sadaqat*); fasting (*sawm*); and livestock offering.

◘ Internal acts (feeling of reverence and adoration for God)

These acts include to remember (and contemplate on the creations of) (*dhikr*), trust (*tawakkul*; rely on), thank (*shukr*; be grateful), glorify (*tasbih*) and praise (*hamd*; extol) God; and to repent (*tawba*), resort (*i'tisam*) and supplicate (*du'aa*) to no other than God.

■ **Action: the action injunctions** (*al-ahkam al-'amaliyya*)

Injunctions within this category represent the application mechanism of the Code—as it applies to the followers of the Qur'an. To a large extent, they include injunctions that expound the Code and provide the fine details.

Action Injunctions are of two types:

▶ **Action-Type I** (injunctions on worship)

Injunctions of this category give the fine details of the man-God actions of the Code, particularly the rites. They provide details such as the how, when, and where.

▶ **Action-Type II** (the space-time specific injunctions)

Injunctions that do not fit in any of the previous categories fall into this category. They are injunctions that are affected by space-time. Injunctions of Action-Type II were applicable only to the QMonotheists or would have applied in circumstances when the Prophet was sought to arbitrate.

In this category lie the injunctions that elaborate on (give the fine details in connection with) the injunctions of the Code that operate in the man-world dimension, such as providing punishment for violations (penal code) and implementation details (provide details on contracts, divorce proceedings, etc.). Additionally, instruction that addressed the authority of the Prophet, instruction on political allegiance, along with instruction that reflected social norms of the space-time of the Prophet all belong in this category.

Examples of this category of injunctions include the injunctions that comprise the Qur'anic penal code, the intestate law of inheritance, and injunctions that elaborate on matters of marriage and divorce. For instance, the Code directs that the QMonotheists can only marry Monotheists—this would include people from all Monotheist groups; it specifies the women who a man can marry. Additionally, the Code permits divorce. The Action-Type II injunctions elaborate on the (technical) details, such as the limit on the number of women a man can marry and the proceedings for marriage and divorce.

From here onwards, it will be important to distinguish between the traditional Q.I. classification and the proposed Q.I. classification. When talking about Traditional Islam, it is always the traditional Q.I. classification that is in mind. Otherwise, it is the proposed Q.I. classification that is being referenced. Hence, whenever I mention the non-eternal applicability of the Qur'anic Action-Type II injunctions, the Q.I. classification referenced is the proposed Q.I. classification.

NOTE*1: The Qur'an described God's directives as decrees. For the injunctions of the Code, I understand the Qur'an to have distinguished between two types of directives of God: *al-kitab* and *al-hikma*.

I understand the terms *al-kitab* and *al-hikma* when used together in the Qur'an, in all ten occurrences (with and without the definite particle *al*—equivalent for the definite article "the"), that they represented the Code (Q. 3:48 in 3:42–51, 5:110 in 5:109–120; along with Q. 2:129 in 2:124–134, 2:151–152 in 2:151–157, 3:164 in 3:156–185, 62:2 in 62:1–4; in addition to Q. 2:230–231 in 2:226–242, 3:81 in 3:79–85, 4:54 in 4:44–57, 4:113 in 4:104–114). This proposed word interpretation and usage differs from the known interpretations, both classical and contemporary. When these terms were used in the Qur'an to represent the Code, I understand *al-kitab* and *al-hikma* to depict divine mandate and moral precepts, respectively.

A divine mandate is specific and directive, whereas ethical precepts offer a general framework for moral conduct.

To elaborate a bit, a divine mandate consists of specific directives or commands from God, often related to religious duties or moral obligations. These mandates are considered obligatory for believers to follow and are typically specific in nature, outlining particular actions or behaviors expected of individuals.

On the other hand, moral precepts are broader principles or guidelines that guide human behavior towards ethical conduct and virtuous living. Moral precepts encompass a wider range of ethical principles and provide a foundational framework for making moral decisions in various contexts.

It is essential to understand that the described usage of these terms is for when they appeared together, and in such instances, they—together—represent the Code. However, when used separately, *al-hikma* generally retains the same meaning, while *al-kitab* may also depict other meanings depending on the context.

Side note 3.2 The Qur'an's call to fulfill the Code in light of the proposed applicability rules of the Qur'anic injunctions

The Qur'an commanded all peoples to fulfill the Code (Q. 10:104–105, 30:30, 42:13–16). I understand the Qur'an's call to fulfill the Code (to obey and uphold) to involve both man-world and man-God dimensions. Do the proposed applicability rules of the Qur'anic injunctions affect this commandment? According to the proposed applicability rules, all injunctions appearing under the category "the Code" are of eternal applicability. Thus, the proposed applicability rules do not affect the applicability of the injunctions of the Code.

One must distinguish between the Code and the application mechanism of the Code. They are not one and the same thing. When it comes to the applicability mechanism (to apply the Code in a specific space-time), this is where the proposed applicability rules have consequences. Let us look into how the proposed applicability rules affect the actions category of the Qur'anic injunctions:

- The Action-Type I injunctions

Injunctions detailing how to apply the injunctions of the Code on worship are considered to be of eternal applicability: details on worship cannot change with space-time.

- The Action-Type II injunctions

All injunctions within the Action-Type II category without exception (including those that expound on the ethics injunctions) are not considered to be of eternal applicability but are rather space-time specific. Hence, the proposed applicability rule for this category affects the injunctions that specify how to apply the part of the Code on morality.

Law and space-time dependent implementation details are restricted by space-time and cannot be assumed to be of eternal applicability. How to apply the part of the Code on morality is best left to societies across space-time to figure out for themselves. That is to say, it is best to leave for societies to come up with implementations that realize the Qur'anic moral code according to the best (relative) understanding of fairness in their space-time.

4. What is the Qur'an saying? An interpretation of the Qur'anic revelation

An initial general outline of the proposed interpretation of the Qur'anic revelation was presented in the last chapter of Volume 1. This outline marks where the first volume ended and where this book resumes in presenting the proposed interpretation of the Qur'anic revelation.

I have reproduced this initial outline here for the reader to see how the following chapters discussing the stance of the proposed interpretation of the Qur'anic revelation on law build on it. And to understand how the view on law fits in within the proposed interpretation of the Qur'anic revelation and why it constitutes an essential component of it.

For the curious and true believer alike, it is intriguing to try to figure out what the Creator of all things and beings wanted His creation to know in the last of His revealed scriptures. The proposed interpretation of the Qur'anic revelation is an attempt in that direction. In essence, what the Qur'an is saying can be distilled down to this: Believe in the one and only God, live a moral life, and do not divide amongst yourselves.

In the big picture, when attempting to understand what the Qur'an is and what it is saying (the gist of), taking into consideration the proposed understanding of what the term *al-islam* signified (the Code), the existence of two main groups of Monotheists, and the proposed classification of the injunctions of the Qur'an, a high-level interpretation of the Qur'anic revelation is formalized.

Part of the general outline of the proposed interpretation of the Qur'anic revelation is identical to what we find in all interpretations of the Qur'an that we know about, yet another part is not.

The part that the proposed interpretation of the Qur'anic revelation shares with previous interpretations is that the Qur'an was a communication from God—it relayed the speech of God verbatim— that was revealed to a non-Israelite, an Arab from the clan of Hashim of the tribe of Quraysh, Prophet Muhammad ibn 'Abdulla.

The Qur'an came confirming the previous revealed scriptures. It was delivered to peoples who were never addressed directly by scripture in a language they could understand, the Arabic language (not Hebrew, Aramaic, or Greek). It was directed to all beings, to

Israelites and non-Israelites, to those who already had scripture and to those who did not.

The Qur'an declared that God was the sole deity and commanded not to associate with God by taking any other as deity.

The Qur'an asserted that it was the same message that all the revealed scriptures had come with; however, the Qur'an identified various followers. It was the followers who had divided amongst themselves and it was not that there were different messages.

The Qur'an made clear to the peoples of previous scriptures that whereon they had differed. The Qur'an asserted in connection with the peoples of previous scriptures who divided amongst themselves and fell into variance that their case rested with God to judge between them on the Day of Resurrection. The Qur'an declared that Prophet Muhammad's task was to deliver God's message and that the Prophet had no contention or concern with the disbelievers from the peoples of previous scriptures.

The Qur'an emphasized that those who choose not to accept the Qur'anic revelation from the peoples of previous scriptures, as all others who reject the revelation, would be doomed in the hereafter. And those who believe and do righteous deeds would be (forever) in Paradise.

As for the part of the proposed interpretation of the Qur'anic revelation that I believe to be unique to it, let me begin with that, the Qur'an commanded that the one—and only—deity should be the sole source of divine instruction. More about what this particular commandment entails is elaborated on in both Volume 2 and this volume of this series, i.e. the proposed interpretation of the Qur'anic revelation's view on the sources of religious knowledge and its view on law, respectively.

Furthermore, about what already has been addressed in Volume 1—of the unique characteristics of the proposed interpretation of the Qur'anic revelation—I list the main features to be: The message of the Qur'an constituted a call to believe in the one and only God, to fulfill His code of ethics and worship, *al-islam*, and not to be divided. Those who believe in God and the last day (true believers)—irrespective of the scripture they follow; who abide by the Code; who perform acts of worship and do good in their lifetime would be rewarded in the afterlife an abode in Paradise. The Qur'an tells us that true believers are not to impose (coerce) what they believe on others,

70

nor are they to impose the Code on others. All beings will return to God; God will be the judge.

God's code of ethics and worship takes center stage in the Qur'an. This code, *al-islam*, is in harmony with the higher eternal human nature. It provides universal moral principles that guide human behavior. Moreover, it tells us how God is to be worshiped. The Qur'an affirmed the Code to be the basis for life and judgment on the last day. It also purified the Code from any alterations that had been made to it by men who falsely attributed such alterations to God.

The Qur'an called all believers in God back to the way of Abraham. It called to bring together all those who chose the same path to God: it called for the encompassing of all those who followed the same path to God regardless of the revealed scripture they followed. This is what I have referred to as the inclusive quality of the Qur'anic message. Yet the Qur'an did not call all believers in God to have a single religion. It did not require the followers of the previous scriptures who accepted the Qur'anic revelation to abandon their religious affiliations.

The Qur'an brought together the followers of the different revealed scriptures. It declared food and marriage permissible amongst the Monotheists. Those who accepted the revelation from the peoples of previous scriptures maintained their religious identities; nevertheless, aside from accepting the belief system of the Qur'an (the five articles of faith), accepting the revelation brought about significant changes to their practices.

The Qur'an's call to follow the way of Prophet Abraham was a call to return to the origins—that too applied to dietary restrictions and acts of worship. For those who accepted the revelation from the peoples of previous scriptures, their dietary restrictions would have become the same as those of the QMonotheists: no dietary restrictions beyond the four divine prohibitions. The observance of the Sabbath was also lifted. Moreover, these peoples were to give the *zakat* (20% of income), as did the QMonotheists, directly to Prophet Muhammad and not to the religious leaders of their respective communities.*1 Other rites would have continued to be observed as per each scripture.

In conclusion, I see—as supported by the findings of the proposed interpretation of the Qur'anic revelation—all three major monotheistic religions, Judaism, Christianity, and Islam, as we know them today, to deviate from the essence of God's revelations. The proposed interpretation of the Qur'anic revelation can be seen as bringing reform to these monotheistic religions.

We now proceed to the stance of the proposed interpretation of the Qur'anic revelation on law. Chapters 5 through 9 introduce this understanding about law. Furthermore, Islamic law and its relationship to Traditional Islam is explored.

NOTE*1: In the Qur'an *sadaqat* (giving) took two forms: obligatory giving (the *zakat*; 20% of income) and voluntary giving.

My understanding of the Qur'anic term *al-zakat*, a technical term describing the amount of obligatory giving due, to represent 20% of income is not how Traditional Islam understands the amount due by obligatory giving. The Qur'anic terms *sadaqat* and *zakat* are discussed in Volume 1 of this series.

Obligatory giving in the space-time of the Qur'anic revelation after the capture of Mecca—due on Monotheists living in a Monotheist state—could be pictured as modern-day income tax that was due on nationals living in a nation-state—where the nation is defined in terms of religious following, in this case, Monotheism. A good portion of the proceeds of the *zakat* would be spent on social causes; it would also cover state related expenses of administrative and military nature.

On the other hand, Islamic law declared the *zakat* to be paid by a Muslim individual to depend on the type of asset (different percentages applied). For example, speaking in general terms since there are numerous interpretations of Islamic law: For money, the *zakat* due was 2.5% on assets continuously owned over one year that are in excess of a minimum monetary value. Thus, aside from the significantly reduced rate of 2.5%, for money, the *zakat*, according to Islamic law, was not due on total income beyond a certain threshold, but rather, it was due on savings that surpass a certain threshold during the past year.

5. Islamic law: A case study

The proposed interpretation of the Qur'anic revelation does not see religion to be the source of law, but rather, it sees religion to be a source of ethics. It sees that any acceptable interpretation of religion that is based on revealed scripture should have no law component. It rejects religious law altogether and calls for the implementation of secular law. In consequence, the proposed interpretation of the Qur'anic revelation would be redefining the role of religion and its domain of operation.

It has been proposed earlier that the composition of any Qur'anic-based interpretation of religion reflects the injunction categories of eternal applicability of the associated classification of the Qur'anic injunctions (Q.I. classification). Therefore, to justify that the interpretation of religion associated with the proposed Q.I. classification should not have a law component, we need to verify that the proposed Q.I. classification's Action-Type II category of injunctions does not have eternal applicability.

Starting with this chapter, Islamic law will be used as the vehicle to study the eternal applicability of the Action-Type II injunctions of the Qur'an and the *Hadith*. This is facilitated since the action injunctions of the Qur'an and the *Hadith* are the primary sources of Islamic law.

Islamic law constitutes a crucial component in any of the classical and dominant interpretations of Islam, a component that has shaped all interpretations of Islam. Besides the objective stated above to study Islamic law, the study of Islamic law serves the purpose of allowing the reader to gain a better understanding of this component that has long shaped the various interpretations of Islam. It will allow the reader to understand how man has influenced and still influences the interpretations of Islam.

In the study of Islamic law, we will examine: Islamic law from a cause and effect perspective; the religious legitimacy of Islamic law; the concept of eternality; arguments to reject the eternal applicability of the Qur'anic Action-Type II injunctions; Islamic law's two components; along with introducing the approach to be adopted in the next two chapters to reject both components of Islamic law.

5.1 Terminology: Islamic law versus the *Shari'a* and *Fiqh*

What is of principal interest to us in this book is to understand the relationship between religion and the making of law: religion as a source of law. But before we get to that, we need to understand some basic terminology and what is what.

To begin with, we need to understand the difference between what we understand law to be today and the term Islamic law—putting aside any associated religious connotations. Let me start by defining what I mean by "law" today. We understand (Western) law, today, in its generic sense, to be "a body of rules of action or conduct prescribed by controlling authority, and having binding legal force." (Black et al. 1979, 795)

We need to keep in mind that the modern era is the era of the modern state. The concept of the modern state (and its systems) has affected how we perceive and understand numerous other concepts that have existed in the past to organize society. Therefore, to superimpose our modern understanding of law on the legal culture of Islam would simply not be very helpful if we really seek to understand.

It was not until recent history that what is commonly called Islamic law was prescribed by a controlling authority (the state or its representatives), and had binding legal force. In pre-modern times, the Muslim state was not involved in the making of law (legal authority was held independently from the state), and the body of law of the legal culture of Islam—if we can call it that—did not have binding legal force. The body of law of a particular school of jurisprudence, basically, served as a juristic guide for the judge. Furthermore, this body of law so-to-speak was not codified. It was not until a judge—who was never involved in the making of the law—made a verdict on a case that the ruling was binding (and only) to the parties involved.

In the following subsections we will look into how the term Islamic law relates to the terms *Shari'a* and *Fiqh*. And what the terms *Shari'a* and *Fiqh* represent, today and in the past.

5.1.1 On Islamic law

We hear the term *Shari'a* used a lot. To many it represents Islamic law. To many the *Shari'a* represents (is imagined to be) a uniform, comprehensive, and codified body of law that is the same wherever it is applied (constant over space), and which has been the same over the centuries (constant over time). Most also equate the *Shari'a* with another Arabic term, *Fiqh*; both understood to mean and to represent the same thing. But is any of this accurate? First, the *Shari'a* is not Islamic law, neither is *Fiqh*. Second, the *Shari'a* is not *Fiqh*.

Before we get to what the *Shari'a* and *Fiqh* are, let us look into that which I have claimed they are not: neither of them is Islamic law. But what is this Islamic law, and what does this book mean when using the term Islamic law?

I find the term Islamic law to be rather problematic even from a linguistic point of view, or as put by Hallaq (2005b, 151–152), the term poses a linguistic predicament. Hallaq (2005b, 152) states: "[T]he very use of the word law is a priori problematic, for to use it is to project, if not superimpose, on the legal culture of Islam notions saturated with the conceptual specificity of nation-state law, a punitive and surveillance-oriented law that by comparison to Islam's jural forms, lacks (note the reversal) the determinant moral imperative." Hallaq (2005b, 153) goes on to say: "'Islamic law' almost never signifies a geography or a material-institutional culture but a religion, a religious culture, a religious law, a religious civilization, or an irrationality (hence the presumed 'irrational nature' of this law). By the rules of linguistic entailment, therefore, the 'religious' emerges as oppositional to such concepts as 'rationalism' and, more starkly, 'secularism'. In other words, the very utterance of the word 'religious' speaks of the absence of the secular and the rational. With this essence-based, yet language-driven, conception of 'Islamic law', the emphasis would continue to be on the religious, irrational and un-secular 'nature' of 'Islamic law', and much less on how it functioned in social contexts, and what its 'religiosity' practically meant to the actors involved in its production, application, and reception."

As problematic as I find the term Islamic law to be, yet it is the term I will use to depict what Islamic law has become commonly accepted to represent: the body of law of the legal culture of Islam. Furthermore, in examining Islamic law, I have assumed Islamic law (the body of) to be a uniform and comprehensive body of law.

NOTICE: In more accurate terms, today, Islamic law is perceived to be codified. And the term Islamic law is perceived as to represent the codified version of the uniform and comprehensive body of law of the legal culture of Islam.

As stated in Chapter 1, for the purposes of our analysis, I have assumed the existence of a uniform body of law that represents the general consensus of all schools of jurisprudence (and modern realizations of Islamic law). Though, such existence is fictitious from a reality perspective, since there are numerous schools of jurisprudence each with its own interpretation of Islamic law (the same applies to the modern realizations of Islamic law). Consensus on every point of law never existed among the different schools of jurisprudence (inter-school consensus), nor did it exist within the bodies of law of the schools themselves (intra-school consensus): within each school's body of law we find pluralist views on different points of law (non-codified body of law).

Furthermore, none of the classical bodies of law of the various schools of jurisprudence constitutes a comprehensive body of law, since with changing space-time new problems arise that the classical bodies of law did. not address. Accordingly, new space-time dependent (Islamic) laws are required to be developed on an on-going basis in line with the principles of each school of jurisprudence (its doctrinal legal methodology, positive legal principles, and hermeneutics). Yet in modern times, we find bodies of law that are not based on the principles of only one of the classical schools of law, and on numerous issues they do not even follow the principles of any of the classical schools. Most of the newly developed Islamic law falls into this category. This applies to the interpretations of law of the numerous contemporary groups, movements, and states.

In the following sections and chapters, whenever the term Islamic law is used, it is a uniform and comprehensive interpretation of Islamic law (the body of) that is implied unless explicitly stated otherwise. Moreover, in modern times, Islamic law is perceived, or rather is imagined, by most Muslims and non-Muslims alike to be codified. Hence, whenever codified Islamic law is assumed, I will use the term "codified Islamic law" in reference to a codified version of the abovementioned uniform and comprehensive interpretation of Islamic law.

Chapters 6 and 7 thoroughly address how the terms *Shari'a* and *Fiqh*, as this book uses these terms, fit in with our study of Islamic law. Nonetheless, the following two subsections discuss the pre-modern conception of *Shari'a* and its transformation. I discuss this matter for the reader to be aware of the transformation that has come upon pre-modern *Fiqh* and its application. I hope this brief introduction, even in its succinct form, serves to demonstrate how politics, in this case, initially through colonialism and later—and ongoing—through the modern state, has affected the religion of Islam (particularly the conception of *Shari'a*).

I find the work of Wael B. Hallaq, a leading scholar of Islamic law and Islamic intellectual history, in the field of the study of *Fiqh* to be intriguing. In the following two subsections I make additional reference to the earlier cited article by Hallaq, "what is *Shari'a*?" In this article Hallaq (2005b) discussed the historical and transformative impact of colonialism on *Fiqh* and its application. Hallaq explored the profound transformations and challenges faced by the pre-modern conception of the *Shari'a*, particularly *Fiqh*, due to the impact of colonialism, modernization, and entexting, which ultimately led to reshaping the nature and function of pre-modern *Fiqh*.

5.1.2 *Shari'a* and *Fiqh*: The pre-modern conception

To begin with, we need to understand, in general terms, what Traditional Islam means by the terms *Shari'a* and *Fiqh*. The *Shari'a* refers to the divine law derived directly from the Qur'an and the *Sunna* (originating from the primary sources). It encompasses not only legal principles but also moral and ethical guidelines. *Fiqh*, on the other hand, is a human effort to comprehend and apply the divine principles of *Shari'a*. It is the human endeavor to understand and interpret the *Shari'a*, translating divine principles into specific legal rules and ethical guidance. The *Shari'a* sets the moral and legal framework, while *Fiqh* addresses specific legal issues, rulings, and methodologies for legal interpretation.

Hallaq (2005b) discussed the challenges in representing and understanding the pre-modern conception of the *Shari'a*, i.e. pre-modern *Fiqh* and its application. This was the era prior to when modernity and colonialism had impact on Muslim legal systems.

Hallaq rejected the notion that the pre-modern conception of the *Shari'a* can be fully grasped through modern conceptual and linguistic frameworks. The pre-modern conception of the *Shari'a*, according to Hallaq's account, can be described to be a complex and multifaceted concept that encompassed various aspects of legal, moral, social, cultural, and institutional dimensions. The pre-modern conception of the *Shari'a* was not confined to a fixed set of legal texts but was a comprehensive system embedded in dynamic socio-legal relations within diverse social, moral, and cultural contexts.

Fiqh in the pre-modern era, according to Hallaq (2005b), served as a legal and jurisprudential framework that is characterized by dynamism, diversity, and adaptability to diverse social, cultural, and geographical contexts. It was a comprehensive system that aimed to maintain social order, justice, and moral balance within the Muslim community.

Fiqh encouraged intellectual diversity and recognized different legal interpretations. Within the framework of *Fiqh*, there existed numerous schools of jurisprudence, and within each school, we find multiple legal opinions on specific issues. This flexibility was crucial for adapting to the diverse social, moral, and cultural exigencies within the Muslim world. Legal decisions addressing legal issues were a result of a dynamic process of understanding and interpreting the principles of the school doctrine within specific socio-cultural contexts. This flexibility and adaptability resulted in context-specific legal decisions that allowed for a nuanced approach to legal issues. Legal decisions aimed to ensure social harmony and the well-being of the community by addressing legal matters within the broader context of community values, adapting to local conditions, and allowing for a diversity of opinions in the pursuit of justice and moral well-being (151–168).

For insights on the nature of pre-modern *Fiqh*, I quote Hallaq (2005b, 168):

> It would be [a mistake] to equate *fiqh* with law in the sense we use this term in modern contexts. *Fiqh* was a process of understanding, which is what the Arabic term literally and lexically means and what its technical and professional corollary implies; it was the study (*ishtighal*) and intellectual engagement (*tahqiq, tanqih*) of the school doctrine, intended to understand all possible ways (*aqwal*) of reasoning on, and interpretation of, a particular case. It was not the case that was important, but rather

the principle illustrated by the case as well as other cases which constituted an illustration of how the principle is to be defined, delimited, refined, articulated, restricted, and, very importantly, distinguished from another group of cases that yield another cognate principle, and yet not allowed to overlap with another. It was the principle (*asl*; pl. *usul*) of the *fiqh* which mattered, not the individual cases and opinions, which were more illustrative than prescriptive. Individual opinions, strictly speaking, did not constitute law in the sense modernity forces us to understand either "law" or "case law", nor was it the "legal effect" of stating the will of a sovereign that the Muslim jurists intended to accomplish in the first place. Their law was an interpretive project, not "a body of rules of action or conduct prescribed by [a] controlling authority". It was not a "solemn expression of the will of the supreme power of the state", for there was no state in the first place. It was the intellectual and hermeneutical work of private individuals, jurists whose claim to authority was primarily epistemic, but also religious and moral. It was not political in the modern sense of the word, and it did not involve coercive or state power.

Furthermore, the law was not an abstraction. It did not apply equally to "all", for individuals were not seen as equal to each other. Each individual and circumstance was deemed unique, requiring *ijtihad* that was context-specific. This explains why Islam never accepted the notion of blind justice, which also explains why there was no point in *stating* the law *in the sense* we see in today's legal codes. Rather, the law was an *ijtihad*ic process; a continuously renewed exercise in hermeneutics; an effort at mustering principles *as located in life-situations*; a mission requiring the legists to do what is right in a particular moment of human existence. The *fiqh*, even in its most detailed and comprehensive accounts, was no more tha[n] a juristic guide that directed the judge and all legal officers on the ground to resolve a situation in due consideration of the unique facts involved therein. The *fiqh* as a *shar'i* manifestation, as a fully realised and realisable "law", would not be revealed until the jural principles meshed with social reality and until the dialectic of all human, social, moral, material, and other types of relations involved in a particular case was to come to full circle.

(The second set of square brackets, the "[a]" in the citation above, appears in the original.)

5.1.3 The conceptualization of *Shar'ia* in the modern era

Today we find the Arabic terms *Shari'a* and *Fiqh* to be commonly depicted in English as Islamic law. To understand what the term "Islamic law" represents and how it came to be we need to go back in history.

Hallaq (2003) argues that in the pre-modern era, for over a millennium, *Fiqh* and its application represented a manifestation of self-governing. The state was not the carrier of legal authority—or strictly speaking, legal power. However, juristic sovereignty was something that the modern-state required and won, which in turn led to the demise of *Fiqh* as Muslims knew it and lived it until about two centuries ago. With the advent of the modern nation-state in Muslim societies there has been a transformation of legal authority. In the modern nation-state we find a fundamental reversal of principles, where the traditional arrangement in which legal authority rested with jurists (*faqaha'*, singular *faqih*), gives way to the nation-state's assertion of the authority to dictate and shape legal norms. The state's legislative interference, centralization of legal control, and adoption of codification are significant departures from the traditional separation of legal and political authority. This shift represents the loss of epistemic authority by religious scholars and the rise of state-dominated legal power (243–258).

The transformation of the pre-modern conception of *Shari'a*, according to Hallaq (2005b)*1, began in the late eighteenth century CE with the colonial interventions in regions like British India. The British colonial authorities initiated a process of entexting, where certain Muslim legal texts were translated, codified, and restructured according to European legal frameworks.*2 This transformation severed *Fiqh* from its traditional socio-epistemic foundations, stripping it of its dynamic and context-specific nature. Moreover, the colonial authorities imposed their own legal and administrative structures, replacing indigenous systems of governance and justice with European models. As a result, the traditional role of figures like jurists and judges in interpreting and applying *Shari'a* was marginalized, and the authority to define and enforce law was consolidated in the hands of colonial administrators. This transformation marked the demise of the traditional *Fiqh* as it was known and practiced for centuries, replacing it with a colonial legal regime that served the interests of imperial powers rather than the needs of local communities. Moreover, this transformation reflects broader colonial ambitions to reshape colonized societies in ways that served colonial interests while simultaneously eroding indigenous autonomy and identity.

These imposed changes by the colonial authorities not only affected legal practices but also had far-reaching and permanent impact on the nature and practice of *Fiqh*, along with broader cultural and epistemic implications.

By isolating and extracting legal rules from their interpretive and socio-epistemic contexts, the term "Islamic law" came to be associated with a fixed and unchanging set of rules, divorced from the diverse interpretive traditions and social complexities within Muslim societies (151–176).

As for Muslim-majority states, (also) until modernity, *Fiqh* was neither codified nor was it under the control of the ruling powers. The initial attempts by a Muslim state to codify and promulgate selected parts of *Fiqh* as law, that aligned with a single school of jurisprudence (in this instance, the Hanafi school), began in the nineteenth century CE under the Ottomans, taking the form of codifications based on civil law—in contrast to British India that started in the late eighteenth century CE and was in the form of common law.

Furthermore, according to Anderson (1966, 244–246), the first example in Muslim history of codification that did not necessarily depict the (dominant) opinion of a single school of law (the Hanafi school in this case), was the codification and promulgation of the law of "obligations" (contract, tort, etc.) of the Hanfi school by the Ottomans in 1876 CE.

NOTE*1: In the article "What is *Shari'a*?" Hallaq (2005b) provided a critical examination of the colonial legacy on Islamic legal traditions and the broader socio-political implications of colonialism on Muslim societies. Hallaq discussed how colonialism, particularly in the context of British rule in India, profoundly transformed the pre-modern conception of *Shari'a* and paved the way for the emergence of the modern nation-state. He highlights how colonial powers imposed European legal systems like Anglo-Muhammadan law, eroded traditional sources of legal authority, and fundamentally altered the relationship between law, society, and state. This process, starting in the late eighteenth century CE, involved entexting Islamic legal doctrine, detaching it from its socio-epistemic foundations, and integrating it into European-style legal frameworks. Through the use of cultural technologies of colonialism, colonial authorities fundamentally altered the legal landscape, leading to the decline of traditional *Fiqh* and the establishment of codified, bureaucratic legal systems aimed at state control and social engineering. These transformations had far-reaching implications for the legal, social, and political landscapes of Muslim-majority countries, as they transitioned into modern nation-states influenced by European legal frameworks and cultural paradigms imposed during colonial rule. The remnants of Islamic legal thought, now enshrined in the civil codes of modern Muslim-majority countries, are characterized as a distorted version lacking the vitality and adaptability of their predecessors.

NOTE*2: Entexting in this context is the process of extracting *Fiqh* from its socio-epistemic foundations and transforming it into a detached, codified genre—thus altering its original function and significance. This was done through taking legal concepts out of their original interpretive and commentarial traditions, and turning them into fixed, written texts (systematized into a legal code). This, in essence, turned *Fiqh* into a tool for social engineering within the bureaucratic state.

This entexting process was facilitated by colonial powers like the British, who sought to impose their own legal frameworks and institutions onto colonized societies. By codifying *Fiqh* into a standardized textual format, colonial authorities could more effectively control and administer legal systems according to their own norms and principles, rather than those of the indigenous populations.

5.2 Scope of study

When discussing Islamic law, this work tackles Islamic law's components and sources that involve man-world affairs. In more exact terms, the scope is limited to examining the Action-Type II injunctions of the Qur'an and the *Hadith* and the laws extracted directly and indirectly from them. This work does not address the Action-Type I injunctions of the Qur'an and the *Hadith* and the laws extracted directly and indirectly from them.

From here onwards, any usage of the term "primary sources" will denote the Action-Type II injunctions of the Qur'an and the *Hadith*, unless explicitly stated otherwise. And any reference to Islamic law will only relate to its components that deal with the worldly realm.

5.3 The dilemma caused by Islamic law and its consequences

5.3.1 Islamic law is more than a legal code

The interpretations of Islamic law are represented by the works produced by the various schools of jurisprudence, any of which tackles issues related to all aspects of human existence that go far beyond what a legal code is expected to cover (civil and penal codes, among other areas of law).

Traditional Islam considers Islamic law to be a way of life—it addresses both ethical standards and legal rules. This has had a profound role in shaping individual and collective identities. According to Traditional Islam, besides the spiritual and ethical roles that religion plays in a Muslim's life, religion is considered to be the source of all laws. As a result, Islamic law is not confined to matters of religious worship and ethics, but its scope extends to cover all worldly matters, including but not limited to matters related to living things, nonliving things, tangible and intangible products of man, systems (such as legal, political, economic), etc.

NOTICE: In this work I use the term "body of law" in referring to the works produced by the various schools of jurisprudence. This is because this work is primarily concerned with the law component of these works (involving man-world affairs), and this is what is being referred to by "body of law." However, it is acknowledged that the scope of these works covered more than law.

Traditional Islam considers Islamic law as the spectacles through which Islam is to be observed; in other words, Traditional Islam considers Islamic law a manifestation of what Islam is perceived to be. To demonstrate, Islamic law, as Traditional Islam sees it, can be modeled in three-dimensional space as consisting of two components, each operating in a separate plane. A vertical component operating in the vertical plane—representing the relationship between man and God; and a horizontal component operating in the horizontal plane—representing the relationship between man and the world around him. Islamic law can be viewed as the link that connects man (regulates the relationship of), in each of these planes, with God and the world, respectively. From this representation, it can be seen that Traditional Islam considers Islamic law to operate in both planes, hence, having two components. Traditional Islam has further considered Islamic law's components in both these planes to be eternally applicable, i.e. it assumes an unbreakable link.*1

The proposed interpretation of the Qur'anic revelation does not accept religious law to have a component in the horizontal plane far beyond the space-time of the revelation, and only sees religious law to operate in the vertical plane (pertaining to acts of worship). The proposed interpretation recognizes the role religion plays in the horizontal plane to be that of guidance rather than regulation: a role for ethics not law. And it sees ethics (represented in the Code), not Islamic law, to be the link that connects man with the world (guides the relationship of).

NOTE*1: The representation of Islamic law as two components operating in three-dimensional space is a metaphorical representation of the relationships of man (the regulation of). It demonstrates the role of religion in a Muslim's life by visualizing how religion relates man to the creator on one hand and to the creation on another. This model does not attempt, nor does it suggest in any way, to confine our understanding of God or to limit it in space.

5.3.2 The effect on the Muslim individual

At the individual's level, Muslims in modern times are faced with a dilemma when it comes to law. What law is suitable for modern times? When answering this question, Muslims are unable to reconcile the inner conflict that they experience due to the difference between the answer given by Traditional Islam and what they have come to believe from living in the fifteenth century after the first revelations of the Qur'an.*1

Modern-day Muslims become in conflict when they refuse to blindly follow what they are told by the supporters of Traditional Islam: Muslims are told that they must only accept legal systems based on Islamic law.

Modern-day Muslims are told time and time again that they are religiously obligated to accept and follow Islamic law across space-time. They are told so by the obligatory Islamic religious education they receive in school, by the religious authorities/representatives in their communities and the media, and even by the state in Muslim-majority countries that implement any form of Islamic law in their systems. However, the message varies, as to what extent of Islamic law they are to accept and follow—whether it is just in private life or is it also to include public life. The message also varies as to which interpretation of Islamic law is to be followed.

NOTE*1: It is believed that the first verses of the Qur'an were revealed around 610 CE.

Side note 5.1 Traditional Islam is not the Qur'an

An example of the dilemma caused by Islamic law (and/or legal codes based on) can be seen when considering the following issues—that although derived from the Qur'an (interpretation of), most Muslims do not find acceptable or applicable in current times: slavery (not prohibited), *slb* (crucifixion) as a form of punishment, and two women's testimony to be equal to the testimony of a single man.

There are those who point out that not every Muslim will find accepting slavery, crucifixion, or the testimony of two women to be equal to the testimony of a single man as absurd or morally unacceptable. Yes, for sure not every Muslim will. Yet the majority, if asked such questions directly (outside or away from religion), will not find any of the mentioned issues acceptable. Muslims, who currently accept such issues, say that they do so because it is written in the Qur'an. In saying that, they are making two assumptions. First, they assume everything in the Qur'an to apply across space-time. Second, they assume Islamic law's interpretation about the issue mentioned in the Qur'an to align with what the Qur'an was saying in regard to the issue.

Accepting everything written in the Qur'an to be eternally applicable is merely a proposition forwarded by Traditional Islam. One should keep in mind that Traditional Islam is not necessarily correct in such a claim. And any proposition should be weighed against reason. It must be made clear that Traditional Islam is not the Qur'an: Traditional Islam is a religion based on an interpretation of the Qur'anic revelation. The same principle applies to all other claims made by Traditional Islam, including its interpretations on issues mentioned in the Qur'an. Just as with any interpretation, these interpretations are not necessarily correct. And any claim should be weighed against reason.

This work will show the implications of not accepting the views of Traditional Islam on the abovementioned issues. It puts forward an alternative interpretation of the Qur'anic revelation where not everything in the Qur'an is accepted to be eternally applicable. As a result, the proposed interpretation does not accept slavery, crucifixion, and that the testimony of two women is equal to the testimony of a single man (which by the way is an Islamic law legal rule and was not directly stated in the Qur'an—as noted in Chapter 6), in addition to not accepting many other issues that Traditional Islam takes for granted.

Side note 5.2 Muslim-majority countries

As of 2010, there are 49 countries where Muslims constitute over 50% of the population (Pew Research Center. and Pew Forum on Religion & Public Life. 2011, 26).

It is to be noted that the statistics about the percentage of Muslims in the so-called Muslim-majority countries do not reflect data about practicing Muslims. Nor do they even represent data about those who identify as Muslims. These figures represent statistics about individuals categorized as Muslims by the countries in which they reside.

5.3.3 The effect on society in Muslim-majority countries

Law adopted by Muslim-majority countries is a reflection of the different approaches undertaken to tackle the dilemma encountered by the Muslim individual. There are Muslim-majority countries that have all-secular or all-religious legal systems (some of which lack a codified legal system), with all-secular or all-religious legal codes in place, respectively. And there are Muslim-majority countries whose legal codes are more or less a mix of laws from both religious and secular sources (Anderson 1959, 17–37, 81–100), what can be described as mixed legal codes, in which all law is codified.

In the Muslim-majority countries that adopt mixed legal codes, law is based entirely on secular law, but to some extent with a special flavor from Islamic law. Proponents of mixed legal codes consider them to be based on interpretations of Islamic law that are most suitable for modern times ('Ashmawi 1996, 15–44)—such mixed legal codes can be regarded as products of liberal interpretations of Islamic law.

The Islamic law flavor described to be present in the mixed legal codes can be best observed in cases involving death or injury. In such cases, according to Islamic law, the victim or his legal representative is directly involved in the legal process (specifics vary: he has the choice to legally pardon and/or is entitled to receive material compensation, *diyya*). In modern-day Muslim-majority countries that have mixed legal codes, when it comes to cases involving death or injury, the Islamic law flavor is manifested in their legal codes in that victims (or legal representatives) are allowed to waive their personal rights in such cases, yet the prosecution is still allowed to charge the offenders for violating public rights. However, in Muslim-majority countries with mixed legal codes, when it comes to family law or what is known as personal status issues (which covers matters such as marriage, divorce, child custody, adoption, and inheritance), law in the family category is still based entirely on Islamic law, and is applied solely on Muslim citizens.

Through tying the application of Islamic law to religion, there are those who argue that since Muslims believe abiding by Islamic law to be part of religion, then no legal system other than that based on Islamic law should be adopted. This is the argument that religious political parties use in an attempt to convince the Muslim public to adopt all-religious legal systems. Some even reject having codified legal systems.

Similarly, some radical religious movements use the same argument, but add to it—besides calling for more conservative interpretations of Islamic law—that not only is it a religious obligation to implement an all-religious legal system, but (religion through Islamic law also dictates) that such an implementation should be within a religion-based political system. These radical movements claim that a caliphate-like system is what should be in place, despite the fact that beyond the time of the Prophet the Qur'an did not specify any particular type of political system that should be followed.

In a way, the argument reduces to be more or less of an argument on what each party considers to be an acceptable interpretation of Islamic law, and to what extent Islamic law should be implemented (solely in the legal system or in all systems). From this perspective, Islamic law is the window (to power) used to get through to the hearts and minds of the Muslim populations. Both in non-violent and violent forms, these religion-based parties/movements can be described as advocating Islamism, the belief that politics is an extension of the faith.

NOTE: In Muslim-majority countries, the transition from the pre-modern conception of *Shari'a* to state-dominated legal power and modern legal systems has profoundly impacted the Muslim community's perception and experience of law, emphasizing challenges such as alienation from cultural and religious heritage, erosion of trust in the legal system, and questions regarding the compatibility of state-imposed laws with Islamic values (Hallaq 2003). I would say this applies regardless of the extent to which Islamic law is incorporated into the legal system (the modern state remains to be the carrier of legal authority in contrast to pre-modern times).

Side note 5.3 The impact of Islamic law on Muslim communities and societies

The impact of Islamic law on Muslim communities and societies is rooted well into the cultures of the people, and it involves all aspects of life. Legislative reform at the state level is but a first step towards any reform. The sought reform is one that would influence religious thinking and the role of religion in a Muslim's life.

According to al-Nuwayhi (2010), the Ottomans (1299–1922 CE) in the mid-nineteenth century CE started the trend of secularization of law in response to arising circumstances in which the adopted religious legal system at the time was incapable of handling. From then on, this trend continued in [numerous] Arab countries. [Certainly, this was not the case for all Arab countries, since a minority of Arab countries to this day remains to have religious legal systems in place.]

The Ottomans initially started their legislative reform by incorporating law from secular sources into the commercial and criminal areas of law, which later followed into other areas. However, Islamic law was maintained to be the basis for law dealing with family matters or what is called personal status issues (165). As of January 1, 2007, there are 22 countries in the Arab league (League of Arab States), all of which are Muslim-majority countries (Wikipedia 2007). The combined population of Muslims in these countries forms about 20% of the global Muslim population.

The Ottomans move was surely a step in the right direction, but one that was rather late. To demonstrate the vast influence of Islamic law on Muslim societies, I cite as an example the effect of law on one such aspect of society, its economy. Kuran (2011) studied the economic ramifications of adopting Islamic law in the Middle East, and argues that the long adoption of Islamic law in these countries reflected negatively on their economies, and is the reason behind the economic underdevelopment of Middle Eastern countries in current times. Kuran (2011, book flap) states, "starting around the tenth century [CE], Islamic legal institutions, which had benefited the Middle Eastern economy in the early centuries of Islam, began to act as a drag on development by slowing or blocking the emergence of central features of modern economic life--including private capital accumulation, corporations, large-scale production, and impersonal exchange. By the nineteenth century [CE], modern economic institutions began to be transplanted to the Middle East, but its economy has not caught up."

Side note 5.4 What is *diyya* (material compensation for death or bodily injury)?

Al-Fawzan (2005) describes *diyya* (plural *diyyat*) to be a specified amount of compensation—depending on harm inflicted—paid to the victim or his legal representative as legal compensation (Q. 2:178–179, 4:92–93). According to Islamic law, *diyya* varies according to the victim's religion, sex, and legal status (free or slave); *diyya* could be pardoned partially or completely. Islamic law identifies the following situations to require *diyya*:

- Pre-meditated murder

If the offender is pardoned rather than killed in *qisas* (retaliation in kind—as per the orthodox interpretation of the word), then *diyya* is paid directly from the offender's own wealth.

- Quasi pre-meditated murder (kill when initially having the intention to cause harm rather than death) and manslaughter (kill although having no intention to harm or kill—also applies to crimes committed by the insane and minors)

No *qisas* (retaliation in kind) in this case. However, *diyya* is paid by the offender's agnate relatives, *al-'aqila* (his supporters and backers, which includes all male relatives from his father's side, the *'usba*: father and sons, brothers and their sons, uncles and their sons, father's uncles and their sons, grandfather's uncles and their sons). [Not all schools of jurisprudence include father and sons in *al-'aqila*. Additionally, some schools of jurisprudence require the offender to pay with *al-'aqila*]. Otherwise, if the offender has no *'usba* then *diyya* is paid from the Muslims' house of wealth (*bayt al-mal*). If there is none, then the offender is obligated to pay himself.

Expiation (*kaffara*) is required in this case, but is the responsibility of the offender. Expiation is either in the form of emancipation of a believing slave, or in the form of fasting two consecutive months in repentance.

■ Non-fatal injuries in parts of body and wounds—covers body organs, senses or functions, wounds and fractures

[As to whether *qisas* (retaliation in kind) is required or not, schools of jurisprudence differ. Some schools differentiate based on intention, while others do not, and consider all such crimes worthy of *qisas*.] Those who differentiate require *qisas* only in cases when pre-meditated harm was inflicted; otherwise, only *diyya* would be required. However, in all situations when *qisas* is required, if pardoned, then *diyya* is paid instead of *qisas*. As for the party obligated to pay *diyya*, the situation is similar to who is obliged to pay *diyya* in cases of crimes leading to death (2: 515–577).

Regarding the above Islamic law interpretation of *diyya*, the tribe or clan when obligated to pay *diyya* can be viewed to play two roles: The tribe is acting as the counterpart of today's insurance companies; in addition to that, the tribe can be viewed to have a role in deterring violence. From the perspective of the offender's clan or tribe, the ones who pay (in) *diyya*, it is not of their best interest to keep on paying compensation because some members of the tribe choose to resort to violent measures when it comes to settling disputes. Therefore, it would be plausible to assume that the tribe would likely take measures to influence its members to change their ways (social impact against violence). The tribe would oblige its members to go for more civil measures to resolve disagreements, to choose arbitration.

The *diyya* in such a scenario reflects an unpleasant fact of life that remains to this day. For some, it is not right or wrong that would influence them to take action. For some, or probably for most people, it is only the financial consequences directly affecting their pockets that would move them to take action. Hence, as far as the tribe was concerned (the community in that space-time was but several tribes), besides the ethical implications and the reducing of harm effect, there would be an additional motivation to deter violence, one with financial consequences, the *diyya*.

If looking into historical reports, according to 'Ali (1993), *diyya* was already in practice in pre-Islamic Arabia, though with different standards for different communities: for the same offense different amounts were paid in compensation. Each community or sometimes even each tribe had its own standard for *diyya*. For example, Jewish communities of pre-Islamic Arabia applied *diyya* as did non-Jewish Arab communities; however, (apparently) with a different standard for each of the Jewish tribes (6: 534–535).

The reader is cautioned that the aforementioned interpretation of the Qur'anic penal code entry on loss of life and injuries is that of Islamic law, and it is my view that such an interpretation does not necessarily reflect what is stated in the Qur'an in this regard. Addressing the penal code of the Qur'an is beyond the scope of this book. However, it can be said that a *diyya* based solution for settling blood related disputes can be thought of as a bespoke solution designed specifically for clan-based societies (patriarchal clan systems): the whole extended family pitches in to pay *diyya*. Nowadays, even if considering only Muslim-majority states, society composition and structure, mostly, is not based on tribes—it is not tribal societies, as it was in the space-time of the Prophet.

Side note 5.5 A perspective on how *diyya* relates to Islamic law of inheritance

This side note presents the prevalent perspective of some Muslims who call for religious law reform regarding matters of inheritance. The perspective presents arguments for why the Islamic law of inheritance is no longer appropriate in current space-time.

Speaking about *diyya* opens up the opportunity to look into Islamic law of inheritance, which is one of the areas of Islamic law that is still being applied in most Muslim-majority countries with the exception of the Muslim-majority countries that have secular legal systems.

In trying to understand why the Qur'an differentiated in the fractional shares of inheritance between a woman and her male counterpart, al-Nuwayhi (2010) argues that in the space-time when the Qur'an was revealed, women did not have fixed inheritance rights. The Qur'an affirmed the right of women to inherit (Q. 4:7 in 4:7–14) and gave women fractional shares, though in most cases less than those of men (Q. 4:11–12 in 4:7–14, 4:176). For instance, [as per the orthodox interpretation,] a daughter's share would be half the fractional share of a son. This can be regarded as an attempt in the direction to improve the rights of women in society as best as possible in that space-time. Society in the time of the Prophet was that of tribal nature, where male kinship (*'usba*) played a role in the tribe's survival and prosperity. It was a time when men were obligated to provide beyond the usual financial responsibilities that one would expect in this day and time. Men had financial responsibilities towards their tribe, like in cases of collecting *diyya*, supporting allies, paying for tribal penalties, or when members of the tribe were in severe debt. In addition to fulfilling customs of honoring guests, taking care of neighbors, helping stranded travelers, and other situations. Whereas at that time, women were not expected to participate in these additional financial obligations. The higher a man's ranking in his tribe, the more obligations he carried. This describes the social environment of the particular space-time when the Qur'an was revealed (155–161).

Modern times, however, can be characterized as an era when men, in most if not all Muslim communities and societies, do not carry any of the extra financial burdens that were required by the tribal men of Arabia in the seventh century CE. Modern times can also be characterized as an era of women's economic empowerment, where the number of women entering the workforce is continuously on the rise. Globally, the gap between labor-force participation rates of women and men is narrowing (UNSD 2015). It is a time when dual-income households have become more of an economic necessity; in many households, it is even the women who are the breadwinners. In today's societies, we often find single-income households where women support the family financially, while men stay at home to care for the

90

children. Times have changed, alongside so have societies; therefore, Islamic law of inheritance should no longer be considered applicable in current space-time.

On the other hand, it is the view of the present author that the Qur'an's verses on fractional shares of inheritance related only to intestate succession in the space-time of the revelation. The reader is referred to side note 9.1 for more on this topic.

Furthermore, it is my view, that for Islam, it is total religious reform that ought to be sought and not to limit religious reform to religious law reform. The proposed interpretation of the Qur'anic revelation does not consider law to be a component of religion. It rejects religious law altogether and calls for the implementation of secular law. The topic of religious reform beyond religious law reform is discussed in Chapter 9.

5.3.4 The approach to resolve

The mere existence of religious law, or in more accurate terms, the acceptance that religious law has the right to exist is the reason behind the Muslim's dilemma of not knowing what law to follow. Moreover, Traditional Islam's considering Islamic law to be a way of life intensifies this dilemma: it has the authority to control all aspects of human life.

To some Muslims, the importance of Islamic law goes even further. In their eyes, Islamic law is Islam. To them, the interpretation of Islamic law that they follow overshadows all other components of their interpretation of religion. For some of these groups, their radical interpretations of Islamic law reflect ideologies that propagate violence and destruction. Such interpretations make it permissible for them to kill anyone who does not follow their same interpretation of Islamic law—Muslims and non-Muslims alike—or in some cases it even obliges such killings. Such interpretations of Islamic law oppose the Qur'an itself by obliterating the sacredness the Qur'an gives to the human life (Q. 4:29–31, 5:27–34, 6:151 in 6:151–153, 17:33 in 17:22–39, 25:68 in 25:63–77). To such (delusional) fanatics, in their understanding, it is Islam that instructs them to do so. It is God's law that orders it. Of course, there exists, and has existed throughout Muslim history scores of these groups, each of whom sees its own interpretation of Islamic law exclusively as the only correct manifestation of God's law. These fanatics do not differentiate between Islamic law and Islam; to them, it is one and the same thing. What they follow is the true Islam, the only Islam, all else is false.

The proposed interpretation of the Qur'anic revelation sees that the interpretation of religion associated with the proposed Q.I.

classification should not have a law component. It rejects religious law altogether and calls for the implementation of secular law. The study of Islamic law will help us realize that what is claimed to be eternal religious law is nothing but a man-made attempt to eternalize law originally produced for specific spaces and times. Understanding the non-eternal nature of Islamic law and all its sources will bring us to separate law from religion.

Armed with the understanding of the particulars of Islamic law, Muslims would as a result be able to identify, express, and act on their standpoints, guided by their moral principles and values, without confusion or fear of being in contradiction with archaic laws and regulations. Muslims would be able to put worldly matters in their proper perspective, and would be able to call them by their proper names. Matters that have been wrongfully associated with religion century after century would no longer be allowed to be associated with the Qur'an or with the legacy of the last of the prophets. They would be known for what they really are, and would be called by their actual names, such as inequality, customs, murder, politics, etc.

What qualifies as law for a Muslim is not a question that only concerns and affects the Muslim individual, but rather, it extends to society and even to humanity as a whole. Muslims are not limited to a race, ethnicity, or geographic location, and do not live in isolation, but interact and live in this world along with people of other faiths and beliefs. Muslims constitute around one-quarter of the world's population. What qualifies as law for a Muslim affects the choices that Muslims make when selecting or establishing systems (legal, political, economic, etc.) and legal codes within the countries in which they live. It even affects the policies and relations that their countries have with other countries. The notion that only Islamic law qualifies to be the basis for all laws that are to be accepted and followed by Muslims has been, and is still being used and abused for political as well as for other motives.

The proposed interpretation of the Qur'anic revelation not only resolves the inner conflict that the modern-day Muslim struggles with, but its effect also extends to resolve conflicts beyond the level of the Muslim individual. It works to tackle both violent and non-violent religious-oriented parties/movements that call and advocate for political systems that implement Islamic law (conservative/traditionalist; neomodernist; neorevavalist; or Islamist

92

often referred to as fundamentalist). Such voices need to be challenged in the same way that they approach the Muslim individual, and that is through religion. Muslims need to be convinced that states and religious-oriented parties/movements that base themselves partially or entirely on religious grounds—through claiming that they seek to uphold and implement the *Shari'a*—only do so from illusion, and do not have any religious justification whatsoever. Accordingly, Muslims are not religiously obligated to accept such ideologies, to any extent, once it has been made clear that there is no religious legitimacy or justification to their claims. Muslims would thus be free from being politicized by those who attempt to use religion as an excuse to gain or to maintain power. In the end, it is the Muslim individual who needs to be addressed and convinced by this thesis.

Side note 5.6 Muslims in % of world population

Muslims speak hundreds of languages and come from diverse ethnic backgrounds. In 2010, Muslims accounted for 23.4% of the estimated global population of 6.9 billion (Pew Research Center. and Pew Forum on Religion & Public Life. 2011, 13). This figure does not represent practicing Muslims, nor does it represent those who identify as Muslims. Rather, it represents individuals categorized as Muslims by the countries in which they reside.

5.4 Stating the problem

5.4.1 The religious legitimacy given to Islamic law

Traditional Islam religiously justifies the legitimacy of Islamic law and declares Islamic law mandatory by religion. The following depicts an approach that Traditional Islam uses to religiously justify the legitimacy of Islamic law:

■ Traditional Islam claims that only God has the right to legislate.

There have been several arguments made to support this claim, one of which can be pictured to go as follows: A Muslim believes in the oneness of God; there is no deity but God. A Muslim believes that God, who has no associates, is the only deity worthy of worship. It follows from believing in the oneness of God that no entity can share any of the rights owned by God. The right to be worshiped thus is exclusive to God. Traditional Islam claims that all man's actions in accordance with God's commands are in worship of God. And since only God gets to dictate (command) how He is to be worshiped, it is concluded that only God has the right to legislate.

■ Traditional Islam considers the Action-Type II injunctions of the Qur'an and the *Hadith* to constitute God's eternal law.

REMINDER: As stated in Section 5.2 (scope of study), in the study of Islamic law, the term "primary sources" denotes the Action-Type II injunctions of the Qur'an and the *Hadith*.

■ Islamic law is law that is derived directly and indirectly from God's eternal law, i.e. the primary sources.

▶ Islamic law considers the Qur'an to be a primary source of law.

▶ Islamic law considers the Prophet's *Sunna* to be a primary source of law—often to explain, restrict, or to expand on the Qur'an. This was mainly due to interpreting verses of the Qur'an commanding the QMonotheists to obey God's Messenger as commands from God directing followers of the Qur'an to follow the Prophet's *Sunna* (Q. 4:59 in 4:59–70, 4:80 in 4:71–84, 24:51–52 and 24:54 in 24:46–57, 59:7 in 59:1–10). However, historically, not all Muslim scholars agreed to consider the *Sunna* to be a source of law (al-Bardisi 198-?, 195–197). Moreover, there were Muslim scholars who did not agree that the *Hadith* (or part of) represented the *Sunna*; accordingly, they did not agree that the *Hadith* (or part of) be considered a source of law (Amin 1969, 225–251). This work follows the broad consensus in that the *Sunna* reflected in the *Hadith* (or part of) is a primary source of Islamic law.

REMINDER: It is to be noted that all interpretations of Islamic law do not recognize the inclusive quality of the Qur'anic message that has been proposed in Volume 1. And in consequence, they do not look into the possibility that there could have been laws declared in the Qur'an and *Hadith* (for those who recognize *Hadith* to be a source of law) that were addressed to Monotheists in general.

As far as Traditional Islam is concerned, in the time of the revelation, all those whom the Qur'an described as being believers from the peoples of previous scriptures were converts who had become Muslims. Traditional Islam does not recognize people

94

from the peoples of previous scriptures to have preserved their religious identities while at the same time accepted the revelation.

Side note 5.7 On considering abiding by Islamic law to be in worship of God

The confusion surrounding Islamic law, worship, and their interrelation can be attributed to Traditional Islam's:

- Misinterpreting the verb *u'bud* appearing in the Qur'an

In Volume 1 it was proposed that in the Qur'an the verb *u'bud* (in its numerous grammatical forms) was used to direct to take God as the sole source of divine instruction. On the other hand, Traditional Islam interpreted this term to mean "worship," although the Qur'an was explicit in using distinct actions verbs (and not the verb *u'bud*) when instructing the QMonotheists or others about rites, good deeds, etc. (Q. 2:83, 22:77–78, 53:59–62, 98:5 in 98:1–8). Worship in Traditional Islam's interpretation includes obedience in addition to feeling or expression of reverence and adoration for God.

- Not distinguishing between the injunctions of the Qur'an

Traditional Islam considers adhering to all action injunctions of the Qur'an to be in worship of God, instead of limiting worship solely to performing acts of worship.

- Not distinguishing between the Qur'anic injunctions and Islamic law

Traditional Islam initially considered adhering to the Qur'an's man-world action injunctions to be in worship of God, then went on to eventually consider adhering to Islamic law's man-world action injunctions to be in worship of God. To this day, Traditional Islam considers all man's actions when following Islamic law to be in worship of God, and considers the classification of actions into man-God actions and man-world actions to be but a technical classification as described by Dasuqi & Jabir (1999, 64–67). Hence, Traditional Islam eventually considered abiding by laws made by men to be in worship of God (the making of which is in itself an on-going process across space-time). This point will become more evident once we discuss the two components of Islamic law in Chapters 6 and 7.

Side note 5.8 Al-Shafi'i and the principles of jurisprudence

Al-Shafi'i (d. 204 AH / 820 CE), a prominent jurist, who is considered the eponymous founder of one of the major Sunni schools of jurisprudence, is recognized to have established the basis for the principles of jurisprudence (*usul al-Fiqh*)—to systemize the methods used to derive religious law.

Coulson (1978) pointed out that in the jurisprudence realm, al-Shafi'i established the Prophet's *Sunna* to be a source of law (*hujiyyat al-sunna fi al-tashri'*) by interpreting and associating the word *al-hikma* (commonly means "wisdom") that was mentioned in the Qur'an with the *Sunna*. As a result of his interpretation of the term *al-hikma*, al-Shafi'i considered the actions of the Prophet (legal decisions) to be divinely inspired and to be complementary to the Qur'an. That is to say, al-Shafi'i considered the *Sunna* to be revelation. Moreover, he argued that as a matter of form, the *Sunna* could be properly ascertained and established only in the form of *Hadith*. The authority of *Hadith* became binding once (its attribution to the Prophet was) accepted and would not be open to objective criticism (53–61). Coulson noted: "Although nominally the *sunna* (or practice of Muhammad) was for ash-Shafi'i the second source of law, in fact it was bound to assume a primary importance. The Qur'an was to be interpreted in the light of the *sunna*, and since the function of the *sunna* was to provide an explanatory commentary on the Qur'an it was naturally vested with a superseding authority." (Coulson 1978, 57)

It is the viewpoint of this author that al-Shafi'i's interpretation of the term *al-hikma* conflicts with how the Qur'an used *al-hikma*. I understand the term *al-hikma* surely not to be the *Sunna* as claimed by al-Shafi'i. To debunk al-Shafi'i's interpretation of *al-hikma*, I reiterate what I had proposed in Volume 1 to be my understanding of the Qur'an's usage of the term *al-hikma* (with and without the definite particle *al*— equivalent for the definite article "the"):

> The term *hikma* comes from the word-root *hkm* (*hakama*, a transcription showing short vowels). I understand the word-root *hkm* to mean: to give a decisive word on a matter or issue.

> I interpret the term *hikma*—used in the Qur'an for both singular and plural— to mean: God's decisive word on a matter (*qawl fassl*)—that distinguishes and separates between truth and falsehood. It was used in the Qur'an in connection with moral precepts. It is a form of divine instruction, God's ruling on a matter.

> I see that the common usage of the term *hikma* to mean "wisdom" was not how the term was used in the Qur'an. I understand the interpretation of *hikma* to mean wisdom to have been a later usage, and it was never a Qur'anic usage of the term. That is to say, over time, the word's usage evolved to encompass the meaning "wisdom."

> The Qur'an's moral precepts were a form of instruction from God. It is to be noted that in the Qur'an, God's instruction is a decree; it is God's ruling on a matter.

> The ethical precepts, *al-hikma*, serve as a universal moral code comprehensible to humanity. These precepts are considered universal truths that reflect the divine will and are binding on believers as moral imperatives. These precepts encompass universal values such as compassion, justice, honesty, and love, guiding believers in leading virtuous lives aligned with their faith.

> These guiding principles, grounded in fundamental values, offer clear standards for discerning right actions from wrong ones, thereby shaping the ethical conduct and moral decision-making of individuals and communities.

> We find associated with the term *hikma* the terms—in their various grammatical forms—revealed (*awha*), sent down (*anzal*), given (*aata*), and teach (*yu'alim*), along with reference to God and the prophets (including *luqman*, whom I understand to have been a prophet). This explicitly shows that these moral precepts were not the products of the prophets mentioned in the verses but were divinely revealed to them from God.

96

I cite here a single occurrence of *al-hikma* in the Qur'an that clearly shows beyond doubt that the term does not mean the *Sunna*. Q. 17:22–39 explicitly gave examples of *al-hikma* (what is considered to be of). These verses listed several ethics injunctions, which were described by the last of these verses, Q. 17:39, to be of *al-hikma*, what I interpret, as aforementioned, the moral precepts: a form of divine instruction.

5.4.2 To challenge Islamic law

Let me first clarify an important issue. In Volume 1 I proposed that the usage of the verb *u'bud* in the Qur'an was in connection with divine instruction. When saying "*u'bud* entity A," a commandment appearing in the Qur'an where entity A was never other than God, the commandment would constitute a call to take as master entity A—on matters of instruction (Q. 9:31 in 9:29–35).

The Qur'an used the verb *u'bud* (and other patterns sharing the same root) when:

- The Qur'an commanded to take God as the source of instruction on the Code (Q. 39:11 in 39:1–18, 98:5 in 98:1–8)
- The Qur'an declared that the sole source of instruction in the Code, *al-islam*, was God (Q. 3:79–85, 10:104–105, 12:39–40, 109:1–6)
- The Qur'an commanded not to take divine instruction from other than God: the one (and only) deity should be the sole source of divine instruction (Q. 3:64 in 3:64–74, 9:31 in 9:29–35, 18:110 in 18:99–110)

One might ask, wouldn't this mean that only God has the right to legislate? I understand the Qur'an's usage of the verb *u'bud* (and other patterns sharing the same root) to be in connection with divine instruction about those things that should or should not be done (the dos and the don'ts), the permissible versus the prohibited, i.e. it was about the Code. Therefore, the commandment to take divine instruction only from God (*alla ta'budu illa iyah*)—in its different forms—was in connection with instruction about the Code. And, for matters beyond the Code, I do not see the Qur'an's usage of the verb *u'bud* to involve such issues.*1

Notwithstanding how the verb *u'bud* was used in the Qur'an, the known linguistic meaning of the verb *u'bud* goes beyond identifying the direction of instruction flow as in "be a slave to (on matters of instruction)" to include the demand to comply with and carry out the instruction: obey with submission. Traditional Islam even went further beyond. The verb *u'bud* has been incorrectly interpreted by Traditional Islam to mean "worship." Worship, in Traditional Islam's interpretation, includes obedience in addition to feeling or expression of reverence and adoration for God. Traditional Islam uses the word *'ibadat* (a noun, plural), a word which does not appear in the Qur'an, to collectively refer to acts of worship. Using such a term to represent acts of worship has contributed to the erroneous association of acts of worship with the verb *u'bud*. Muslims, most if not all, whenever they encounter the verb *u'bud* in the Qur'an incorrectly associate with it acts of worship.

For the sake of argument, in what follows, I follow along with Traditional Islam in its assumption that the usage of the verb *u'bud* in the Qur'an meant "worship"—unless explicitly stated otherwise.

I shall not delve into challenging the different arguments raised by Traditional Islam to religiously justify the existence of Islamic law, nor will I challenge Islamic law's choice in sources. The approach undertaken to challenge Islamic law is by challenging the (claim of) eternal applicability of the sources it has declared for itself. In other words, the approach is to explore whether or not the Qur'an and the *Hadith* can be considered as sources of eternal law (do they constitute God's eternal law?). Once it has been established that the applicability of the primary sources of Islamic law is non-eternal, then it follows that the Qur'an and the *Hadith* cannot be considered to constitute God's eternal law, and cannot be used as sources of (man-world) law suitable to establish law across space-time. As a result, Traditional Islam would be unable to justify the legitimacy it gives to Islamic law.

If the primary sources of Islamic law themselves were space-time specific, then it follows that law derived directly or indirectly from them would accordingly not necessarily be the best law for all space-time—by ethical and humane standards. Hence, acknowledging and enforcing law derived from the primary sources would not result in law that is appropriate to be used across space-time. And doing so would go against one of the main pillars of the Qur'an, the pillar of justice. Accordingly, once the applicability of the primary sources of Islamic law is proven to be space-time specific rather than eternal, the primary sources cannot be considered to constitute God's eternal law since according to the Qur'an, God is just. As a result, Islamic law would lose its legitimacy and the justification behind its existence.

NOTE*1: To get a feel of the Qur'an's usage of the verb *u'bud*, I cite three examples:

(1) I find Q. 39:11 in 39:1–18 to clearly present the relationship between divine instruction and the Code. In this verse we find the Prophet to state that he was commanded to "*a'bud allah mukhlisan lah al-din* (take God as Master—on matters of instruction; His code exclusively)."

Q. 39:11 stated, Say (oh Muhammad) I was commanded to take God as Master—on matters of instruction; His code exclusively.

(2) Furthermore, we find the same commandment to appear in Q. 98:5. I find Q. 98:5 in 98:1–8 to sum up what was required to be considered one of the Monotheists. In this verse we find the phrase "*ya'budu allah mukhliseen lah al-din* (take God as Master—on matters of instruction; His code exclusively)." Q. 98:5 was talking about the associators and those who did not accept the revelation from the peoples of previous scriptures.

Q. 98:5 stated that they ("the disbelievers from the peoples of previous scriptures" and "the associators") were not enjoined but to take God as Master—on matters of instruction; His code exclusively; to revere the prohibitions; to uphold the prayer and give the *zakat* (obligatory giving; 20% of income); and that is the benchmark code (that matters are measured against).

(3) I find the paragraph Q. 3:79–85 to further assert that the commandment to take divine instruction only from God was about the Code. Q. 3:79 talked about not to take divine instruction from other than God. Q. 3:83 talked about God's code of ethics and worship in the form of an exclamatory question: Is it other than God's code that they (the peoples of previous scriptures) seek, although to Him submitted all creations and to Him all return? In Q. 3:85, the Qur'an confirmed that whoever followed other than *al-islam* for a code, it would not be accepted from them on Judgment Day.

Side note 5.9 Challenging the claim that no one has the right to legislate but God

Challenging the premise that (man-world) law expressed in the Qur'an and the *Hadith* is eternally applicable would refute the claim that no one has the right to legislate but God:

> The claim that no one has the right to legislate but God necessitates, as a consequence, that God's law is eternal: the Action-Type II injunctions of the Qur'an and the *Hadith* are applicable across space-time. Showing this not to be the case, through demonstrating that (man-world) law within the primary sources is not applicable for all space-time—even if for a single account—proves that the claim proposed by Traditional Islam, that no one has the right to legislate but God, is wrong. It also proves that (man-world) law within the primary sources was not meant to be used across space-time: assuming it to be eternal was wrong. Accordingly, law derived directly or indirectly from the primary sources would not bring about best solutions for man-world affairs across space-time, since such law would always be based on sources that they themselves were space-time specific.

As demonstrated, contesting the claim of the eternal applicability of the primary sources disproved the specific trail of reasoning cited as an example of the arguments made by Traditional Islam to justify the existence of Islamic law. And I re-iterate: Best solutions for changing space-time can only be produced by law that is adapted to changing space-time; in other words, man would need to legislate for himself in changing space-time.

5.5 The eternality of the Qur'an

Muslims are used to saying or hearing that the Qur'an is eternal. Eternal according to the dictionary means: always existing (without beginning or end); lasting forever (without end). But what does eternal mean when referring to the Qur'an—is it in terms of lifespan, applicability, or both? How does this relate to the injunctions of the Qur'an?

Historically, there has not been any differentiation between the Qur'anic injunctions of the various categories when it comes to their lifespan and applicability horizon. Traditional Islam claims that all Qur'anic injunctions have both eternal lifespan and eternal applicability. This work presents a different viewpoint in this regard.

In this section an attempt is made to answer the abovementioned questions and to present this work's understanding of the concepts involved. We shall examine the eternality of the Qur'an from the angles of both lifespan and applicability. We will look into each, and see how and if they interrelate.

Our journey starts with looking into the traditional view of the applicability of the Qur'an and how it relates to the different understandings of the lifespan of the Qur'an. The historical debate that led to such understandings is then introduced. From there, this work's understanding of lifespan and applicability as they relate to the Qur'an is presented.

5.5.1 The applicability and the lifespan of the Qur'an

Throughout Muslim history there was never disagreement about the applicability of the Qur'an. I understand the applicability of the Qur'an, historically, to have derived its legitimacy from the Qur'an's being divine speech. It is divine speech that, throughout Muslim history, has been interpreted to directly address all audiences, including and beyond its original audience in the space-time of the revelation. Therefore, the applicability of the Qur'an—and its injunctions—was recognized to persist (to remain valid) within the boundaries of the Qur'an's lifespan.

To start with, let me be clear about what I mean by the Qur'an's lifespan. Lifespan here means life or lifetime: the period during which the Qur'an exists. Now, when it comes to the duration of the Qur'an's lifespan, we find disagreement. We find more than one understanding.

One might wonder as to why there would be different possibilities for the duration of the Qur'an's lifespan. The reason for having more than one possibility is that it all depends on how one understands the Qur'an.

From here onwards, when using the phrase "the Qur'an's lifespan," it is the duration of the Qur'an's lifespan that is intended, unless explicitly stated otherwise.

Now, back to our discussion. We will get to the reasoning behind the various understandings of the Qur'an's lifespan; however, for now, considering all possibilities, the lifespan of the Qur'an could be represented by:

- An unbounded interval (without beginning or end): To be co-eternal with God.

- A left-bounded interval (without end): There is a specific point in time for the starting of the lifespan; hence, the lifespan extends from a specific point in time onwards.

From a practical perspective, and from the standpoint of those who first received the Qur'an, the beginning of the left-bounded interval would be the time of revelation of the Qur'an rather than any prior time.*1

- A bounded interval (with both beginning and end): Limited by a lifespan window, from the revelation of the Qur'an up until the last day.*2

The lifespan in this case constitutes a finite interval (both ends are finite), as opposed to the previous two cases that represent infinite intervals. When saying the lifespan of the Qur'an constitutes an infinite interval, it is the same as saying the lifespan of the Qur'an is eternal.

NOTE*1: I said "prior time" in reference to the time of its alleged creation in a guarded tablet in the heavens, as per how some interpret Q. 56:75–80, 85:21–22 in 85:17–22. I would like to point out that what is referenced in these verses is "*qur'an*," without the definite particle *al* (equivalent for the definite article "the"), which refers to that which was being read of the divine speech. I disagree with the aforementioned interpretation in that the referenced verses referred to the creation of "the Qur'an" in the heavens. I understand these verses to be referring—whether it be figuratively or not—to the state in which the divine communication was transported by the angel(s) (it could be touched only by the purified, *la yamassahu illa al-muttaharun*): it was a communication—that was transported—in tablet form (protected and preserved); and sent down by God. The transport of the Qur'an involved—it included but possibly was not limited to—the archangel Gabriel (Q. 16:102 in 16:98–105).

In Q. 42:51–53, the verses tell us that the divine communication was revealed (*wahy*) to the Prophet via God's messenger, the archangel Gabriel. I understand this to mean that the Qur'an was read to the Prophet in Arabic by the archangel Gabriel. This understanding is also supported by other Qur'anic verses: Q. 2:97 in 2:97–99, 26:192–195 in 26:192–227, 53:1–18, 81:19–25.

NOTE*2: When saying "revelation" or "time of revelation," I would like to point out that the revelation of the Qur'an to Prophet Muhammad was over several years that ended with the death of the Prophet in 11 AH / 632 CE (Q. 17:105–106, 25:32–33). The Qur'an itself mentions that it was revealed gradually, rather than all at once (Q. 17:106 in 17:105–111, 25:32 in 25:4–34). Most traditional sources consider the revelation of the Qur'an to have been over a period of twenty-three years.

NOTE: The Qur'an directly addressed the beings in the space-time of the revelation, the space-time of Prophet Muhammad. Later generations interpreted how the Qur'anic revelation applied to them. For anyone living outside the space-time of the revelation, one can only interpret (attempt to) what the Qur'an is saying, and how the Qur'anic revelation applies in one's own space-time. When it comes to interpretation—being a matter of probability not certainty—no party can claim its interpretation to be the truth. There is no truth but the Qur'an, everything else is relative.

5.5.2 Historically: The divine attributes and the createdness of the Qur'an

The applicability of the Qur'an has always been directly associated with its lifespan. The various understandings of the lifespan of Qur'an can be traced to how the speech of God, and consequently the Qur'an, was considered to relate to the nature of God. These viewpoints have historical roots that go back to the early third century AH (ninth century CE) and before. This brings us to two important topics in the history of Islamic theology: the divine attributes and the createdness of the Qur'an. Contemporary scholars differ in what led to what, whether it was the study of the divine attributes that led to the controversy over the createdness of the Qur'an, or was it the other way around. As for the discussion herein, I will go over both topics regardless of which chronologically came first.

5.5.2.a The divine attributes

When it came to describing the divine, there was vast disagreement among the Muslim schools of theology. Three main views can be identified. The groups behind them were: the literalists, the rationalists, and the mediators.

The literalists (early traditionalists) believed that how God described Himself in the Qur'an should be taken word for word. Some of these literalists believed in *tashbih wa tajsim*, affirming similarity between God and His creations whether in characteristics or behaviors. This included and was not limited to anthropomorphism (the attribution of human form and/or attributes to a deity), while others of them said: we don't know, we believe in what is in the Qur'an without asking why or how (*bila lima wala kayfa*).

The Qur'an contains depictions of God in which God is described to have a face (Q. 28:88), hands (Q. 38:75 in 38:67–88), eyes (Q. 54:14 in 54:9–17), and to sit on the throne (*istiwa' 'ala al-'arsh*) (Q. 20:5)—corporeal depictions. God is also described as "the Light of the heavens and the earth" (Q. 24:35). Moreover, we also find the divine attributes (*al-sifat*), the adjectives the Qur'an employs to describe God (to describe the essence of God), those on which the names (*al-asma'*) of God are based. For each of the names of God given in the Qur'an, there exists a corresponding attribute, for example: when saying God is "the all-Merciful," "the all-Powerful," "the Living," the corresponding attribute for each of these names, respectively, would be mercy, power, and life.

On the opposing side, there were the rationalists, led by the Mu'tazila, who rejected the view adopted by the literalists. The Mu'tazila rejected the reality of any of the descriptions of God found in the Qur'an. The Mu'tazila believed that when God described Himself in the Qur'an as that there was nothing like Him (Q. 42:11) and there is none equal with Him (Q. 112:4), that then necessitated considering all descriptions of God found in the Qur'an to be figurative. Accordingly, the Mu'tazila gave metaphorical interpretations to all anthropomorphic and other depictions of God found in the Qur'an.

I find it imperative to expand upon the Mu'tazila's understanding of the divine attributes. The Mu'tazila denied the existence of divine attributes in God. According to the Mu'tazila, the divine attributes were identical with the divine essence: God's essence and attributes are one. In other words, the divine attributes had no real existence, but were merely descriptions of God's essence. Goldziher (d. 1921 CE) eloquently described the Mu'tazila's stand on ascribing attributes to God. I quote Goldziher here. As far as the Mu'tazila were concerned, to ascribe attributes to God, Goldziher writes, "would, after all, introduce multiplicity into His one and indivisible being. And even if we think of these attributes (as, given the nature of God, we must) as being in no way distinct from God's essence, as being inherent in His essence from all eternity and not superadded to it--even then the mere positing of such existents, eternal even though inseparably joined to God's essence, would imply the admission of eternal entities besides the one eternal God. But that is *shirk*, 'association.' *Tawhid*, the pure belief in God's unity, therefore demands that one reject the supposition that God has attributes, whether eternal and inherent, or additional to his essence. This consideration had to lead to the denial of divine attributes; to the view that God is all-knowing but not by a knowledge, all-powerful but not by a power, living but not by a life. There is no distinct knowledge, power, and life in God; all those things that strike us as attributes are indivisibly one, and not distinct from God Himself. To say that God is knowing is no different from saying 'God is powerful' or 'God is living.' Were we to multiply such statements to infinity, we would still not be saying anything but 'God is.'" (Goldziher 1981, 95–96)

Then there was a later group, the mediators—mainly the Ash'arites and the Maturidites (major Sunni schools of theology)—who tried to mediate between the viewpoints of the traditionalists and the rationalists. For the mediators, all attributions of human form were rejected; however, they accepted that God had real divine attributes. The mediator subgroups differed in how they classified the divine attributes, and in how these attributes were interpreted in relation to the divine essence.

5.5.2.b The Mu'tazila—what makes them special?

Before moving on and talking about what I believe to be, probably, the most important theological topic that historically has had extensive consequences on shaping the religion of Islam, the createdness of the Qur'an controversy. I stop here to talk about one of the groups directly involved in this controversy. It is the Mu'tazila, a unique group in Muslim history who are known for having adopted a rationalistic approach in their interpretation of religion.

The Mu'tazila (Arabic for "those who withdrew themselves"), or the Mutazilites as they are known in English to some, are of particular interest to us here because of their unique stance on the divine attributes.

This Muslim group, the Mu'tazila, described themselves as the people of unity and justice (*ahl al-'adl wa al-tawhid*). The Mu'tazila thought held to five theological principles, the two most important of which were the unity of God and divine justice. The first of which led them to deny the reality of divine attributes (as being distinct entities) and that the Qur'an was uncreated, and the second led them to assert the existence of free will. The Mu'tazila's opponents included the literalists (believed in no metaphors in the Qur'an), determinists (believed everything to be predetermined), and traditionalists (believed the only sources of truth to be the Qur'an and the *Sunna*). The Mu'tazila were called numerous names by their adversaries, one of which was "the deniers of the attributes."

I find it worthwhile to expand on the Mu'tazila's understanding of the depictions of God found in the Qur'an. Robinson (1998), writing about Ash'ariyya (a major Sunni theology) and Mu'tazila in the Routledge Encyclopedia of Philosophy, described the Mu'tazila's position on depictions found in the Qur'an apparently implying that God had a body. Robinson stated that the Mu'tazila insisted "that God is not merely numerically one but also that he is a simple essence. This led them to deny that he has a body or any of the characteristics of bodies such as colour, form, movement and localization in space; hence he cannot be seen, in this world or the next. The Mu'tazila therefore interpreted the Qur'anic anthropomorphisms as metaphors – God's 'hands' are his blessing, God's 'eyes' are his knowledge, his 'face' is his essence and his seating himself on his throne is his omnipotence[.]" (Robinson 1998, 1: 522)

Moreover, in the same article, and regarding the divine attributes in the Qur'an, Robinson writes about the Mu'tazila: "When we speak of God as 'living', 'knowing', 'powerful' and 'eternal', we are, in their opinion, merely considering him from different points of view.

God's 'attributes of essence' (*sifat al-dhat*), as they are generally called, are a product of the limitations and the plurality of our own intellectual faculties; in reality, they are identical with God's essence. Thus, according to al-Ash'ari (Maqalat: 484), Abu al-Hudhayl [a leading Mu'tazilite] maintained that 'God is knowing by virtue of a knowledge which is His own essence' and that he is likewise powerful, living and eternal by a power, a life and an eternity which are none other than his own essence. Al-Nazzam [a leading Mu'tazilite] expressed this even more forcefully when he said, 'If I say that God is knowing, I merely confirm the divine essence and deny in it all ignorance. If I say that God is powerful, living and so forth, I am only confirming the divine essence and denying in it all powerlessness, mortality and so forth' (Maqalat: 484)" (Robinson 1998, 1: 522). Robinson goes on to say: "In addition to the attributes of essence, the Qur'an employs a whole series of adjectives such as 'providing' and 'forgiving', which describe God in relation to his creatures. It is easy to imagine a time when God did not have these attributes. The Mu'tazilites called these 'attributes of action' (*sifat al-fi'l*) because they deemed them to come into being when God acts. In their reckoning, God's 'speech' belongs to this category of attributes, for it does not make sense to think of his commandments as existing before the creation of the beings to whom they are addressed. Thus the Qur'an itself, although the Word of God, is temporal and not eternal." (Robinson 1998, 1: 522)

5.5.2.c The createdness of the Qur'an controversy

The debate concerning the nature of divine speech was of particular importance since, to the followers of the Qur'an, the Qur'an aside from being recognized to be a revelation from God (Q. 2:97, 16:102 in 16:98–105, 26:192–195 in 26:192–227), it is believed to be the speech of God (verbatim) (Q. 2:75 in 2:75–82, 9:6, 42:51–53). But how is one to understand the attribution of speech to God? This brings us to the notorious controversy over the createdness of the Qur'an.

In the createdness of the Qur'an controversy, we have on one side the Mu'tazila, and their opponents on the other. The opponents of the Mu'tazila were of two groups (Amin 1964, 3: 37–40). The first group said, we only know that the Qur'an is the speech of God and we will not enter into the discussion whether it was created or not. The second group considered the speech of God to be a divine attribute of essence, and as all attributes of essence, they considered divine speech to be co-eternal with God, i.e. to be uncreated; hence, they concluded that the Qur'an was uncreated.

Historically, the createdness of the Qur'an controversy brings us to events of the early third century AH (ninth century CE); though, the notion of the createdness of the Qur'an started around a century earlier, around the end of the Umayyad era in the early second century AH (Amin 1964, 3: 161–163). In the early third century AH, it is reported that the Abbasid caliph, al-Ma'moun (d. 218 AH / 833 CE), who had adopted the Mu'tazila's view on the createdness of the Qur'an declared it to be the official state doctrine. Moreover, he instigated an inquisition where prominent religious scholars and employees of the government were queried on the createdness of the Qur'an. The question of importance was whether the Qur'an was considered to be created or was it considered to be uncreated (preexistent). Those who did not concur to the Mu'tazila's view were persecuted.

The Mu'tazila considered only God to be non-changing, independent of, and above space-time. The Mu'tazila, based on their understanding of monotheism, which adhered to both reason and scripture, denied the existence of divine attributes—whether as distinct qualities of the divine essence or as additions to it. To the Mu'tazila, the speech of God was not, nor was anything else, co-eternal with God. The Mu'tazila emphatically refused to consider the Qur'an uncreated (to be co-eternal with God), since in their view claiming the Qur'an to be uncreated would be equivalent to saying that the Qur'an was (a) God. In a manner of speaking, to the Mu'tazila, for one to say the Qur'an was God, was no different from saying Jesus Christ was God (Q. 5:17–19, 5:70–79), i.e. it constituted believing in other deities, or in believing that God had associates, which goes against the Mu'tazila's theological principle of the unity of God.

The rationalism of the Mu'tazila appealed to the more liberal, learned classes of the Muslim society of the time. Needless to say, the idea of an abstract God did not find popularity among the masses. The inquisition (known as the *mihna* in Arabic, meaning "ordeal") was imposed by three successive Abbasid rulers and lasted around 15 years, 218–234 AH / 833–849 CE. However, it had much longer consequences. The masses rejected the Abbasid inquisition. They saw it as an attempt to suppress the freedom of religious belief and as a means of control rather than reform. As a reaction against the extremism of the Mu'tazila's view they went to the other extreme. Hence, in the aftermath, the inquisition brought traditionalist theology into the forefront and resulted in its support and adoption by the masses (eventually leading to what became the orthodox Sunni view on the createdness of the Qur'an: The Qur'an is uncreated). This ultimately led to the abandonment of the Mu'tazila thought and for the Mu'tazila to eventually die off as religious group.

The belief in the uncreated nature of the Qur'an is a point of agreement between the two major branches of Islam, both Sunni and Shi'a. For over a thousand years, Sunni Muslims have regarded the Qur'an as co-eternal with God. Historically, certain elements within Shi'a theology shared specific theological positions with the Mu'tazila, including the doctrine of the createdness of the Qur'an. However, the majority of Shi'a Muslims today, particularly the Twelver Shi'a, reject the Mu'tazila doctrine and adhere to the belief in the divine and uncreated status of the Qur'an, aligning more closely with Sunni orthodoxy on this particular issue.

NOTE: On the nature of divine attributes, the Mu'tazila did not believe in real divine attributes, the Mu'tazila believed God's essence and attributes were inseparable, with no distinction between them. Essentially, what this means is the divine attributes were perceived as merely descriptive terms or metaphorical depictions of God's essence rather than distinct qualities or entities. Hence, the Mu'tazila maintained that the divine attributes were not independently existing entities but rather conceptualizations or descriptions of God's essential being. Unlike the Mu'tazila, Orthodox Sunni theology believes in the reality of divine attributes. There is a belief in the existence of real, distinct attributes in God alongside His essence (a way of expressing their coexistence and inseparability). However, the relationship between these attributes and God's essence is understood in a way that maintains His transcendence and unity. On the divine attributes, the two major Sunni theologies, the Ash'ari and Maturdi theologies, say (Ali 1963, 270; Hye 1963, 227): Divine attributes are not the divine essence nor are they other than the divine essence (*la huwa wa la ghairuhu*).

In Sunni theology, the divine attributes are considered intrinsic qualities that emanate from God's essence, helping to define His nature and reveal aspects of His being. While divine attributes are considered inherent aspects of God's being, they are also understood to be distinct from His essence in the sense that they represent different qualities or characteristics of God. These attributes are not separate entities but rather expressions of God's essential nature.

The divine essence refers to the core, intrinsic nature of God, which is considered transcendent and beyond human comprehension. Divine attributes, on the other hand, are qualities or characteristics that are attributed to God, such as His mercy, knowledge, or power. While these attributes are inseparable from God and are inherent to His essence, they are distinct concepts from His essence itself. In other words, the attributes describe aspects of God's nature without being identical to His essence.

The divine attributes offer glimpses into aspects of God's nature that are comprehensible to humans, but the totality of God's essence remains beyond our full understanding. It's a nuanced concept within theological discourse, emphasizing both the accessibility of certain aspects of God's nature and the recognition of the inherent limitations of human understanding when it comes to grasping the divine essence in its entirety.

Sunni scholars affirm both the reality of these attributes and the oneness (*tawhid*) of God, emphasizing that God's essence transcends and is beyond the attributes. This distinction is made to safeguard the idea that God is unique and incomparable, and His essence is beyond human comprehension.

Side note 5.10 The Trinity in Christianity and the divine attributes in Islam

The createdness of the Qur'an controversy in the ninth century CE (in the matter of the nature of the Qur'an) finds its equivalent in Christendom—within Christology (the field of study within Christian theology concerned with the nature and person of Jesus Christ)—in the great controversy between Arius and Athanasius that occurred in the fourth century CE. As it turned out, the dominant denominations in the Christian community accepted that Christ was co-eternal with God the Father. And the Sunnis of the Muslim community accepted that the Qur'an was uncreated (eternal) divine speech.

Is there more to say about the similarities in the orthodox views of these two religions?

The concept of the Trinity in Christianity and the concept of divine attributes in Islam are distinct theological ideas with fundamental differences. In Christianity, the Trinity refers to the belief in one God existing in three persons: the Father, the Son (Jesus Christ), and the Holy Spirit. Each person of the Trinity is understood to be fully God, possessing the divine nature completely, yet they are distinct from one another in their roles and relationships within the Godhead. The Father is seen as the creator and sustainer of all things, the Son (Jesus Christ) as the savior who took on human form to redeem humanity, and the Holy Spirit as the divine presence and active force within believers. The doctrine of the Trinity asserts that these three persons are co-equal, co-eternal, and together form one Godhead.

On the other hand, in Islam, there is a strict monotheistic belief in one God, with no concept of plurality within the divine essence. God is considered the sole creator, sustainer, and ruler of the universe, with no equals or associates. Islamic theology emphasizes the transcendence and oneness of God, rejecting the concept of the Trinity or any form of polytheism. According to Islamic theology, the divine attributes refer to the qualities or characteristics of God that reflect His nature and essence. These attributes are not considered distinct persons within God but rather facets of His singular divine essence. Islamic theology emphasizes the absolute oneness of God, without any partners or divisions.

There are those who assume the concept of the (divine) Trinity not to be far from that of the divine attributes (the orthodox Sunni understanding of). The famous Muslim exegete al-Razi (d. 606 AH / 1209 CE), a Sunni himself and a follower of the Ash'arite theology, long ago argued against this notion (examples found in his commentary on Q. 2:221, 4:171, 5:17) (al-Razi 1981, 6: 60, 11: 118, 11:195). Al-Razi argued that the personas (from the Latin "persona"—face or mask) in the Trinity are not attributes (*sifat*), but rather, they are distinct essences (*thawat*). His argument was that: They are distinct essences since they are accepted to be embodied in others and to separate from those others; if these personas were not distinct essences their ability to move would not have been possible (moreover, the movement of attributes is not possible). Al-Razi concluded by saying: Hence, even if those who believe in the Trinity call them attributes, in reality, they prove to be multiple essences existing in themselves.

5.5.2.d On the right of religious freedom: Reflecting on the *mihna* and what is going on in modern times

When recalling the createdness of the Qur'an controversy, and if we were to imagine the so-called *mihna* (ordeal or inquisition as commonly translated) not to have occurred, that is to say, if the debate on the createdness of the Qur'an had remained outside the political circle, as had been the case for all other issues of religion, then matters would probably not have gotten out of hand and the aftermath of this controversy would probably not have been as drastic as it had been. But the state intervened and that was what enraged the masses. What did the state do? From the events of the *mihna* we understand that the state attempted to impose on the masses one theological interpretation—its interpretation about the nature of the Qur'an—over other interpretations.

The state at the time of the Abbasid caliph al-Ma'moun (d. 218 AH / 833 CE) adopted the Mu'tazila school's stance on the createdness of the Qur'an to be the official state doctrine and instigated an inquisition where prominent religious scholars and employees of the government were queried about their position in its regard. The inquisition continued into the reign of the following two Abbasid rulers, and lasted around 15 years, 218–234 AH / 833–849 CE. Those who opposed the state's view were persecuted. The people saw this as state meddling in religious matters, and their response was that it was not for the state to decide on matters of religion. As a result, the inquisition brought traditionalist theology into the forefront and resulted in its support and adoption by the masses.

Let us come back to the present era, and look into what is happening today in a good number of, if not most, Muslim-majority states in connection with what I argue to be meddling in religious affairs. Let me highlight three points in particular:

(1) The state records the religion of its citizens

The state (non-secular Muslim-majority states) assumes religion to be inherited from one's father and registers the religion of each citizen accordingly. This goes against the right of religious freedom, where one should be able to choose whatever religion one chooses to follow or none at all.

What business is one's religion to the state? The answer is that so the state knows what personal status law to enforce on this citizen. For citizens who are registered by the state as Muslims, this amounts to imposing the state's interpretation of Islamic law on them. This complicates matters especially when citizens from different religions choose to marry and have children, and in cases of inheritance and the last will and testament, among many others. For example, if a Muslim woman and a Christian man wanted to marry, then the man would need to convert. And the children would be considered Muslims by the state. This creates a lot of social pressure on the husband-to-be, and many choose either not to get married or to immigrate to somewhere where they could get married without requiring the groom to convert and where they would avoid imposing a religion upfront on their children.

(2) The codification of Islamic law

We find the state (Muslim-majority states of mixed legal systems) to be choosing what interpretation of Islamic law it sees fit on each point of law (mostly in personal status law), and it is imposing this codified interpretation of Islamic law on its Muslim citizens (those citizens whose parents are listed by the state as Muslims).

Let us assume for the sake of argument that having religious law is acceptable, it is my understanding then, that the codification of Islamic law would be against the right of religious freedom of the Muslim citizens of such states: imposing one interpretation of

Islamic law—that of the state—over all other interpretations on any point of law.

(3) To include the subject of religion in school curriculums: the obligatory religious school education for Muslim children

The state (non-secular Muslim-majority states) is once again violating the right of religious freedom of its Muslim citizens. It is choosing the interpretation of Islam that it sees fit and it is teaching it to children whose parents are listed by the state as Muslims.

There is no single interpretation of Islam. And the state, the modern nation-state, to assume the role of the gatekeeper of religion, and to impose its interpretation of Islam on its citizens (whether it be by teaching it to the young or by enforcing the laws it has chosen to represent its own interpretation of Islamic law) goes against the right of religious freedom to which citizens of such states should be entitled.

In a manner of speaking, keeping in mind article 18 of the universal declaration of human rights (UNCHR n.d.), modern-day so-called Muslim-majority states are far less honoring the right of religious freedom of their Muslim citizens than were the Abbasids at the time of the *mihna*. And look where that got us!

NOTE: Amin (1964, 3: 202–207) commented on what the Muslims lost with the fall of the Mu'tazila almost a century ago, in 1933 CE. He made a similar remark to the one I mentioned above about how things could have been different if the state had not meddled (intervened) in religious issues. However, Amin did not address the issue of modern Muslim-majority states' meddling in religious affairs.

This was probably due to the anticipated repercussions if he had done so, or perhaps because he did not envision the same solution that I propose: the need for secular states. It is important to note that during Amin's time, most Muslim-majority states were under colonial rule, including his home country, Egypt. Subsequently, when these states later gained independence, the three points highlighted above were widely prevalent in most cases, as these new states were often non-secular modern nation-states.

Taking into account what has been discussed about state meddling in religious affairs, whether historically or in the modern era, it only makes sense that the modern nation-state should be secular to prevent the abuse of religion and the infringement on the rights of its people.

5.5.3 More on divine speech and the consequences of how it was understood

Looking back at the createdness of the Qur'an controversy, to summarize: Both parties considered the Qur'an to be divine speech. One party considered divine speech to be an attribute of essence (eternal); the other party considered divine speech to be an attribute of action (temporal, created).

As far as our discussion is concerned, in regard to the eternality of the Qur'an, we are interested to explore how createdness versus uncreatedness relates to lifespan and applicability. It is my understanding that the whole controversy was about lifespan and not applicability. Applicability was directly associated with lifespan: applicability was recognized to persist (to remain valid) within the boundaries of lifespan.

The consequences of the assumption of createdness or uncreatedness on the lifespan and the applicability of the Qur'an are explored next.

5.5.3.a Createdness versus uncreatedness and consequences on understanding lifespan

The lifespan of an instance of divine speech has to do with the instance itself, it depends on the subject matter of the instance. As I see it, the debate was over the lifespan of the Qur'an, as a whole, and it did not get into the lifespan of the instances of divine speech within the Qur'an.

From the words used to describe the controversy, "the createdness of the Qur'an," we understand that both parties initially differed as to the whether the Qur'an was "created" or "uncreated" (preexistent). This tells us that both parties were debating its starting point, when the Qur'an came to exist, and not its end-point. Though, they did not discuss lifespan; nevertheless, from the createdness of the Qur'an controversy one can deduce each party's position on lifespan.

The opponents of the Mu'tazila's assuming divine speech to be an attribute of essence, would lead us to understand lifespan from their perspective to be represented by an unbounded interval. As for the Mu'tazila's position on lifespan, the Mu'tazila considered the Qur'an to be created and did not comment on its end-point. However, the term "created" in itself implies that the entity is not endless. Thus, it would be reasonable to assume the lifespan of the Qur'an in the Mu'tazila's case to be a bounded interval. Now from a rationalistic perspective, the last day would be the end of the Qur'an's lifespan, since when the last day arrives, according to the Qur'an, the offer made by God in the Qur'an for the beings to believe would no longer be valid. However, for all practical purposes, since the date of the last day is unknown, the lifespan of the Qur'an could be represented by a left-bounded interval (without end).

NOTE: The Mu'tazila believed that the Qur'an, the literal word of God, was created at a specific point in time. They did not provide a specific temporal point for the creation of the Qur'an in their theological framework. This meant that the Qur'an came into existence when God chose to create it, thereby making it temporal rather than eternal. The exact timing was not a central issue in their theological framework; the key point was its created nature.

The emphasis was on the principle that the Qur'an had a beginning and was brought into existence by God's will, rather than existing eternally alongside God. According to their view, the Qur'an was not considered eternal but had a temporal origin, distinct from the eternal essence of God. They held that the Qur'an was created by God's will and command. This view rejects the notion of the Qur'an existing prior to its creation and underscores its status as a divine creation rather than an inherent aspect of God's eternal being.

NOTE: It is important to realize that speech in itself is made up of instances of speech. Hence, to consider divine speech to be created or uncreated would impact all and each of the instances of divine speech.

The Qur'an's passages and paragraphs all constitute instances of divine speech. Moreover, even if saying the Qur'an as a whole constitutes an instance of the speech of God, we must realize that the Qur'an does not constitute all instances of the speech of God. We can understand this concept from the Qur'an itself, as expressed in Q. 18:109.

Q. 18:109 (Pickthal): Say: Though the sea became ink for the Words of my Lord, verily the sea would be used up before the words of my Lord were exhausted, even though We brought the like thereof to help.

How does Sunni theology understand instances of divine speech within the context of its uncreated nature?

In Sunni theology, particularly within the Ash'ari and Maturidi schools, divine speech, like the Qur'an, is seen as a reflection of God's eternal speech, which is believed to be uncreated. This means that while the Qur'an itself is considered eternal and uncreated, each passage within it is regarded as a manifestation of God's eternal speech. Sunni scholars stress that, even though the Qur'an was revealed over time, its words convey the timeless nature of God's speech, which exists eternally. Consequently, the Qur'an is viewed as the literal word of God, gradually revealed but always existing in the divine realm. This perspective underscores the eternal

114

and unchanging essence of the Qur'an, representing God's will and guidance throughout time.

The view of the Qur'an as always existing in the divine realm affirms that the Qur'an is not a created entity but rather an eternal aspect of God's being, existing alongside His divine attributes. This concept emphasizes the timeless and unchanging nature of the Qur'an, implying that it has always been present in the divine realm as an expression of God's eternal speech.

5.5.3.b Createdness versus uncreatedness and consequences on understanding applicability

The createdness versus uncreatedness controversy was a significant point of contention, and was played out in early Muslim history. The ramifications of this controversy can be realized even in our current times: the createdness of the Qur'an controversy only helped Muslims—both Sunni and Shi'a—affirm that all Qur'anic injunctions were of eternal applicability.

Regardless of whether the Qur'an was considered created or uncreated, the Qur'an and consequently all Qur'anic injunctions were considered eternal in both lifespan and applicability. This helped to further assert the status of the Qur'an as the source of law.

To understand how this came about, let us take it step by step—I attempt to outline the logic involved:

- In the createdness of the Qur'an controversy both parties considered the Qur'an to be divine speech

One party considered divine speech to be an attribute of essence (eternal); the other party considered divine speech to be an attribute of action (temporal, created).

- Consequences on understanding lifespan

Depending on how each party considered divine speech, whether it be created or uncreated, this would affect the lifespan of the Qur'an—be it an unbounded or a left-bounded interval. However, both left-bounded and unbounded intervals represent infinite intervals. In other words, both are eternal, it is just that they differ in the starting point.

All injunctions of the Qur'an follow the Qur'an in lifespan. Hence, the respective understanding for the lifespan of the Qur'an would also apply to the lifespan of the injunctions themselves.

■ Consequences on understanding applicability

For the debating parties (and for Muslims throughout Muslim history), I understand the applicability of the Qur'an to derive its legitimacy from the Qur'an's being divine speech. Moreover, it is divine speech that was interpreted to directly address all audiences, including and beyond its original audience in the space-time of the revelation. Accordingly, both parties considered the Qur'an to be applicable within and throughout the relative lifespan each recognized for the Qur'an.

It is my understanding that what was under debate in the createdness of the Qur'an controversy was the lifespan of the Qur'an and not its applicability. That is to say, each of the two parties considered the Qur'an applicable within the relative lifespan recognized by each party. The lifespan of the Qur'an can be seen to define the boundaries of the Qur'an's applicability. Therefore, both parties came to understand the Qur'an to be eternally applicable.

▶ For those who considered divine speech to be an attribute of essence (eternal)

To claim the speech of God to be an attribute of essence, and to reflect this on the Qur'an, allowed those who believed in this claim to consider the Qur'an in applicability to transcend space and time. Since to them the divine attribute of speech being an attribute of essence (as the divine essence itself) transcended space and time.

▶ For those who considered divine speech to be an attribute of action (temporal, created)

Claiming the Qur'an to be created tells us that divine speech, like any speech, has its limitations depending on context (and it is not above space-time). However, I understand the discussion—at the time—to have been limited to the Qur'an as a whole. And it was not about the instances of divine speech within the Qur'an.

Looking back at history and analyzing how the Mu'tazila regarded the Qur'an, it can be understood that the Mu'tazila considered the Qur'an to be applicable within what they understood to be its lifespan.

116

Hence, we find that assuming the Qur'an to be created had no effect on the applicability of the Qur'anic injunctions. In practice, the applicability horizon of the Qur'anic injunctions was assumed to be within the Qur'an's lifespan; consequently, all Qur'anic injunctions were considered eternally applicable.

To consider the injunctions of the Qur'an to be applicable across space-time has been the standard practice in the making of Islamic law. Furthermore, this assumption has led Muslim jurists to openly take out of context, Qur'anic injunctions that were meant for a specific context, as that in which they were used in the Qur'an, and to consider them to be applicable across space and time.*1

NOTE*1: We find this understanding about the eternal applicability of the Qur'an—and its injunctions—to be explicitly clear in the jurist maxim "what counts is the general meaning rather than the particular context (*al-'ibrah bi 'umum al-lafz la bi khusus al-sabab*)," which claims to look into what has been known as the (alleged) *asbab al-nuzul* (what is alleged to be the causes of the revelation—some prefer to call it the occasion of the revelation), and to apply the Qur'anic injunctions beyond the (alleged) cause of the revelation.

We also find this understanding about the eternal applicability of the Qur'an to have been followed in interpreting the Qur'an (*ta'wil*) and not just in the making of Islamic law.

Side note 5.11 The Mu'tazila: Qur'anic createdness and the applicability of the Qur'anic injunctions

Although the Mu'tazila considered the Qur'an to be the speech of God, they did not consider the Qur'an co-eternal with God. The Mu'tazila did not consider the Qur'an uncreated, but rather, that it was temporal or created. Historically, it appears that even though the Mu'tazila considered the Qur'an to be created, they accepted the Qur'an to be the source of law.

The Mu'tazila's approach to interpreting and deriving legal principles from the Qur'an was influenced by their theological views, particularly the belief in the createdness of the Qur'an. They emphasized the role of reason in interpreting religious texts, and their legal methodologies often reflected a rationalistic and ethical approach.

NOTICE: The Mu'tazila believed that the Qur'an was created by God, rather than being an eternal and inseparable aspect of God Himself. This distinction allowed them to assert that God's will was separate from the Qur'an, meaning that that God's will, or divine commands, existed separately from the Qur'an. According to this view, the Qur'an, while conveying divine guidance, was not considered inherently divine in the sense of being an eternal aspect (expression) of God's essence. This is in contrast to the orthodox view that the Qur'an is considered to have always existed as an essential attribute or expression of God

Himself, existing alongside His divine attributes. Consequently, the Mu'tazila were more inclined to subject religious texts to rational analysis, using human reason alongside scriptural sources.

It is reasonable to assume that according to the Mu'tazila, the Qur'an is an expression of God's will, but not necessarily a direct or exhaustive representation of it. Seeing the Qur'an as a separate creation from God's direct will suggests that it may not reflect every aspect of God's will with absolute accuracy. Therefore, humans are not bound by every command in the Qur'an as if it were directly dictated by God. This implies that while the Qur'an is considered the speech of God, human interpretation of its commands may vary, and not every command may apply universally or in the same way across different contexts. Therefore, humans may not be bound to interpret and apply every command in the Qur'an in a literal or rigid manner, as if each command were directly dictated with precise instructions for every situation. This perspective allows for more flexibility in interpreting and applying its teachings, enabling humans to act according to their own understanding of God's will and allowing for a broader range of choices and actions.

Law was part of the Mu'tazila's interpretation of religion. Generally speaking, many Mu'tazila favored jurisprudence of the Hanafi school, yet there appeared Mu'tazila scholars who had their own views in jurisprudence. The specific nuances of the Mu'tazila's legal theories and applications varied among Mu'tazila scholars.

As for the relationship between the doctrine of the createdness of the Qur'an and the applicability of the Qur'anic injunctions, a topic that historically does not appear to have been explicitly addressed, the reader needs to be aware that most of what we know about the Mu'tazila—the earlier theologians in particular—comes from heresiographers and polemics written by their opponents, as hardly any of the Mu'tazila's original early works survived. Therefore, one can only speculate on how the doctrine of the createdness of the Qur'an influenced the Mu'tazila's viewpoints regarding the applicability of the Qur'anic injunctions.

■ Historically: The Mu'tazila accepted the Qur'an to be the source of law; otherwise, polemics would have surely mentioned anything to the contrary. That being the case, then to the Mu'tazila, the whole createdness-uncreatedness controversy was limited to the discussion of the divine attributes: the doctrine of the createdness of the Qur'an was concerned with the unity of God (theology related).

It is clear that law was part of the Mu'tazila's interpretation of religion. Although the doctrine of the createdness of the Qur'an had theological consequences on the Mu'tazila's interpretation of religion, it did not change their belief that the Qur'an, including its injunctions, remained applicable throughout its lifespan. While their view on its applicability was unchanged, the Mu'tazila's belief in the createdness of the Qur'an influenced their interpretation of its applicability, emphasizing human reason and free will in understanding and adhering to its teachings.

■ Theoretically: In theory, the mere fact that the Mu'tazila considered the Qur'an to be created, leaves the possibility open for them, at some point in time, to reject the applicability of certain injunctions within the Qur'an if proven to contradict reason. Yet to the best of my knowledge, there exists no Mu'tazila work—of the later surviving Mu'tazila works—that mentions this theoretical possibility.

5.5.4 Lifespan and applicability: The traditional versus proposed view

Looking back into Muslim history and learning about the createdness of the Qur'an controversy and the different standpoints regarding the divine attributes has helped us glean perspective on the position of Traditional Islam with respect to the lifespan and the applicability of the Qur'an and its injunctions.

Traditional Islam has assumed the lifespan of the Qur'an to be eternal, to comprise an infinite interval, and the lifespan of all injunctions within the Qur'an to have the same lifespan as the Qur'an itself. Furthermore, Traditional Islam has assumed the lifespan and the applicability horizon of the injunctions to be one and the same thing. Accordingly, Traditional Islam considers the applicability of all Qur'anic injunctions of the various categories to be eternal. Such assumptions have led to consider Islamic law a cornerstone in any interpretation of religion based on Traditional Islam.

This work differs with the traditional view on the lifespan and the applicability of the Qur'an and its injunctions. It accepts that all contents of the Qur'an share the same lifespan as the Qur'an itself; however, it recognizes this lifespan to be a bounded interval—similar to what was assumed to have been the Mu'tazila's view—and not an unbounded interval. Furthermore, it views the applicability of the Qur'anic injunctions to vary. It views the applicability of the injunction categories related to belief, ethics, and worship to be equal to the bounded interval of the Qur'an's lifespan, while it views the applicability of the Action-Type II category of injunctions to be space-time specific. This leads to reject religious law as to comprise a component of any acceptable Qur'anic-based interpretation of religion.

But how did I arrive at this reformed view of the lifespan and the applicability of the Qur'anic injunctions? In what follows I clarify the reasoning involved, some of which has already been touched on when exploring the position of the Mu'tazila on lifespan (Section 5.5.3.a).

As has been stated previously, the Qur'an is a communication from God. The Qur'an can be viewed as an offer from God delivered through Prophet Muhammad. The offer constituted an invitation for all beings to believe in, submit to, and worship the one and only God; however, as per the offer, belief, submission, and worship are not enough to win an abode in Paradise. For an everlasting abode in Paradise, true believers must also do good in their lifetime (Q. 4:122–126, 13:18–26, 53:31–42). This offer is a time-limited offer; it ends with the last day or with one's death, whatever comes first (Q. 17:61–65, 23:99–104 in 23:91–118, 63:9–11). Accordingly, the lifespan of the instance of God's speech manifested in the Qur'an is from the time of revelation up until the last day (a bounded interval: bounded at both beginning and end). Hence, the lifespan of the Qur'an comprises a bounded and not an infinite interval. In view of that, the lifespan of the injunctions of the Qur'an cannot be assumed to be eternal.

NOTICE In view of the Qur'an to represent a time-limited offer from God to us beings, one could ask: What utility would the Qur'anic injunctions on belief, worship, or even ethics be after the last day? For the Qur'an described the opportunity to believe and to do good to be confined solely to before the last day.

For simplification purposes and for easier comparison with Traditional Islam on the injunctions, I will assume this bounded lifespan of the Qur'an to be a left bounded interval (since the date of the last day is unknown). Although, strictly speaking, I maintain that the lifespan of the Qur'an is a bounded interval. Be that as it may, the lifespan of the Qur'an still determines the lifespan of all injunctions within the Qur'an. Thus, all Qur'anic injunctions equally have an eternal lifespan. When it comes to the applicability of the Qur'anic injunctions, unlike Traditional Islam, this work does not make the assumption that applicability is necessarily equal to lifespan. This work is of the viewpoint that the applicability from the time of revelation onwards applies solely to the injunctions that address belief, ethics, and acts of worship. However, when it comes to the injunctions of Action-Type II, which elaborate on regulating worldly matters, this work considers their applicability to be space-time specific.

The reasoning behind rejecting the eternal applicability of the Qur'anic Action-Type II injunctions is given in the next section.

Side note 5.12 The Medina implementation

The Qur'an included stories of God's prophets/messengers from Adam to Muhammad passing through Noah, Moses, Jesus, and many others. It is my understanding that for any space-time after the death of Prophet Muhammad, the particulars of the story of Prophet Muhammad and the peoples of Medina, its social norms and laws, as mentioned in the Qur'an, are of mere historical significance.

After the death of the Prophet, the particulars of the story of the Prophet became not any different from any of the other stories (examples) of prophets/messengers of God mentioned in the Qur'an. The particulars of the story of Prophet Muhammad were expressed in numerous verses of the Medina era, where many of the Medinan verses were addressed directly to the peoples of that particular space-time. Such verses reflected specifics relevant only to the Medina implementation in the time of the revelation. The Medina implementation is an implementation that, for us today, should be of mere historical significance, rather than as Traditional Islam considers it to transcend space-time.

Law declared in the Qur'an can be described as being in harmony with the social norms in the space-time of the revelation. Yet at the same time, it included progressive reforms in the direction of the Qur'anic ethics. However, social norms and law evolve, by humane and ethical standards, and are not fixed. Assuming them to be fixed, on the account that they were mentioned in the Qur'an, is an assumption made by men.

Side note 5.13 On social norms and social roles at the time of the revelation

An example on social norms and social roles at the time of the revelation can be observed in Q. 3:14–15. In these verses, when addressing the patriarchal society of the space-time of the Prophet, the Qur'an cited examples of worldly desires relevant to that society, the utmost of what they could desire.

In Q. 3:14, the Qur'an declares that it is adorned to people the love of lusts for (desires of) women, sons, and wealth (expressed as stored-up heaps of gold and silver), in addition to tillage, livestock, and marked horses; all of which reflect enjoyments (also translated as: pleasures, comforts, possessions, provisions, or belongings) of the worldly life. However, in the end of the verse and in the following verse, Q. 3:15, it is stated (roughly) that what awaits the pious with God is better.

By listing love of certain desires in particular, Q. 3:14 reflected the norms prevalent in the patriarchal society of the space-time the Qur'an was revealed. It should be understood that Q. 3:14 does not imply that the norms prevalent in the space-time the Qur'an was revealed would continue to be prevalent across space-time. Additionally, Q. 3:14 does not ask to preserve such norms throughout space-time.

The idea behind Q. 3:14–15, by citing examples of desires relevant to the society of the space-time the Qur'an was revealed, was for people of that particular space-time to understand (and hopefully for people of other space-time to also understand), that whatever one considered to be optimal desires in the worldly life, what awaited the pious in the afterlife would be better.

By the same logic, laws declared in the Qur'an suitable to manage and organize the society when the Qur'an was revealed, a society with norms as depicted in Q. 3:14, were meant explicitly for that society within that particular space-time, and cannot be expected to apply to societies across space-time.

Side note 5.14 An insight on the form of society and the injunctions of scripture

In an interview with the late orientalist William Montgomery Watt (d. 2006 CE), during his 90th year in 1999 CE (Maan and McIntosh 2000, 2011), while answering one of the questions posed, Prof. Watt expressed his viewpoint on the relationship between the form of society and the injunctions of the Qur'an and the Bible: "[T]he precise commands which God gives to believers depend on the form of society in which they are living. Traditionally Muslims have argued from God's eternity that the commands he gives are unalterable, and they have not admitted that social forms can change" (Maan and McIntosh 2000, 10). He adds, "I therefore do not believe that either the Bible or the Qur'an is infallibly true in the sense that all their commands are valid for all time. The commands given in both books were true and valid for the societies to which the revelations were primarily addressed; but when the form of society changes in important respects some commands cease to be appropriate, though many others continue to be valid." (Maan and McIntosh 2000, 10)

I find it worthwhile to cite the original question and the complete response given by Prof. Watt (Maan and McIntosh 2000, 10):

Islam maintains that the word of God is final and we can't change it. Christianity, with its understanding of the dynamic presence of the Holy Spirit is in constant flux. Where do you stand on this difference?

I would be inclined to say that the Qur'an is the word of God for a particular time and place and will not therefore necessarily suit other times and places. The prohibition on usury may have been good for a certain time and place but that doesn't mean it will always be good.

[According to Fernando (2020, sec. 2), "Historically, the term usury was used to describe all forms of lending involving the payment of interest by the borrower. In recent times, however, the term is generally used to describe only those loans which carry particularly high rates of interest."]

Watt, in the footsteps of Traditional Islam, assumed the Qur'anic term *al-riba* to mean "usury" in the traditional sense, representing any interest-based lending. Moreover, he considered usury to be acceptable today. However, I would like to point out that usury, in the modern usage of the word, referring specifically to providing loans at unreasonably high interest rates, is illegal today in most, if not all, countries around the world. The following side note discusses the Qur'anic term *al-riba*.]

You see, I think that Muslims need help in reaching a fresh understanding of the Qur'an as God's word, but comparison with the Bible does not help much. The Qur'an came to Muhammad in a period of less than 25 years, whereas from Moses to Paul is about 1300 years. Christians could perhaps show from the Bible that there is a development in God's relation to the human race. For

122

example, Moses was told to order the death penalty by stoning for anyone who broke the Sabbath by gathering firewood on it. Joshua was told to exterminate the whole population of various towns, men women and children. Could the loving God taught by Jesus have given such barbaric and bloodthirsty orders? To say "No," as one would like to do, throws doubt on the inspiration of the Bible. We seem to have to say that the precise commands which God gives to believers depend on the form of society in which they are living. Traditionally Muslims have argued from God's eternity that the commands he gives are unalterable, and they have not admitted that social forms can change.

I therefore do not believe that either the Bible or the Qur'an is infallibly true in the sense that all their commands are valid for all time. The commands given in both books were true and valid for the societies to which the revelations were primarily addressed; but when the form of society changes in important respects some commands cease to be appropriate, though many others continue to be valid. I do, however, believe that Muhammad, like the earlier prophets, had genuine religious experiences. I believe that he really did receive something directly from God. As such, I believe that the Qur'an came from God, that it is Divinely inspired. Muhammad could not have caused the great upsurge in religion that he did without God's blessing.

The diagnosis of the Meccan situation by the Qur'an is that the troubles of the time were primarily religious, despite their economic, social and moral undercurrents, and as such capable of being remedied only by means that are primarily religious. In view of Muhammad's effectiveness in addressing this, he would be a bold man who would question the wisdom of the Qur'an.

Side note 5.15 What is *al-riba*?

The term *riba* is derived from the word-root *rba* (*raba*, a transcription showing short vowels) that basically means: to grow, to increase, to augment. In the Qur'an the word *al-riba* (with or without the definite particle *al*—equivalent for the definite article "the") has a negative connotation to it. It was used to refer to a practice that the Qur'an prohibited.

Traditional Islam considers *al-riba* to be any interest-based lending. There are those who consider *al-riba* to be debt slavery: defaulters in *al-riba* would end up as slaves ('Ali 1993, 5: 574, 617–620; 'Ashmawi 1995; Kuran 2011, 144–147; Martin 2004, 2: 596–597). However, based on the usage of the term *riba* in the Qur'an, I interpret the Qur'anic term *al-riba* to represent a lending practice that has unreasonably high rates of interest.

Let us go back to the Qur'an to see how the Qur'an used this term—what does the Qur'an say about *al-riba*?

From the Qur'an the following can be understood about *al-riba*:

■ It involved a capital investment that yielded return for the lender (Q. 2:278–280 in 2:275–281)

It is a lending practice where the borrower has to pay back the original amount borrowed plus an additional amount (accumulated interest).

- It returned multiples of the original amount loaned (double or its multiples) (Q. 3:130 in 3:130–137, 30:39 in 30:36–40)

It was double the original amount borrowed that was required to be paid back, and it was redoubled in the event of default and the extension of the loan for another period, and so on.

Q. 30:39 stated that in the balance with God, what multiplies is what is given out in *zakat* and not what is lent out in *riba*. In this verse the Qur'an contrasted between the revenue from lending out in *riba* and the revenue from giving the *zakat*. What should really matter is reward in one's balance with God if one sought true reward.

I interpret the *zakat* or obligatory giving to be 20% of income. I understand the paying of the *zakat* in the time of the revelation to represent the equivalent of paying taxes to the state (on income and other taxes), that a good portion of its proceeds would be spent on the poor, the needy, and other social worthy causes.

Q. 30:39 was the only instance in the Qur'an where the term *riba* appeared without the definite particle *al* (equivalent for the definite article "the").

- The Qur'an prohibited the practice of *al-riba*: it was not a new prohibition (Q. 2:275–281, 3:130–132 in 3:130–137, 4:161 in 4:160–162)

The practice of *al-riba* was—unconditionally—prohibited in the Qur'an (regardless of whether or not the borrower was a believer). From the Qur'an we understand that the prohibition of *al-riba* was not new, the Qur'an stated that previously it had also been forbidden: the Qur'an explicitly stated that the followers of the Torah had been forbidden it.

After considering the occurrences of the term *riba* in the Qur'an (with or without the definite particle *al*), as previously pointed out, I interpret this term to represent a lending practice with unreasonably high rates of interest—which we understand existed in the space-time of the revelation. Therefore, it is my view that not all interest-based lending was prohibited by the Qur'an; rather, it was specifically *al-riba* that was prohibited. Today, most states around the world have laws to protect against providing loans at exorbitant interest rates, which place a cap on interest rates for loans.

5.6 Can the Qur'an be considered a source of eternal law? (arguments against)

In this section I present arguments to support the reasoning behind rejecting the eternal applicability of the Qur'anic Action-Type II injunctions. It is important to realize that this held view, to regard the applicability of Action-Type II injunctions to be space-time specific, does not oppose the Qur'an. The Qur'an never declared its Action-Type II injunctions to have eternal applicability. To consider the Action-Type II injunctions of the Qur'an to be eternally applicable was based on a claim made by men; it was a claim made by Traditional Islam.

Six arguments are presented that refute the claim of the eternal applicability of the Qur'anic Action-Type II injunctions, and consequently refute the religious justification given to all law based on or derived from them.

The reader is to note that the arguments presented do not have to refute the eternal applicability of every single injunction within the Action-Type II category of injunctions. Actually, if only a single injunction within the Action-Type II category is shown to be of non-eternal applicability, then that goes to prove that the claim made by Traditional Islam about the eternal applicability of the Action-Type II injunctions was false.

5.6.1 Inter-scripture abrogation

It is to be argued that acceptance of inter-scripture abrogation implies acceptance of the non-eternal applicability of law that manages man-world affairs.

All Muslims accept and acknowledge inter-scripture abrogation (abrogation between the revealed scriptures where certain injunctions in later scripture abrogated those in earlier scriptures) (Q. 3:50 in 3:45–51, 7:157 in 7:155–159, 13:36–41). The view presented in this work accepts inter-scripture abrogation, not intra-scripture abrogation (within a scripture: within the Qur'an), and recognizes inter-scripture abrogation as the abrogation in question when interpreting Qur'anic verses that explicitly mention abrogation (Q. 2:106, 13:36–41, 16:101–102).

It is my understanding that the various revealed scriptures were versions of the same message (Q. 7:43 in 7:40–43, 87:9–19), each delivered in the language of the peoples it was originally sent to (Q. 14:4, 41:44, 42:7, 46:12). The variation in the law injunctions across the revealed scriptures indicates that the injunctions within each scripture that elaborated on regulating worldly matters were not meant to be eternally applicable. As far as injunctions go, the Code was pretty much the same across all the revealed scriptures; however, each scripture had its unique set of laws. That is to say, the Code was realized differently in the laws included within each of the different scriptures.

One could interpret inter-scripture abrogation of the law injunctions to have occurred so that the new (modified) law injunctions would better suit the social norms of the new space-time—which is what is expected of law. The newer scripture came with laws to realize the (constant) ethics in ways that best suited the space-time of the revelation of the new scripture. And if we accept this abrogation occurring to law injunctions of the earlier revealed scriptures, the law injunctions of the Qur'an would be no different. Not that there has been new revelation to abrogate them, but rather, it is that, change in space-time has rendered a good number of these laws invalid. This stems from the simple fact: For law to be just, it should change with space-time, i.e. law regulating worldly matters simply cannot be assumed to be eternal.

As aforementioned, it is my view that abrogation of the older law injunctions occurred since the social norms of society changed over space-time. This brings us to talk about change in social norms. To say the least, change in social norms is slow—as to be discussed in Section 6.6. For instance, let us take an example closer to our time, maybe the idea would be easier to grasp. Not until the middle of the twentieth century CE, was there a universal adoption of human rights law that banned slavery. Moreover, not until the twentieth century CE, or more accurately, the second half of it, did states start to give women equal political rights. And not until then were there (universal) laws that prohibited discrimination against women. There are so many other examples on the development of humane ethical laws that we nowadays take for granted. Laws that call for equality irrespective of race, ethnicity, gender, religion, or country of origin are relatively new. In effect, over the history of mankind, change in social norms occurred slowly, and inertia kept old norms alive within cultures over long periods of time. The slow change in social norms could help explain the time gap between the different scriptures. This could also help explain why not all inter-scripture laws were abrogated: some norms did not change since societies remained to be patriarchal.

It is worthwhile to reflect on the fact that the Qur'an required Prophet Muhammad to always revert to the Qur'an whenever he was asked to arbitrate in disputes—even when the disputes involved Monotheists who were followers of other scriptures (Q. 5:48–49 in 5:41–50). This could be understood in that, since the Qur'an was the last (and latest) of the divine communications; therefore, the laws it included represented the most up to date laws most suitable for that space-time.

There is more I would like to say about inter-scripture abrogation before we move forward with the next argument in support of rejecting the eternal applicability of the Qur'anic Action-Type II injunctions. However, what will be addressed is not directly related to the topic of rejecting the eternal applicability of the Qur'anic Action-Type II injunctions, yet I find it important to include in order to build a more comprehensive understanding of inter-scripture abrogation.

Let us look at inter-scripture abrogation from a different or wider perspective. Let us go back to the Qur'an and try to answer a couple of questions that should give new insights and provide us with a better understanding of inter-scripture abrogation. One might ask: Why would God, an omniscient omnipotent deity (Q. 2:255, 18:109–110, 36:77–83), send newer scripture abrogating earlier divine injunctions? The question here is twofold: Why the new scripture, and why abrogate?

5.6.1.a On why send new scripture(s)

As for why the new scripture part, an answer to this question that I understand from the Qur'an, that it was to make clear that whereon the peoples of previous scriptures had differed and to bring the followers of God's message together.

The Qur'an tells us, that initially, people—the followers of God's message—were one community, then they fell into variance and divided amongst themselves (Q. 2:253, 3:18–19, 3:105, 10:19, 10:93, 11:110, 16:124 in 16:120–128, 19:34–37 in 19:16–40, 32:23–25, 41:45, 42:13–14, 45:16–17, 98:4 in 98:1–8). Therefore, later messengers were sent to make clear that whereon the followers of God's message had differed (Q. 2:213, 16:63–64, 27:76–81, 43:63–65 in 43:57–89). Moreover, according to the Qur'an, in the communications delivered by the messengers of God, from Noah, passing through Abraham, Moses, Jesus and Muhammad, followers were enjoined—through the messengers—to fulfill God's code and not to be divided (Q. 42:13–16 in 42:1–26).

The Qur'an explicitly stated that it had been revealed so as to explain clearly all that had been bestowed before (Q. 16:43–44,

16:89). It contained verses that addressed convictions and practices of those who had gone astray from the peoples of previous scriptures (Q. 5:12–19, 5:70–79, 9:29–35). It also shed light on some false practices of other peoples besides the (known) peoples of previous scriptures and made clear what had truly been ordained by God (Q. 5:103–105, 6:136–153).

Furthermore, as a new scripture, the Qur'an called on all followers of the revealed scriptures to fulfill the Code and not to be divided (Q. 42:13–16). The Qur'an confirmed the message of the earlier revealed scriptures (Q. 2:41 in 2:40–46, 2:89–91 and 2:97–101 in 2:83–103, 3:3–4, 4:47 in 4:44–57, 5:48 in 5:41–50, 6:92, 35:31, 46:12), as did the previous messengers and scriptures in connection with what had come before them (Q. 3:81–82, 3:39 and 3:50 in 3:33–63, 5:46 in 5:41–50, 61:6 in 61:5–9). The Qur'an called for exclusive monotheism (Q. 2:255, 3:18, 7:158, 20:1–8, 23:116–118, 28:88)—bringing guidance, mercy, and good tidings to those who submit and warning all others (Q. 18:1–8, 25:56, 27:1–6, 41:1–8).

The Qur'an asserted in connection with the peoples of previous scriptures—both pre-revelation (historical) and contemporary—who divided amongst themselves and fell into variance that their case rests with God (their affair was with God to judge between them on the Day of Resurrection) (Q. 2:113, 10:93 in 10:93–109, 45:16–17). Furthermore, regarding the contemporaries of them, who additionally did not accept the Qur'anic revelation, the Qur'an declared that the Prophet's task was to deliver God's message, and that the Prophet had no contention or concern with them (Q. 3:20 in 3:18–20, 5:67 in 5:65–69, 6:159 in 6:154–160, 42:15 in 42:1–26)—the Prophet was sent as a witness, a herald of good tidings, a warner and a summoner (of all men) to God by His leave (Q. 33:45–48, 34:28, 48:8–9, 73:15–19). The Qur'an emphasized that those who choose not to accept the Qur'anic revelation from the peoples of previous scriptures (as all others) would be doomed in the hereafter, and those who believed and did righteous deeds would be (forever) in Paradise (Q. 4:56–57 in 4:44–57, 4:150–152 in 4:150–175, 11:17 in 11:1–24, 42:16 in 42:1–26, 98:6–8 in 98:1–8).

5.6.1.b On why abrogate some of the earlier injunctions of the previous scriptures

For the second part of the question, on abrogation, note that the Qur'an indicated that God knows very well what He is sending down (God knows what is appropriate) (Q. 16:101 in 16:98–105), and that among the things that newer scripture had come with was to make permissible part of what previously had been prohibited (Q. 3:50 in 3:45–51, 7:157 in 7:155–159). Therefore, the answer to why abrogate could be: To make matters easier for the followers of the different scriptures.

The Qur'an indicated that some injunctions in the earlier scriptures were prescribed in response to wrongdoings of the peoples, as in the case of the additional dietary restrictions (Q. 4:160–161 in 4:153–162, 6:145–147, 16:118 in 16:114–119)—the additional restrictions beyond the four divine prohibitions (Q. 3:93–95). Even the Sabbath was described to have been ordained on those who differed (Q. 16:124 in 16:120–128). All these injunctions were abrogated in the Qur'an and the prohibitions were lifted.

> NOTE: As discusses in Volume 1, the Qur'an brought together the followers of the different revealed scriptures (the inclusiveness aspect of the Qur'an's teachings). It declared food and marriage permissible amongst the Monotheists. Those who accepted the revelation from the peoples of previous scriptures maintained their religious identities; nevertheless, aside from accepting the belief system of the Qur'an (the five articles of faith), accepting the revelation brought about significant changes to their practices. This is the realm of inter-scripture abrogation. The change in the practices of those who accepted the revelation from the peoples of previous scriptures primarily related to dietary restrictions and the Sabbath. Moreover, there was an administrative change, when it came to giving the *zakat*, they were required to give the *zakat* (20% of income) to Prophet Muhammad, on par with the QMonotheists.
>
> The Qur'an called to follow the way of Prophet Abraham. It called to return to the origins—that too applied to dietary restrictions and acts of worship. For those who accepted the revelation from the peoples of previous scriptures, their dietary restrictions would have become the same as those of the QMonotheists (no dietary restrictions beyond the four divine prohibitions). The observance of the Sabbath was also lifted. Moreover, these peoples were to give the *zakat*, as did the QMonotheists, directly to the Prophet and not to the religious leaders of their respective communities. Other rites would have continued to be observed as per each scripture.

5.6.2 Legal vacuum

The society in the space-time of the revelation could be described as being simple in terms of structure and composition. The model of the state implemented at the time of the Prophet, after the capture of Mecca, was one in which different religious communities would self-govern according to their own community laws. The laws needed to organize each community were simple and limited too. We find that the Qur'an did not come with laws for communities that did not believe in the Qur'an. The laws found in the Qur'an were only for the QMonotheists, apart from a few that also affected other Monotheists.

The laws found in the Qur'an are laws limited in both number and scope. These laws are mostly related to what can be categorized under family law and penal law. If taking the laws found in the Qur'an out of the model of the state in which they were implemented, and if we were to attempt to apply them in today's states, we would find there is a legal vacuum. This goes to show that the laws within the Qur'an—a component within the Qur'an's Action-Type II injunctions—were meant for the space-time of the revelation and cannot be assumed to be eternally applicable.

In an attempt to understand the context of implementation of the Action-Type II injunctions of the Qur'an in the space-time of the Prophet, as an example, I will reference the penal code of the Qur'an. A detailed study of the penal code of the Qur'an is beyond the scope of this book. However, it is suffice to know that the penal code of the Qur'an handled only a handful of offenses—dealing in matters related to loss of human life, bodily injury, property theft, illegal sexual acts, and what could be described as acts of corruption in the land (traditionally interpreted as "brigandage"). The Qur'an's penal code was meant for a small community in a time long ago. The Qur'an's penal code would not suffice the needs of most societies of the present era.

When it comes to penal codes, it is my understanding that in the space-time of the Prophet there was differentiation between penal codes; moreover, different penal codes would apply to different communities.

After the capture of Mecca, in the territories under the rule of the QMonotheists, I assume the following penal codes would have been upheld:

■ The penal code of the QMonotheists

The penal code of the Qur'an would have been applied solely on the QMonotheists. Followers of previous scriptures who accepted the revelation would have applied laws according to their own scriptures (Q. 5:41–50, 5:65–69). In disputes that involved Monotheists who did not follow the same scripture, or in cases of disputes amongst Monotheists who followed the same scripture but who wanted to escalate, it is my reckoning these Monotheists would have resorted to the Prophet to arbitrate (Q. 3:23, 4:59–70, 42:15 in 42:1–26). In such incidents, the laws of the Qur'an would have been upheld if and when applicable (Q. 5:48–49 in 5:41–50, 16:126–127 in 16:120–128, 17:33 in 17:22–39, 42:39–43 in 42:35–43).

■ The penal code of the disbelieving communities of the peoples of previous scriptures (under the rule of the QMonotheists, Q. 24:55)

Under the new order of affairs upon the capture of Mecca, the Qur'an prescribed that these peoples would have been required to pay the *jizya* (commonly interpreted to mean "poll-tax") (Q. 9:29 in 9:29–35). As for the penal code or any other laws to be applied within such communities after the capture of Mecca, no explicit mention was given in the Qur'an. It only makes sense that they would have continued to apply their own community-laws.

Furthermore, the Qur'an clearly stated that there would be no compulsion in the choice of code; after all, the right path had been distinguished from the paths that lead people astray (people were free to choose; they were made aware of their options—and the consequences involved) (Q. 2:256–257). Amongst the objectives of such a directive, as I see it, would be to protect against religious persecution (in this case: to protect the communities under the rule of the QMonotheists from religious persecution and to protect against persecution from within these same communities). Hence, I would assume that members of such communities would have continued to follow their own code and community-laws. Yet if amongst them, there were those who wanted to accept the Qur'anic revelation, then they would have been allowed to do so even if it had been originally forbidden under their local laws, i.e. they would have been given the opportunity to accept the Qur'anic revelation away from being persecuted by their own communities.

Aside from the Qur'anic injunctions that have been discussed in Volume 1, in relation to food, marriage and acts of worship, the Qur'an mainly specified laws only for the QMonotheists. Nevertheless, in many cases, it did mention what God had prescribed in the previously revealed scriptures (Q. 5:32 in 5:27–34, 5:44–45 in 5:41–50).

The penal code of the Qur'an only addressed situations in which both offender and victim were from the QMonotheists. For example, when discussing the offense of killing another human being, in the specific cases of murder and manslaughter, the Qur'an described how to act when both the killer and the victim were from the QMonotheists (Q. 2:178–179, 4:92–93). This is not to be understood that it was legitimate for the QMonotheists to kill others who were not QMonotheists. On the contrary. In the ethical system of God (the guideline behind all laws), the taking of any human life (*al-nafs*) was prohibited unless for a rightful reason (Q. 6:151 in 6:151–153, 17:33 in 17:22–39, 25:68 in 25:63–77): only as punishment for deliberate killing or punishment for "corruption done in the land"—traditionally interpreted as "brigandage" (Q. 5:32 and 5:33 in 5:27–34).

For inter-community killings that involved subjects from the QMonotheists and other communities, I assume arbitration would have been in order, as arbitration was the approach adopted in that space-time to resolve disputes (Q. 2:188).*1

The concept of the state has evolved over time. Nowadays, there are hardly any states whose citizens all follow the same religion; furthermore, there are very few states with tribal based societies of the same religious following. Modern states and their societies have different structure and composition from those of the space-time of the Prophet and are more complex in almost every aspect. Citizens living in modern states come from diverse racial, ethnic, and religious backgrounds. At present, and in the era of the modern state, it would neither be practical nor efficient for each (religious) community within the state to have its own set of laws. Aside from the fact that

132

surely for any religious community there does not exist a corpus of divine law (I am not talking about man-made law that is claimed to be divine law; I am talking about divine law originally included in scripture) that covers the present era's complexities and intricacies. This goes to show that laws stated in the Qur'an were not meant to be eternally applicable.

NOTE*1: Q. 17:22–39 represents a passage that listed ethics injunctions. However, in this passage we find a single law injunction that appeared within Q. 17:33 that gave authority to the *waly* (partner—of kinsmen or others) of the one killed unjustly (not in the course of justice) to kill the murderer in return.

I find interesting that within listing the ethics injunctions, we only find this particular punishment (course of action given for the case of unjust killing). I understand this course of action to have applied—in the space-time of the revelation—in the case of a murder where both the victim and the perpetrator were Monotheists. (This punishment appeared within entries of the Code. Monotheists accept the Code; thus, they would have accepted this punishment.)

5.6.3 The absence of a unique interpretation of the Qur'anic Action-Type II injunctions

It is to be argued that if there does not exist a single and unique interpretation of the Qur'an's Action-Type II injunctions, then how can any interpretation of the Action-Type II injunctions claim that it is the right interpretation that should be applied across space-time?

The classical schools of jurisprudence differed in interpreting the Qur'an's Action-Type II injunctions. As an example, the classical schools of jurisprudence differed in interpreting the penal code of the Qur'an, particularly the effect of repentance on applying punishment (Kuwait Ministry of Awqaf and Islamic Affairs 1995, 17: 133–134). Moreover, the schools of jurisprudence did not agree on almost all particulars regarding the offenses covered in the Qur'anic penal code. Sometimes even disagreeing on the form of punishment to be applied; whether or not the punishments would be applied on non-Muslims; and the criteria for applying the punishment, etc. (Kuwait Ministry of Awqaf and Islamic Affairs 1995, 17: 129–152; Madkur 1996, 136–137). If this proves anything at all, it proves that the penal code of the Qur'an was only intended for the space-time of the Prophet, when the Prophet was alive, and when there could be no contradicting interpretations.

There has always existed a multitude of interpretations of Islamic law. If Islamic law were truly God's law as claimed by Traditional

Islam, then only a single and unique body of Islamic law would exist—overlooking momentarily for the sake of argument the crucial fact that the authorship of the complete bulk of law should be that of God alone for it to be correctly labeled God's law. Otherwise, which of the interpretations of Islamic law constitutes God's law—especially with the vast differences amongst these interpretations on almost each topic and specific of law? Apparently, for the followers of these schools of jurisprudence, it does not matter much what the Qur'an is saying, what counts is what the school's jurists interpret the Qur'an to say. Eventually, what the jurists say about a matter is what makes it into the bulk of law of a particular school of jurisprudence.

5.6.4 The mortality of the Prophet

There are Qur'anic Action-Type II injunctions that dealt with the distribution of spoils (whether gained with or without fighting). These injunctions included the Prophet as a rightful beneficiary (Q. 8:1–4, 8:41, 59:6–10). How the Prophet's share in spoils was to be dealt with after the death of the Prophet was not addressed in the Qur'an.

Muslim scholars and schools of jurisprudence disagreed on how the Prophet's (potential) share of the spoils was to be distributed (al-Tabari 2001, 11:184–200 1/10, 22:515–520 37/28; Kuwait Ministry of Awqaf and Islamic Affairs 1995, 20:12–20, 31:302–321, 32:227–234). If such injunctions were intended to be eternal sources of law, then the Qur'an would have explicitly declared what should happen after the death of the Prophet, and would not have left it for the different interpretations to decide.

5.6.5 Judgment Day perspective regarding the application mechanism of the Code

It is to be argued that on Judgment Day, for those of us who believed in God and who hoped for an abode in Paradise, what matters is: Whether or not one upheld the Code in the earthly life. And not what punishment was applied in the earthly life—for those of us who acted counter to what the Code had instructed.

Believing in Judgment Day requires believing that on Judgment Day our faith and our actions would be judged. The way we lived our lives would be judged according to a set standard. This set standard is the Code, God's code of ethics and worship—as communicated to the beings through the messengers of God. In the first chapter of the

134

Qur'an, Judgment Day is even called "day of the Code (*yawm al-din*, Q. 1:1–4)."

As explained in Volume 1, to be described as being *muslim* involves submitting to God's code of ethics and worship, the Code—as conveyed through the messengers of God until the last of the messengers and revealed scriptures. However, each of the scriptures we are aware of, in a way, has its own application mechanism in connection with each of the two dimensions of the Code, the man-God and man-world dimensions.

To understand the applicability of the action injunctions that give the fine details for each of the two dimensions of the Code (to understand the applicability of the Action-Type I and Action-Type II injunctions), let us imagine it is already Judgment Day. That is to say, let us think in terms of the Judgment Day perspective regarding the application mechanism of the Code.

On Judgment Day, would it make any difference if we had observed the rite of fasting according to how fasting was prescribed in any of the previous scriptures or should we have observed fasting only according to how it was prescribed in the Qur'an? Each was prescribed by God. Followers of each of these scriptures fast, each at a different time. But all the followers fast because they were instructed to do so in the Code. Now on Judgment Day, when asked about fasting, followers of each scripture would answer: "We performed fasting according to how we were instructed in the scripture revealed to the Prophet we follow." From this, it can be deduced that the Action-Type I injunctions of the Qur'an (and the other revealed scriptures) that give the fine details for acts of worship are eternally applicable. They provide the details that enable us to fulfill the Code. How else would we know how to carry out the acts of worship?

When it comes to the Action-Type II injunctions, taking as an example the Action-Type II injunctions on punishment for violations (the penal codes revealed in the scriptures), do you think it would make any difference that if one had committed an offense in the earthly life (acted counter to what the Code had instructed), and was punished for it in the earthly life, would the form of punishment that one was punished with in the earthly life make any difference on Judgment Day? Whether the punishment was according to the punishments revealed in the scriptures or if it was according to a jail sentence as is customary in modern times, would the form of punishment matter—what difference would it make? Or would it be that what really mattered was that this individual acted counter to what the Code had instructed, and what would really make a difference was whether or not the offender, in her earthly life, had repented for her wrongdoing and had tried to rectify what she had done and/or did good afterwards? Accordingly, it can be deduced that the Action-Type II injunctions of the Qur'an on punishment for violations do not have eternal applicability. By the same token, this would hold true for the other Action-Type II injunctions of the Qur'an: they are not eternally applicable. The same would also be the case for the other revealed scriptures.

5.6.6 Social norms of the past

In any space-time, law is influenced by the social norms of its particular space-time. Laws prescribed in the Qur'an are no exception.

Laws prescribed in the Qur'an are found in the Action-Type II injunctions. The Qur'anic Action-Type II injunctions reflect the social norms of Hijaz (West Arabia), Arabia as a whole, and the region (particularly the norms of the Arab tribes of the region, those of Syria and Iraq—whether settled or Bedouin), that were prevalent in the early seventh century CE, the time of the revelation. For instance, there are Qur'anic Action-Type II injunctions that reflect social norms that accept the institution of slavery, accept physical forms of punishment, and ones that do not give women legal rights equal to those of men. Such injunctions and the social norms they reflect can be described to be unacceptable in modern times. Hence, the Qur'anic Action-Type II injunctions that address such issues cannot be deemed applicable across space-time, but rather, they were space-time specific.

Some might argue that such Action-Type II injunctions contradict the ethics of the Qur'an that demand fairness (Q. 4:58, 4:135, 5:8, 6:152, 7:29 in 7:26–30, 16:90, 17:34–35 in 17:22–39, 42:15 in 42:13–16, 60:7–11 in 60:1–13), and other verses in the Qur'an that serve as a constant reminder that all humans, men and woman alike, share the same origins (Q. 4:1, 6:98, 7:189, 22:5, 30:20 in 3:20–26, 35:11, 39:6, 40:67, 75:36–40, 76:1–2). That surely would be true if one were to consider the Action-Type II injunctions as eternally applicable.

However, if the Action-Type II injunctions were considered space-time specific, then there would be no contradiction. After all, the understanding of fairness and equality (human equality) is affected by space-time. What is considered to reflect fairness and equality in seventh century CE Arabia is different from what is considered to reflect fairness and equality for the different societies in the world of the twenty-first century CE.

As discussed in Volume 1, the objective of the Code was for justice to prevail in this life and the next. The objective of the Code was for us to be just to ourselves and to others. However, as time progresses, for justice to prevail, law needs to evolve in the direction that better reflects the understanding of fairness in the space-time in question. Here I mean relative justice, as absolute justice, in all likelihood, will exist only on Judgment Day.

Since the early seventh century CE, humanity's understanding of fairness has evolved. In the last century in particular, humanity has taken giant steps towards a new understanding of fairness. There has been universal agreement on the abolishment of slavery, the promotion of international human rights standards, and the rejection of discrimination against women, among many other developments. Hence, to be true to the Code, we cannot accept that the Action-Type II injunctions are eternally applicable. Social norms and the Qur'anic Action-Type II injunctions are further discussed in Chapter 6.

5.7 The approach to refute the eternal applicability of the primary sources

In the beginning of this chapter, it was stated that Islamic law would be used as the vehicle to study the eternal applicability of the primary sources. Therefore, the adopted approach to refute the eternal applicability of the primary sources will be through Islamic law, it will be through refuting the eternality of Islamic law.

5.7.1 To refute the eternality of Islamic law

To refute the eternality of Islamic law, we need first to understand Islamic law—starting with its components. By definition, Traditional Islam does not consider all components of Islamic law to be eternal. Yet in practice, more of Islamic law than what is officially declared to be eternal has traditionally been treated as eternal. Hence, our approach to refute the eternality of Islamic law will be in refuting the eternality of all components of Islamic law.

Traditional Islam considers Islamic law to be composed of two components:

- Eternal law: Laws extracted directly from the definitive primary sources.

- Non-eternal law: Laws extracted indirectly from the primary sources.

Even if this section were to explain the approach to refute the eternality of just the eternal component of Islamic law, the reader might wonder, why do that—isn't that what the last section just did? Yes, that is somewhat true. The reasoning behind this objection is valid. In the questioner's mind, since the eternal component of Islamic law is law extracted directly from the definitive Qur'anic Action-Type II injunctions, and since the six arguments presented in the previous section refute the eternal applicability of (all) the Qur'anic Action-Type II injunctions, then the presented arguments have already refuted the eternality of what is considered to be the eternal component of Islamic law. That is to say, if the sources are non-eternal then law derived from them is necessarily non-eternal. Such reasoning assumes that the only source of eternal law is the Qur'an. However, as defined above, the eternal component of Islamic law covers laws extracted directly from the definitive primary sources. The questioner is reminded, that as per the scope of this study of Islamic law (Section 5.2), the primary sources of Islamic law have been recognized to be the Action-Type II injunctions of both the Qur'an and the *Hadith*. Thus, as far as Traditional Islam is concerned, besides the Qur'an, law extracted directly from definitive *Hadith* is also considered to constitute eternal law.*1

Back to the objective of this section: To describe the adopted approach to refute the eternality of Islamic law. To go about refuting the claim of the eternality of Islamic law there are two possible alternatives:

- The top-down approach: This approach stems from rejecting the concept of the eternality of any (man-world) law; subsequently, it rejects all particulars of Islamic law.

It has been argued that assuming the eternality of a divine body of laws would indirectly require humanity to stop progress so that everything would stay static for such laws to always apply. At the same time, assuming the eternality of laws degrades humans to the level of insects, where there is no need for humans to think in order to solve their own problems, since pre-determined solutions have already been divinely prescribed for their monotonous existence (al-Nuwayhi 2010, 106–125, 134). Such arguments have been responded to by proponents of Islamic law in that not all sources of Islamic law are static, but rather some are dynamic, which in turn serve to adapt Islamic law to changes in space-time. However, these so-called dynamic sources of law (dynamic tools) that the proponents of Islamic law consider to be dynamic are in reality not at all that dynamic. First of all, the application of these dynamic tools was put on hold for a millennium or so years. Moreover, the bodies of law that were initially produced by these dynamic tools, over a thousand years back, became to be regarded as static sources of law in themselves. Hence, the bodies of law resulting from the dynamic tools became (also) to be viewed as eternal.*2

■ The sources approach: In this approach all sources of Islamic law are examined, and are proven one by one to be of non-eternal applicability. Thus, if all sources of Islamic law are proven to have non-eternal applicability, then law based on such sources would be non-eternal (the body of Islamic law). Accordingly, the claim of the eternality of religious law is refuted.

I remind the reader that our main purpose in studying Islamic law was to prove the non-eternal applicability of the primary sources. Both of the above approaches accomplish this objective. Out of the two approaches, the top-down approach readily proves the stated objective without requiring us to go into detail and to study each of the sources of Islamic law. That is to say, the top-down approach, besides refuting the eternality of Islamic law proves the non-eternal applicability of the primary sources. To clarify: Accepting the top-down approach to give a valid result (proves the non-eternality of Islamic law), and adopting the argument made by the sources approach yet without examining each of the sources (argument: Islamic law cannot be non-eternal unless all its sources have non-eternal applicability), we reach the conclusion that all sources of Islamic law have non-eternal applicability. Nevertheless, I still choose to take the longer approach: to go over the sources of Islamic law one by one to verify their eternal status. Accordingly, the sources approach is the approach that will be adopted in the remainder of this work to refute the eternality of Islamic law.*3

NOTE*1: By definition, Islamic law declares the definitive primary sources as the only eternal sources of law. However, for all practical purposes, consensus (*ijma'*, agreement of a group on a point of law) is effectively treated as an eternal source of law: almost all interpretations of Islamic law treat consensus as a source of law along with the primary sources in having the authority to produce eternal law. Consensus is explained in Section 7.3.

NOTE*2: It is rather absurd that the bodies of law produced by the so-called dynamic tools became to be regarded as static, and changing them would not at all be permitted. For example, consensus of scholars (*ijma'*) was used as a dynamic tool to produce new laws. However, the bodies of law produced by consensus became to be considered static sources of law in themselves for jurists in later times. The so-called dynamic component of Islamic law, law extracted indirectly from the primary sources—what I refer to in this book as *Fiqh*-based law—is addressed in Chapter 7.

NOTE*3: Not only does the sources approach allow us to better understand the sources of Islamic law and to examine them for eternal applicability—including, of course, the primary sources—but it also provides the reader with the opportunity to better understand the impact of these sources on Islamic law. Additionally, in studying the sources of Islamic law, the reader will be in a better position to appreciate the reform proposed in this work.

5.7.2 The interpretations of Islamic law: Classical and modern

We find Islamic law to be represented in both classical and modern bodies of law, or rather, these bodies of law represent interpretations of Islamic law. The classical bodies of law were produced by the various (classical) schools of jurisprudence. And the modern bodies of law can be seen as modern realizations of Islamic law produced by individuals, groups, and even states.

Two major differentiators distinguish the classical bodies of law from their modern counterparts: the classical bodies of law are the products of schools of jurisprudence, and they are non-codified. Modern schools of law simply do not exist, and unlike the classical bodies of law, modern bodies of Islamic law are by their very nature codified.*1

In spite of these major differences, it is important to point out that modern realizations of Islamic law agree with the classical schools of jurisprudence on the sources of Islamic law. Therefore, in the following sections and chapters of this book, when referencing the sources of Islamic law, I will discuss the sources of Islamic law as set by the classical schools of jurisprudence. Moreover, any classification(s) of Islamic law or its components will follow that of the classical schools unless indicated otherwise.

What enables us to examine Islamic law collectively is that for all practical purposes, all schools of jurisprudence agree on the same sources of Islamic law. However, the resulting body of law from each of the established schools of jurisprudence is different from that of the other schools.

Within each school, over time, there has been variant views on probably every point of law. This pluralism stands in sharp contrast with the spirit of codification. It is to be noted, in this context, historically (from the classical perspective), a body of law of a school of jurisprudence is not a codified representation of the interpretation of law produced by this school of jurisprudence. Official codification simply never occurred.*2

NOTE*1: Associating a body of law with a particular school of jurisprudence means that the body of law is in line with the principles of the school; that is, its doctrinal legal methodology, positive legal principles, and hermeneutics. However, for the modern bodies of law, the law is not based on or according to principles of a unique school's doctrine, simply because no modern schools of jurisprudence exist. The modern bodies of law adopt a pick-and-choose method from the bodies of law of the classical schools, alongside the creation of new laws.

NOTE*2: Anderson (1966, 243) states: "[W]e find no codification of Islamic law whatever, and no enactment of that law by the authority of the State, until quite recent times. On the contrary, the diversity in the interpretation of the law came to be considered a mercy from God while the law as a whole was regarded as a divinely-provided blue-print by which all, Ruler and subject alike, were bound to regulate their behaviour."

The initial attempts by a Muslim state to codify and promulgate selected parts of *Fiqh* as law, that aligned with a single school of jurisprudence (in this instance, the Hanafi school), began in the nineteenth century CE under the Ottomans, taking the form of codifications based on civil law. It should be highlighted that the codification of Islamic law by the British colonial rule in British India started in the late eighteenth century CE and was in the form of common law.

Furthermore, according to Anderson (1966, 244–246), the first example in Muslim history of codification that did not necessarily depict the (dominant) opinion of a single school of law (the Hanafi school in this case), was the codification and promulgation of the law of "obligations" (contract, tort, etc.) of the Hanfi school by the Ottomans in 1876 CE.

5.7.3 The two components of Islamic law (to refute the eternal applicability of)

The adopted approach to refute the eternality of Islamic law will be in refuting the eternality of both components of Islamic law. Despite the fact that the second component of Islamic law is officially declared to be non-eternal by definition, yet in practice, for the most part, it has been treated as eternal. Therefore, there arises the need to study both components of Islamic law.

For each of the different interpretations of Islamic law, the resulting body of law is comprised of two components. These two components of Islamic law are:

(1) Islamic law extracted directly from the definitive primary sources (officially recognized as eternal law)

▶ The Qur'an: Laws were extracted directly from the laws declared in the Qur'an. Yet although stated in the Qur'an, these Qur'anic laws ended up being interpreted differently by the various schools of jurisprudence (mainly due to relying on other sources besides the Qur'an to interpret the Qur'an).

▶ The *Hadith*: Schools of jurisprudence differed regarding what each considered reliable *Hadith*. For each party, it was only reliable *Hadith* that was considered to represent the *Sunna*. A list of laws extracted directly from the *Hadith* supplemented the list of laws extracted directly from the Qur'an. However, the *Hadith* did not complete any of the bodies of law.

(2) Islamic law extracted indirectly from the primary sources (officially recognized as non-eternal law)

Further additions to Islamic law (the bodies of) were added through jurisprudence (*Fiqh*)—via methods not necessarily the same across the different schools of jurisprudence. This portion of Islamic law constitutes its bulk.

In the following two chapters, the two components of Islamic law are studied and their eternal applicability is refuted. Each of the

142

following chapters is dedicated to one of these two components of Islamic law.

5.8 The effect of additions to the sources of religious knowledge on Islamic law

Although this book's main line of analysis is Traditional Islam, a note on the interpretations based on Traditional Islam would prove useful to clarify some ambiguities concerning Islamic law. This would also help clarify the relationships between an interpretation's triad: its recognized belief system, its sources of religious knowledge, and its interpretation of Islamic law.

5.8.1 The sources of religious knowledge and Islamic law (relationship between)

What is considered to be the sources of religious knowledge of an interpretation of Islam directly affect the Islamic law component of that interpretation of Islam, because such sources would also be considered as the primary sources of law for its particular interpretation of Islamic law.

The sources of religious knowledge of Traditional Islam are the Qur'an and the *Sunna*, yet some interpretations based on Traditional Islam add to these sources; they do so by supplementing what they consider *Sunna*. They consider *Hadiths* of certain individuals besides the Prophet to supplement the corpus of the *Hadith*. Sunnis give (varying) importance to the behavior of the first four to rule after the Prophet and others of the close companions. For the Shi'as (most sects), the referenced individuals are the Prophet's daughter Fatima (d. 11 AH / 632 CE) and those whom the Shi'a interpretations of Islam consider to be *imams*, the spiritual and political successors to the Prophet.

Side note 5.16 The non-Qur'anic term *ma'sum* (infallible)

There is a particular term that is relevant to this discussion, it is a term that frequently appears when Muslims describe Prophet Muhammad or any of the other messengers of God to humanity (for most Shi'a sects, usage extends to the Prophet's daughter Fatima and the recognized *imams*), it is the non-Qur'anic term *ma'sum*, which is commonly understood to mean "infallible." Other derivatives of the same root of *ma'sum* appeared in the Qur'an (Q. 5:67, 10:27, 11:43, 12:32, 33:17, 40:33, 60:10), but not the word *ma'sum*.

The root-word of *ma'sum* is *'asm*. According to Omar (2010, 375–376), the root *'asm* (*'asama*, a transcription showing short vowels) means: "To protect, prevent, hinder, defend, preserve, hold fast, abstain, save, keep any one safe from evil, preserve, formally seek refuge." In reference to the Qur'an's usage of a derivative of the root *'asm* with the Prophet, the exegete al-Zamakhshari (d. 538 AH / 1144 CE) interprets Q. 5:67 in 5:65–69, explaining that God commanded His Messenger to deliver all that had been bestowed upon him; otherwise, he would not have delivered God's message. And that God would protect him (his life) from the people (addressing the Prophet: *ya'simuk min al-nas*). Moreover, God would not allow those who reject His message to get their way (in killing the Prophet) (al-Zamakhshari 2009, 300–301).

Both Sunni and Shi'a Muslims consider the Prophet to be infallible. Most Sunni scholars said he was infallible from committing big faults (*kaba'ir*, sins), while most Shi'a scholars (the Twelvers) said he was infallible from all faults. However, there are a few who explain infallible differently, an explanation that makes sense to me—if one had to use such a word—which is that the Prophet was, as the other messengers of God all were, infallible when it came to delivering scripture. In that spirit, it is my view that this trait would only apply to the delivering of scripture (Q. 53:1–5, 69:38–52), and that the messengers of God should not be regarded as infallible humans, acting as sources of truth in themselves.

On the concept of infallibility in Islam, Hasan (1972) argued, "With the demise of the Prophet there remained no such source as divine revelation to ascertain the certitude of the decisions taken by the Muslims themselves in fresh cases. With the passage of time the Islamic society developed far in advance of the seventh-century Arabian society. There was a serious problem before Islam: How to extend the spirit or the divine revelation in order to exercise a check on the individual opinion which is erroneous in character to decide fresh cases, as the resurrection of the physical revelation was not possible? With this situation cropped up the idea of the impeccability of the Prophet of Islam, of the Prophets in general, of the infallibility of the community, and finally of *ijma'* [(consensus)] according to the Sunnis, and of the infallibility of *Imam* according to the Shi'ah. The concept of infallibility in Islam on these different levels is a substitute for divine revelation." (2)

5.8.2 On Shi'a Islam: The belief in *imams* and how it affected Islamic law

I will talk further about the Shi'a interpretations of Islam in particular, since this will give us the opportunity to look into the Shi'a belief in *imama* (imamate; the belief in *imams*; the doctrine of leadership), a belief unique to the Shi'as that is not shared by the Sunnis.

The *imama* is a doctrine which asserts that 'Ali ibn Abi Talib and certain individuals from his lineage—through his wife Fatima, a daughter of Prophet Muhammad—are to be accepted as leaders and guides of the community after the death of the Prophet. To the Shi'a,

144

excluding most Zaidi sects, the *imams* are considered infallible and possess divine knowledge; moreover, they are believed to have been appointed by God to guide the community both spiritually and temporally.*1

NOTICE: For the majority of the Shi'a, including the Twelvers and Isma'ilis, the concept of *imama* entails belief in the divinely appointed nature of the *imams*, their infallibility, and possession of divine knowledge. This belief holds that the *imams* are chosen by God not only to provide spiritual guidance but also to lead the community in political and social affairs, ensuring justice, equity, and the application of Islamic principles in all aspects of life. Furthermore, the *imams* are regarded as infallible and endowed with divine knowledge. Infallibility, in this context, denotes the protection by God from committing sins or errors, particularly in matters of religious guidance and interpretation. The notion of possessing "divine knowledge" refers to the belief that the *imams* are granted profound spiritual insight and understanding by God. This divine knowledge encompasses a deep understanding of religious teachings, guidance on matters of faith and practice, and insights into the spiritual and metaphysical realms.

In the case of the Shi'as, unlike the Sunnis, additions to the sources of religious knowledge were legitimized by the articles of faith recognized by these interpretations.*2

For the Shi'a interpretations of Islam, adding to the belief system of Traditional Islam, for the most part—in terms of religious implications—impacted the sources of religious knowledge, which in turn had a direct effect on Islamic law.

The addition to the articles of faith of interest to us here is the Shi'a belief in *imams*, starting with 'Ali ibn Abi Talib. The effect of this additional belief tenet on Islamic law depends on the Shi'a religious group under study.

There are three main contemporary Shi'a religious groups: the Twelvers, Isma'ilis, and Zaidis. The three groups differ in their understanding of *imama* and the *imams* each group recognizes. All three groups recognize the same first four *imams* (Wikipedia 2001b, sec. 5). Both the Twelvers (this group constitutes the majority of Shi'a) and Isma'ili Shi'a believe the *imams* to be divinely appointed (the living *imam* appoints his successor—through God's guidance).

Furthermore, they believe the *imams* to be infallible and to possess divine knowledge (Wikipedia 2001b, sec. 2). However, for the Zaidi Shi'a, the *imam* is elected not appointed, yet the *imam*—as in the case of the Twelvers and Isma'ilis—has to be a descendent from either of the two sons of the Prophet's daughter Fatima (al-Maghluth 2007, 504). Additionally, the *imam* for the Zaidis is not considered to be infallible (Coulson 1978, 104–108; 1992, 142–146).

For the Twelvers and Isma'ilis, their belief in *imama* affected what they consider to be primary sources, consequently affecting their interpretation(s) of Islamic law; however, that was not the case for the Zaidis. The following outlines how the belief in *imama* affected the interpretation(s) of Islamic law followed by each of the three main contemporary Shi'a religious groups:

■ The Twelvers (the group is named after the number of *imams* it recognizes)

For the Twelvers, the last of the *imams* (the twelfth) is in occultation since 261 AH / 874 CE (Coulson 1978, 106; 1992, 144).

The Twelvers regard the *Hadiths* of these *imams* to supplement the *Hadith* (Esposito 2003, 154; Wikipedia 2001b, sec. 5.1). Hence, in the case of the Twelvers, the belief in *imams* affected what they consider to be primary sources. Consequently, what is regarded as primary sources affects Islamic law.

■ The Isma'ilis (they differed with Twelvers on the seventh *imam*)

The Isma'ilis share the same first six *imams* with the Twelvers. They include religious groups that recognize Isma'il ibn Jafar (d. 138 AH / 755 CE) as the seventh *imam*, though he is not recognized to be the last *imam* by most Isma'ili religious groups. The Twelvers recognize Musa ibn Ja'far al-Kazim (183 AH / 799 CE) as the seventh *imam*.

The Isma'ilis regard the *Hadiths* of the *imams* recognized by them to supplement the *Hadith* (Daftary 2007, 170–172). Hence, Isma'ilis' belief in *imama* affected what they consider to be primary sources, consequently affecting the interpretations of Islamic law that they follow.

The Nizari Isma'ili community has continued with a present living (divinely guided) *imam*. According to the Isma'ilia

Constitution established by the Aga Khan in 1986, Nizari Ismailis recognize the *imam* as having exclusive authority to interpret the Qur'an and provide authoritative guidance on all matters of faith (Wikipedia 2004a, par. 1).

■ The Zaidis (also known as the Fivers; they differed with the Twelvers and Isma'ilis on the fifth *imam*)

For the Zaidis, the imamate continued. They believe that more than one *imam* can exist at the same time, though not in the same place (al-Maghluth 2007, 504). The Zaidis do not regard the *imam* as having any special legislative powers (Coulson 1978, 106; 1992, 144).

The Zaidis' unique understanding of *imama* did not cause them to supplement what they recognize to be the *Sunna*; it did not augment what they consider to be primary sources. The jurisprudence (*Fiqh*) of Zaidis is very similar to that of Hanafi Sunnis (Wikipedia 2001b, sec. 5.2.1 par. 1).*3

NOTE*1: 'Ali ibn Abi Talib was a first cousin of the Prophet. 'Ali was also the son in law of the Prophet—he was married to the Prophet's daughter Fatima (d. 11 AH / 632 CE). 'Ali ibn Abi Tali was the fourth to rule after the Prophet. He was murdered in 40 AH / 661 CE.

Both Sunnis and Shi'as acknowledge that Prophet Muhammad did not have male offspring that lived beyond infancy (the Qur'an stated that the Prophet did not have any male descendant; it is stated in Q. 33:40: "Muhammad is not the father of any one of your men"). The only two male grandchildren of the Prophet—the only sons of 'Ali and the Prophet's daughter Fatima who lived beyond infancy, al-Hasan (d. 50 AH / 670 CE) and al-Husayn (d. 61 AH / 680 CE)—are considered to be the second and third *imams*, respectively.

We understand from the Qur'an that the Prophet had daughters (Q. 33:59 in 33:56–62). The Qur'an does not specify how many. But the word in Q. 33:59 is *banatik* (your daughters), the plural form of *bint* (daughter), which in Arabic is used for three or more daughters. Sunnis recognize the Prophet to have had four daughters from his marriage to his first wife Khadija bint Khuwaylid (from eldest to youngest): Zainab, Ruqayya, Umm Kulthum, and Fatima (Wikipedia 2014a). There are Shi'a that claim that only Fatima was the Prophet's biological daughter, and the others were adopted after the death of Khadija's sister, Hala (Fedele 2019; Wikipedia 2014a). However, I do not agree with that assertion. When referencing the Qur'an, we find that the Qur'an only used the term *banat* in connection with biological daughters (Q. 4:23, 11:79, 33:59). For girls raised in one's household who are not one's biological daughters, the Qur'an used the term *raba'ib* (Q. 4:23; the term was used in this verse in connection with stepdaughters).

The Prophet's grandchildren—who lived beyond infancy—were through two of his daughters: the youngest Fatima and the eldest Zainab. The Prophet's daughter Fatima had four children with 'Ali ibn Abi Talib. And his daughter Zainab had one daughter, Umama bint Abi al-As. 'Ali ibn Abi Talib, after the death of his wife, the Prophet's daughter Fatima, married the Prophet's granddaughter Umama bint Abi al-As who bore him two sons. And after the death of 'Ali, Umama married al-Mughira ibn Nawfal ibn al-Harith and bore him a son (Wikipedia 2005).

NOTE*2: Most interpretations of Islam (both Sunni and Shi'a) add to the Qur'anic belief system: they add to the five articles of faith declared in the Qur'an. The proposed interpretation of the Qur'anic revelation does not recognize any articles of faith beyond the five (unequivocally) stated in the Qur'an. The five articles of faith are: the belief in the one and only God; the angels; the revealed scriptures sent prior to and including the Qur'an; all prophets/messengers of God, and not to make distinction between any of them—this includes believing that Prophet Muhammad was a messenger of God and the last of the prophets; and belief in the last day (resurrection and judgment).

NOTE*3: The Zaidis consider the *imams* not to be divinely appointed, infallible, or possessing divine knowledge; accordingly, they do not consider the *Hadiths* of the *imams* recognized by them to supplement the corpus of the *Hadith*. Nonetheless, Zaidis—as all Shi'as—prioritize the *Hadith* (of the Prophet) that is narrated by the family of the Prophet (*ahl al-bayt*), particularly those transmitted through 'Ali ibn Abi Talib and his descendants.

Zaidi Shi'a Muslims, like Isma'ili Shi'a Muslims, typically recognize their own unique collections of *Hadith*, distinct from both Sunni and Twelver Shi'a collections. These collections contain specific *Hadith* compilations that they consider authoritative. However, it is important to note that the reliance on *Hadith* in jurisprudence varies among the different schools of jurisprudence within each of the main Shi'a sects. Moreover, for the Shi'a, unlike the Sunnis, schools of jurisprudence vary with, and within, a specific Shi'a sect.

5.9 Apostasy law

Those thinking in terms of Islamic law or in terms of Traditional Islam will surely consider this book heresy. An offense that lies within the territory of Islamic law's apostasy law.

What is apostasy law? Apostasy law could be viewed as the means by which Traditional Islam protects itself. It is a law within Islamic law that was produced over a century or so after the Prophet's death. It is a law that considers Muslims who consciously abandon Islam— it includes several acts such as converting to any other religion, or those who reject either type of Islamic law (man-God, man-world), or parts of it—to be apostates (*murtadd,* noun *ridda*). A crime that is punishable by death and confiscation of possessions (Hazm 1983, 1:

73, 2: 144–145, 6: 31, 109–110, 117).*1

Apostasy law goes contrary to the Qur'an, in which it is clearly stated, that people were free in their choice of belief and choice of code. After all, the Prophet was sent to deliver God's message; he was not sent to coerce people to believe: the right path had been distinguished from the paths that lead people astray (people were free to choose; they were made aware of their options—and the consequences involved) (Q. 2:256–257, 5:103–105, 6:100–107, 10:99–109, 17:13–15, 18:27–31, 27:91–93, 39:9–18, 42:6, 42:47–48, 88:17–26, 109:1–6). Moreover, the Qur'an tells us that matters of *milla* (a chosen path in matters of belief, ethics, and acts of worship) were matters for God to assess and reward (Q. 2:62, 2:111–113, 2:135–141, 5:69, 5:104–105, 22:17, 42:15 in 42:13–16).

Apostasy law rests entirely on two *ahad Hadiths* of doubtful authenticity, which could have appeared during the late Umayyad and early Abbasid periods (Lamarti 2002). A time when people under Muslim rule who followed other religions were not forced to convert to Islam and were free to keep/choose their religious affiliations. However, according to apostasy law, if such non-Muslims did embrace Islam and were to revert afterwards, then in such a case they would be considered apostates. Apostasy law could probably have originated, and expanded upon from then onwards, for political reasons in reaction to external or internal political circumstances. Externally, as a reaction to rival rulings against Muslims, like the Byzantine ruling where in Byzantine territories anyone who became Muslim was killed (Amin 1964, 1: 340; Mez 19--?, 1: 76). Internally, as a maneuver to give the ruling authorities a religious justification (excuse) to get rid of their political adversaries, i.e. political apostasy became to be seen equivalent to religious apostasy.*2

Apostasy law, advocated by Islamic law, let alone its going against freedom of religious belief, it restricts freedom of thought and expression by making it sound as if no one has the right to think about the Qur'an but a specific few of self-appointed defenders of God and Islam. Moreover, any thinking about the Qur'an must align with their views, i.e. it must align with their interpretation(s).

On the other hand, a true understanding of the Qur'an would reveal, that the followers of the Qur'an are not supposed to include clergy at all. Needless to say, they should not include those who claim to speak and judge on behalf of God. To add insult to injury, to speak on behalf of God was explicitly prohibited in the Qur'an (Q. 7:33 in 7:31–34). In other words, there should be no middleman between God and man. It was this simplicity that drew people to the Qur'anic revelation to begin with. However, these self-appointed clergy try to present the Qur'anic revelation as something so complex and complicated, to the extent that an intermediary is needed to explain almost every single verse. Yet there is nothing further from the truth. And in their doing so, they repel Muslims and non-Muslims alike away from the Qur'an. Nonetheless, they are only able to drive away those who do not differentiate between the Qur'an and the interpretations of Islam.

To help the reader realize the extent of the restrictions placed by Islamic law on thinking outside what is traditional, and where this work fits into the bigger picture, it is best to try to make sense of some relevant historical events. This takes us to the very beginnings, when the early interpretations based on Traditional Islam were first established (*madhahib diniyya*, interpretations of religion covering interpretations of both theology and law). The first interpretations of Islam grew out of the first civil war that had erupted less than three decades after the death of the Prophet. Additional interpretations followed that did not necessarily evolve from political standpoints. By the end of the first century AH, the established interpretations had their distinct followers, and hardly any new interpretations surfaced afterwards. What followed was a kind of development of the early interpretations and fine-tuning to the norms of the time. Once the era of recording (*asr al-tadwin*) had started, probably around the mid-second century AH, and with the increase in the corpus of religious material, specialization was needed. Each of the main disciplines categorized under religion started to have its own areas of study. Islamic law being one of those main categories started to have its own schools of law (*madhahib fiqhiyya*). Around the mid-fourth century AH, Muslim scholars called for the closing of the gate of interpretation, this applied to interpretations in both theology and law. So basically, ever since the mid-fourth century AH, it has been considered taboo to come up with a new interpretation of law or theology, not to even imagine a new interpretation of the Qur'anic revelation. Today, in the fifteenth century AH, such a historical outline helps the reader understand where this work fits in the overall view of things. This book, along with Volumes 1 and 2, introduce a

150

new interpretation of the Qur'anic revelation. In addition, they argue that the numerous interpretations of Islam are unacceptable representations of the Qur'anic revelation.

We move on to examine the religious laws that are acknowledged in Muslim communities and societies, as put forward by Traditional Islam. According to the report produced by the Pew Research Center's Forum on Religion & Public Life, based on the findings of its survey—particularly on the origins of Islamic law (Pew Research Center. and Pew Forum on Religion & Public Life. 2013, 41–43), "most Muslims believe sharia is the revealed word of God rather than a body of law developed by men based on the word of God" (Pew Research Center. and Pew Forum on Religion & Public Life. 2013, 41). The referenced report utilized the term "sharia" interchangeably with "Islamic law" to indicate the same concept.

What is commonly referred to as Islamic law, is actually separated into two distinct components: law extracted directly from the primary sources and law extracted indirectly from the primary sources, what I refer to in this book as *Shari'a* law and *Fiqh*-based law, respectively.

NOTE*1: According to the aforementioned definition, which is not necessarily the definition of apostasy recognized by all schools of jurisprudence, apostasy law not only covers Muslims who convert to other religions, but it also covers any Muslim—and possibly follower of the Qur'an (any and all interpretations of)—who disagrees with Traditional Islam's interpretation of the Qur'anic revelation or of Islamic law. By this logic, secular Muslims, and even most modern Muslim-majority states (rulers and possibly peoples), would be considered apostates.

NOTE*2: The Arabic term *murtadd* (apostate), linguistically means "he who reverts" (to return to a previous state, practice, etc.)—noun *ridda* (apostacy). On the other hand, the Arabic term commonly known for those who leave one religion for another is *al-sabi'in* (word-root *sba'*). As discussed in Volume 1, the term *al-sabi'in* or its grammatical counterpart *al-sabi'un* were used in the Qur'an (Q. 2:62, 5:69, 22:17), as I understand it to represent, in the space-time of the revelation, Jews who believed in Jesus Christ (they included multiple sects). According to the Jews, these groups left the way of the Jews for another: to believe in Jesus Christ excluded them from being counted as Jews. They were also a distinct group(s) from the Christians: the Christians did not consider them Christians.

Side note 5.17 Apostasy law as a religio-political tool

An example from modern history on the use of apostasy law as a religio-political tool can be seen in the execution of Mahmud Muhammad Taha in 1985 CE by the Sudanese government on charges of apostasy. Taha called for religious reform. At the same time, Taha was politically active in Sudanese politics—founder of the

Republican Party in 1945 CE, later to be known as the Republican Brothers movement. Taha was against the imposition of Islamic law (the Sudanese government's interpretation of) in Sudan in 1983 CE (Packer 2006). Taha believed Islamic law should reflect the fundamentals of the Qur'an: it should reflect equality and social justice regardless of sex, ethnicity, or belief rather than to follow archaic interpretations of Islamic law.

Side note 5.18 On clergy in Islam

Muhammad al-Nuwayhi (d. 1980 CE) was an Egyptian literary scholar and reformist thinker. In his book *Nahwa Thawra fi al-Fikr al-Dini* (Toward a Revolution in Religious Thought), he wrote about this group of people who call themselves men of religion (*rijal al-din*), who had appointed themselves as protectors of Islam (keepers of the truth).

Al-Nuwayhi (2010) describes these individuals to belong to a trend that started following the fall of the Abbasid civilization, in an era that is characterized by backwardness and deterioration, when a certain few in the name of religion gave themselves the right to determine faith, heresy, and to cast verdicts on everything new.

They are a group who gave themselves the right to determine belief and godlessness; who assigned themselves as enemies to freedom of expression and debate; who would judge—besides topics related to religion—theories (and the persons behind the theories) in politics, sociology, economics, and other worldly sciences as to whether they agreed or disagreed with Islam; who call to ban books that do not agree with their interpretation(s) and who actively seek to defame their authors. They are a group whose members nowadays even dress differently and wear distinct (so-called religious) attire. Some make the argument that in every field there is a need for specialization, and religion like any other field needs specialists. Surely, there is a need for specialization in all fields, and religion is no exception. However, the need for specialization does not entitle specialists in religion false sacredness, nor does it entitle them to hold a monopoly over the truth. Specialists in religion, like specialists in any other field, are humans who can be wrong unless they also claim prophetic knowledge or priesthood (110–119).

Side note 5.19 Misconceptions held by Muslims (and non-Muslims)

In addition to the misconception held about Islamic law, where it is mistakenly conceived to be "the revealed word of God rather than a body of laws developed by men based on the word of God" (Pew Research Center. and Pew Forum on Religion & Public Life. 2013, 41), most Muslims—and non-Muslims—do not seem to realize the distinction between the interpretations of Islam and the Qur'an. To most Muslims, the interpretation of Islam that they follow is mistakenly considered to represent the truth. However, all interpretations of Islam are but interpretations of religion that are based on Traditional Islam, which itself represents an attempt at interpreting the Qur'anic revelation. Traditional Islam is not the Qur'an; Traditional Islam is an interpretation of the Qur'anic revelation.

As far as this author is concerned, when it comes to interpretation—being a matter of probability not certainty—and more specifically in relation to the interpretation(s) of the Qur'anic revelation, no party can claim its interpretation to be the truth. There is no truth but the Qur'an, everything else is relative.

6. Islamic law directly from the primary sources: *Shari'a* law

In order to answer why the composition of the interpretation of religion associated with the proposed Q.I. classification does not include a law component, we need to establish that the definitive Qur'anic Action-Type II injunctions do not have eternal applicability.

This chapter looks into what is considered to be the eternal component of Islamic law, what I refer to as *Shari'a* law. Arguing against the eternal applicability of *Shari'a* law gives us the opportunity to examine up front what Islamic law considers to be its eternal sources of law, the definitive laws that were explicitly declared within the Qur'an and the *Hadith*. This chapter will show that the sources of *Shari'a* law, the definitive primary sources, were space-time specific and do not have eternal applicability.

6.1 *Shari'a*, *Shari'a* law, and Islamic law

The previous chapter discussed how the understanding of the term *Shari'a* has been transformed from its pre-modern conception. And how today, in most circles, Muslim and non-Muslim alike regard the term *Shari'a* to be synonymous with Islamic law. Nonetheless, what this work refers to as *Shari'a* law is not Islamic law, the whole of Islamic law, but rather, it is a component of Islamic law.

In this section, we start by looking into the Qur'an where the word *Shari'a* appears, to see what the word meant in the Qur'an. I clarify what this work means exactly by the term *Shari'a* law. And I identify the sources of this component of Islamic law. It is important to know what these sources are, since *Shari'a* law is basically a collection of direct extracts from these sources.

6.1.1 *Shari'a*: More about the word

Shari'a is a term that appeared only once in the Qur'an, Q. 45:18 in 45:12–21. In Q. 45:18, the word *Shari'a* is commonly interpreted to refer to the path that the Prophet was instructed to follow. Linguistically, the noun *Shari'a* is derived from the root *shr'a* (*shara'a*, a transcription showing short vowels), which means "to prescribe."

NOTE: The word *Shari'a* appeared only once in the Qur'an, and that was in Chapter 45. Muslim scholars have consistently considered Chapter 45 to be of the Qur'anic text revealed in the Mecca era. I disagree, and propose Chapter 45 to be of the Medina era. In the Qur'an's Chapter 45, reference is made to the peoples of previous scriptures and their opposition to what the Prophet had come with (and their partnerships), which is consistent with verses we find in the Qur'an's Chapter 5, a chapter clearly revealed in the Medina era.

6.1.2 Terminology: *Shari'a* law versus Islamic law

Both Islamic law and *Shari'a* law are English terms commonly used to represent the Arabic term *Shari'a*. However, in this work I distinguish between these terms.

The term Islamic law will be used to refer to all what is considered religious law, i.e. the body of laws derived directly and indirectly from the primary sources (*al-ahkam al-'amaliyya*). In contrast to common practice, the term *Shari'a* law will be used exclusively to describe that part of Islamic law whose laws are extracted directly from primary sources that are definitive in both attribution and meaning (*qat'iyyat al-thubut wa al-dalala*).

In speaking about law, I have chosen to use the term *Shari'a* law to represent what is considered the eternal part of Islamic law, since I believe this component that I label *Shari'a* law to be the core and heart of the pre-modern understanding of the *Shari'a*. What I call *Shari'a* law has never had a specific Arabic term to reference it. However, despite not giving it a unique name, from early on, Traditional Islam has distinguished what I refer to as *Shari'a* law from the rest of Islamic law. According to Traditional Islam, what it represents is the part of Islamic law that is considered to be eternal since its inputs are (considered to be) eternal (al-Jawziyya 1432 [2010 or 2011], 1: 570–571; Hazm 1983, 5: 2, 5).

REMINDER: When talking about Traditional Islam, it is always the traditional Q.I. classification that is in mind (where all injunctions of ethics, except those of virtue, fall within the actions category). Otherwise, it is the proposed Q.I. classification that is being referenced (where all injunctions of ethics are moved out of the actions category, as described in Chapter 3). Hence, whenever the non-eternal applicability of the Qur'anic Action-Type II injunctions is discussed, it is the proposed Q.I. classification that is referenced.

6.1.3 The sources of *Shari'a* law

Shari'a law has only two inputs (sources):

- The Qur'an

■ The *Sunna*—what is accepted to represent the *Sunna*

In common practice, when referring to the sources of—what I refer to as—*Shari'a* law, they are usually stated to be the Qur'an and the *Sunna*. Effectively though, it is only the definitive action injunctions of the Qur'an and the *Hadith* (what is accepted from the compilations of *Hadith*) that constitute the sources of this eternal component of Islamic law: the sources of *Shari'a* law.

REMINDER: As outlined in Section 5.2 (scope of study), this work's study of Islamic law pertains only to the part of Islamic law (components and sources of) that covers actions to be performed that regulate and are related to organizing man-world relationships and affairs (*al-mu'amalat*).

6.2 Thesis

I propose that *Shari'a* law and the motivation behind it emanate from an effort to produce eternal law based on man's desire to have eternal law, rather than it being a direct directive from God. Thus, I maintain that considering *Shari'a* law as eternal law capable of governing man-world affairs is a mere illusion. In other words, I oppose Traditional Islam's position on *Shari'a* law, argue, and want to prove that *Shari'a* law is non-eternal.

If this claim, *Shari'a* law is non-eternal, turns out to be true, then Muslims would not be religiously obligated to be tied to out-dated solutions for solving man-world affairs. Accordingly, Muslims would be free to explore legislative substitutes that could be more suitable to be used in their current space-time.

6.3 Methodology

You, the reader, will be involved in this endeavor since the adopted methodology is based on reason. We will move forward, together, one step at a time.

In order to go about proving the proposed thesis, the reductio ad absurdum reasoning technique will be utilized. The reductio ad absurdum technique is a line of reasoning where we begin by assuming the opposite of what we want to prove is true. Hence, in order to prove "*Shari'a* law is non-eternal," we assume the opposite to be true: *Shari'a* law is eternal. Then we try to disprove the newly formed assumption by finding an unacceptable outcome or result from it. If we do end up with such an unacceptable result, then we conclude that the assumption was false, thereby proving that what we initially set out to prove was true.

Utilizing the reductio ad absurdum reasoning technique, the opposite of what we want to prove (our reductio ad absurdum assumption) would align with Islamic law's view on the eternality of *Shari'a* law:

Reductio ad absurdum assumption: *Shari'a* law is eternal.
Let us look into this assumption:

■ Eternal law describes law that is considered applicable across space-time. If *Shari'a* law were truly eternal, then none of its laws, without exception, which were originally declared in the primary sources, could be suspended (a substitute for saying "abrogated"), considered unacceptable, or inapplicable in any space-time instance.

■ To produce eternal law *Shari'a* law would need eternal sources. This is exactly how Traditional Islam depicts the sources of *Shari'a* law, where primary sources definitive in both attribution and meaning have been claimed to be eternally applicable.

To refute the reductio ad absurdum assumption "*Shari'a* law is eternal," we need to establish that for the sources of *Shari'a* law, the definitive primary sources, there exists at least a single case in which a source is found not to be applicable across space-time. Law extracted from a source that is not applicable across space-time can by no means be considered eternal. Accordingly, *Shari'a* law would not be eternal.

In Section 5.6 I presented six arguments to support the non-eternal applicability of the Qur'anic Action-Type II injunctions. In this chapter, one of these arguments, the social norms of the past argument, is further explored and used to refute the reductio ad absurdum assumption.

We next look into the two sources of *Shari'a* law to verify whether they are applicable across space-time or not. We start with the Qur'an, and then move on to the *Hadith*.

Side note 6.1 Reductio ad absurdum

The argumentative technique known as "reductio ad absurdum," or "reduction to absurdity," is commonly employed to demonstrate the truth or falsehood of a statement.

"Reductio ad absurdum (Latin: "reduction to absurdity"; pl.: reductiones ad absurdum), ... is a common form of argument which seeks to demonstrate that a statement is true by showing that a false, untenable, or absurd result follows from its denial, or in turn to demonstrate that a statement is false by showing that a false, untenable, or absurd result follows from its acceptance. ... this technique has been used throughout history in both formal mathematical and philosophical reasoning, as well as informal debate." (Wikipedia 2009, par. 1)

6.4 The first source: The Qur'an

6.4.1 Rationale

The Action-Type II injunctions of the Qur'an governed the starting of a community in Medina at the time of the Prophet. These injunctions dealt with organizing the civil society in that space-time.

Law that organizes man-world relationships and affairs is expected to vary across space-time due to changes in social norms across both space and time, it is surely non-eternal. With this understanding, the applicability of the Qur'anic Action-Type II injunctions would be limited to the space-time of the revelation, and assuming the applicability of the Qur'anic Action-Type II injunctions to be eternal is but an assumption made by men.

The Action-Type II injunctions of the Qur'an portray how worldly affairs were managed in the space-time of the revelation; moreover, they serve to give a historical perspective into the norms of that space-time.

6.4.2 Approach

The handling of man-world affairs in the early seventh century CE, within Arabia and its neighboring territories of Abyssinia, Egypt, and the Byzantine and Persian empires, was different from how man-world affairs are approached in modern times. In the described space-time, slavery, physical forms of punishment, and discrimination against women were the norm.

In the discussion to follow, I specifically address these three social norms, shedding light on certain Qur'anic Action-Type II injunctions that are related to these norms. It is argued that in modern times, due

158

to changes in social norms, the solutions presented in the Qur'an in connection with slavery, forms of punishment, and women's rights, cannot be, and are mostly not accepted by Muslims and non-Muslims alike.

6.4.2.a Slavery

Although the Qur'an declared that all humanity was from the same origins (Q. 4:1, 6:98, 7:189, 22:5, 30:20 in 3:20–26, 35:11, 39:6, 40:67, 75:36–40, 76:1–2) and the only differentiator between people was righteousness (Q. 49:13 in 49:11–13), there were no verses in the Qur'an that explicitly banned slavery. Nonetheless, the Qur'an made steps towards reducing and organizing slavery:

■ The captives of war

The Qur'an made a radical change towards eradicating a primary source of slavery known in pre-Islamic Arabia, the enslavement of captives of war. When it came to captives of war, the Qur'an declared that captives of war should either be freed or ransomed (Q. 47:4). Thus, for QMonotheists, the possibility to enslave captives of war, a practice that existed in pre-Islamic Arabia ('Ali 1993, 5: 573) and the region, was no longer an option.*1

NOTICE: In clear conflict with the Qur'anic directive limiting what could be done with captives of war, in that they could either be freed or ransomed (would include prisoner exchange), the enslavement of captives of war was regarded permissible by Islamic law (Kuwait Ministry of Awqaf and Islamic Affairs 1995, 4: 200–206).

NOTICE: To enslave the captives of war was the norm in the lands surrounding Arabia at that time, as observed in both the Byzantine and Sassanid empires (Wikipedia 2014b, sec. 1; 2008b, sec. 2.4). The Arab tribes in the space-time of the revelation were in constant wars with each other (Q. 3:103 in 3:98–120). Hence, in agreement with what has been reported about slavery in pre-Islamic Arabia ('Ali 1993, 5: 570–574), one could rightfully assume that the practice of enslaving the captives of war was also prevalent in the space-time of the Qur'anic revelation. Moreover, it would not be far-fetched to assume this form of slavery—that was not based on religion, color, race or ethnicity—to possibly have been the dominant form of slavery found in the space-time of the revelation. Nevertheless, the Qur'an did not list enslaving the captives of war as an option when it came to handling captives of war (Q. 47:4). Throughout the Qur'an, we find that the Qur'an urged, and in some cases required the emancipation of slaves. Not once did the Qur'an prescribe or encourage enslaving peoples.

■ The emancipation of slaves

There were numerous verses in the Qur'an that encouraged and even prescribed the emancipation of slaves. The emancipation of slaves was cited as a form of obligatory and voluntary giving (*sadaqat*) (Q. 2:177, 9:60, 90:1–20). It was also cited as a form of expiation (*kaffara*) (Q. 4:92, 5:89, 58:3–4).

It is my understanding that the Qur'an further encouraged the emancipation of slaves in what could be referred to as "emancipation by marriage" For a financially-capable QMonotheist free-person to be able to have sexual relations with a QMonotheist slave-person, they were required to be married. And in order to marry a slave-person, the financially-capable free-person would need to emancipate the slave-person. Emancipation by marriage is discussed in side note 6.3.*2

In Q. 90:1–20 the emancipation of slaves was depicted as the impediment (*al-'aqaba*) that the Qur'an urged man to overcome (*iqtaham*)—along with the feeding, on days of severe hunger, those worthy of assistance—probably since it was the right thing to do: it was what ought to be done.*3*4

■ Sexual relations with slave-women

The Qur'an regulated sexual relations involving slave-women. It was only within the framework of marriage (*nikah*) that sexual relations with slave-women were permissible.

In marriages where the slave-woman remained to be a slave, the husband would have been either a slave-man or a free-man (not her owner) who did not have the means to marry a free-woman.

The Qur'an instructed slave-owners to allow their slaves to marry (other slaves) and to help them financially, and not to force slave-women to *bigha'* (transgression) (Q. 24:32–33 in 24:27–34). There is more to say about the Qur'anic term *bigha'*, see side note 6.5.

160

The Qur'an made permissible—yet restricted—for QMonotheist free-men to marry QMonotheist slave-women in a marriage where the slave-woman remained to be a slave and was not emancipated (Q. 4:25 in 4:19–28). In this form of marriage, we have a free-man marrying the slave-woman of someone else; the woman would remain to be a slave owned by the other person. This type of marriage, though permissible, was restricted to those free-men who were financially incapable of marrying free-women. Q. 4:25 in 4:19–28 detailed the procedure involved.

■ Slaves in the household

We find verses that referenced slaves in a way that affirms them to have been part of the household.

Q. 24:27–31 talked about matters in relation to the households of the QMonotheists. Q. 24:31 in 24:27–31 directed QMonotheist free-women that they should be in decent dressing (non-revealing of charms) in the presence of anyone other than certain men from their immediate family and specific others—of which women-slaves were included.

Q. 33:53–55 talked about matters in connection with the Prophet's households. For the Prophet's wives, in their homes, a screen was required between them and anyone other than certain men from their immediate family, their womenfolk, and their women-slaves. Aside from those mentioned, if the Prophet's wives were to be asked for any object it should be from behind a screen.

Q. 24:58 in 24:58–59—with respect to slaves—instructed QMonotheists that slaves in their households should ask permission before coming into their presence at three times: before the prayer of daybreak, when they lay aside their clothes midday (to nap or rest), and after the evening prayer.

In Q. 4:36 the Qur'an instructed that slaves should be treated with kindness. In this verse slaves were included in a list that also named parents, the fatherless, neighbors and several others; the verse ended saying that God loves not the arrogant and the boastful.

When discussing slavery, or any issue from a religious perspective, one should distinguish between what is stated in the Qur'an and what has been reported by other sources. The Qur'an eradicated a major source of slavery known in the space-time when the Qur'an was revealed, the enslavement of the captives of war. However, what has reached us about (alleged) early Muslim history tells a different story, which goes to indicate that if proven to be true, the guidelines of the Qur'an were not implemented (not long) after the death of the Prophet. To make matters even worse, Muslim traditions tell us (allege)—as a general rule—that even in the time of the Prophet, captives of war were taken as slaves; thus, agreeing with pre-Islamic practices. There is blatant contradiction between such sources and the Qur'an.

In order to legitimize enslaving the captives of war, law based on other sources besides the Qur'an was proposed; thus, ignoring the stance of the Qur'an on the matter. Similar is the case regarding the taking of concubines—at least in the outcome. Although in the case of slave-women, the Qur'an's verses were interpreted in a manner to allow such a practice (interpretations that were supported by alleged traditions). I see in both these cases—and in numerous others—that reverting to pre-Islamic practices was to appease the whims of the wealthy and the powerful, even though it stood against what the Qur'an had commanded.

Slavery was commonplace in the space-time of the revelation, and the existence of verses in the Qur'an that described how to manage and deal with slaves implies the Qur'an's acceptance of the institution of slavery in that space-time. Nevertheless, this does not mean that the Qur'an instructed that slavery should be accepted across space-time.

In present time, worldwide accepted norms regarding slavery are reflected in article four of the universal declaration of human rights that prohibits slavery and slave trade in all their forms (UNCHR n.d.). Rejecting slavery in all forms and shapes in modern times necessitates considering the directives of the Qur'an on slavery as inapplicable. Hence, the claim that such Qur'anic Action-Type II directives are eternally applicable is rejected.

NOTE*1: Historically, Arabic words such as *jahiliyya*, *jahili* (without or with the definite particle *al*) have been used to refer to the era before the revelation of the Qur'an. The English language equivalent term "pre-Islamic" is commonly used to refer to this period. Although I find the term "pre-Qur'anic" more fitting to be used; nevertheless, standing with common practice, I have also used the term "pre-Islamic" to refer to the era before the Qur'anic revelation.

NOTE*2: I understand that food and marriage were not prescribed permissible between the Monotheists until the revelation of Q. 5:5. The revelation of Q. 5:5 came after what is known as the Hudaybiyya truce/treaty, which is alluded to at the beginning of the Qur'an's Chapter 5. The historical narrative puts the treaty to have occurred in 6 AH / 627 CE.

I believe the Qur'an's instruction for QMonotheists on marriage and divorce appearing in the Qur'an's Chapter 4 was revealed shortly after the Prophet's emigration from Mecca to Medina in 1 AH / 622 CE. All such instructions involved only QMonotheist relations. The same applies to instruction related to marriage and divorce in Q. 2:221–242.

To my understanding, the Qur'an's instruction on marriage that was specific to the Prophet and issues related to the Prophet's households appearing in the Qur'an's Chapter 33 were revealed around the time of al-Ahzab battle—that was mentioned in the Qur'an's Chapter 33—and shortly after. The historical narrative puts al-Ahzab encounter to have occurred in 5 AH / 626 CE.

Nonetheless, with the revelation of Q. 5:5, in or slightly after 6 AH / 627 CE, marriage between the two Monotheist groups was declared permissible. And for the QMonotheists, the same rules applied to marriage with Monotheists from the peoples of previous scriptures as it did to marriage with QMonotheists: a contract type marriage was required with no time limitation. In Volume 1 of this series, Q. 5:5 is thoroughly analyzed.

NOTE*3: I have not included drawing up a contract of manumission between a master and a slave, what traditionally is known as *mukataba*, among the practices encouraged or prescribed by the Qur'an for the emancipation of slaves. Traditionally, commentators and jurists have interpreted the Qur'anic term *al-kitab* appearing in Q. 24:33 to refer to such a contract. However, my interpretation of *al-kitab* in Q. 24:33 is that it reflected "what God had ordained (among which would be what had been prescribed permissible and prohibited)," which within the context of Q. 24:32–33 in 24:27–34 would refer to marriage.

NOTE*4: The Qur'an banned *al-riba* (Q. 2:275–281, 3:130–132 in 3:130–137, 30:39 in 30:36–40). From the Qur'an itself, we understand that the prohibition of *al-riba* was not new, the Qur'an mentioned that previously it had also been forbidden: the Qur'an explicitly stated that the followers of the Torah had been forbidden it (Q. 4:161 in 4:160–162).

But what exactly is *al-riba*? The term *al-riba* is discussed in side note 5.15. Here is a summary. Traditional Islam considers *al-riba* to be any interest-based lending. However, the term *al-riba*, as I understand it from the Qur'an, refers to a lending practice with unreasonably high rates of interest. It required multiples of the original amount borrowed to be paid back (Q. 3:130, 30:39). But how does *al-riba* relate to the topic at hand—slavery? According to some, *al-riba* is considered to be debt slavery: defaulters in *al-riba* would end up as slaves ('Ali 1993, 5: 574, 617–620; 'Ashmawi 1995; Kuran 2011, 144–147; Martin 2004, 2: 596–597).

Side note 6.2 Marriage in the Qur'an

When considering how the Qur'an addressed its audience—aside from numerous other cues—we understand that in the space-time of the revelation, patriarchy was the norm. The Qur'an was mostly addressing the men. Rarely do we find the Qur'an to address both men and women, or women alone.

It is important to recognize that patriarchy was the prevalent mindset within the communities in the space-time of the revelation. It is within such a social system that the Qur'an presented its progressive directives on so many issues, including but not limited to marriage.

Marriage as presented in the Qur'an, also traditionally in Islamic law, has the basic elements of a contract as we understand contract law today: agreement (offer and acceptance), consideration (of tangible value), capacity (ability to engage in a contract), and legality (legal subject matter).

I understand—from the Qur'an—the outline of the legalities of marriage to be as follows:

> Marriage is a contract between a man and a woman (oral, not necessarily in writing). In this contract the bride is entitled to consideration—of value—from the groom in return for living with the him (exclusive sexual relations). The couple living together—to have sexual relations—represents the affirmation of the arrangement. The arrangement is made known to the public and is not in secret. The parties should either hold together on equitable terms or separate with kindness.
>
> A free-woman would represent herself and would be one of the two parties in the contract. For a slave-woman, it would have been her owner, her legal guardian, who would have represented her in the contract.

With reference to the marriage contract, the Qur'an described the promise the groom makes to the bride to be a solemn covenant (*mithaq ghalith*) that the bride took from him. I understand this to be in regard to his intent—that it was marriage and not any transient motive—and about what the promise entailed (Q. 4:21 in 4:19–21). We find the wording to describe this covenant, for it to be a solemn covenant (*mithaq ghalith*), to have been used in the Qur'an only in two other instances where the Qur'an described covenants: God had taken a covenant from the prophets (Q. 33:7); God had taken a covenant from the Israelites (Q. 4:154 in 4:153–162).

This form of marriage was common—for sure at least in Mecca—in the pre-Islamic era (Q. 60:10–11). However, it is reported, in the pre-Islamic era, there was no limit to the number of women a man could marry ('Ali 1993, 4: 633–637). The Qur'an limited the maximum number of women a man could marry to four. Yet there was a provision: those who were afraid not to be just between their wives should marry only one woman (Q. 4:3 in 4:1–6). The Qur'an further informed its audience that to be just between wives (complete fairness in every aspect) was not something that was attainable, even if one was keen on doing so (Q. 4:129 in 4:127–134). I understand this as to discourage having multiple wives; nevertheless, it was allowed

(Q. 4:128–129 in 4:127–134). I understand the Qur'an's allowing men to have multiple wives to lie within the type II action injunctions.

It is worth mentioning that Q. 4:3, the verse that legitimized for a man to have more than one wife, came within the context of when the Qur'an was talking about caring for *al-yatama*, the fatherless, and ensuring they receive their rightful inheritance and not cheating them out of it (Q. 4:3 in 4:1–6). In Q. 4:3 the Qur'an addressed its audience about marriage to fatherless free-women:

> If you fear that you might not act justly towards the fatherless (with reference to their wealth), then marry others—as you please—instead: some marry two, some marry three, some marry four. Those who are afraid not to be just (between wives) then marry only one; some marry slave-women. That is as such so you will not do injustice to the fatherless.

We find the Qur'an to have used mainly three terms to represent the consideration that is to be given to the bride: *saduqaatihina* (plural of *saduqa*; confirmation for what was promised; the word implies it to be a onetime thing) (Q. 4:4 in 4:1–6), *ujurihinna* (plural of *ajr*; payment) (Q. 4:24 and 4:25 in 4:19–28, 5:5, 33:50 in 33:50–52, 60:10 in 60:10–11), and *farida* (specified portion) (Q. 2:236–237). From the Qur'an we understand that the amount of this consideration was not always specified in the contract (Q. 2:236–237) (al-Razi 1981, 6: 145–156). The giving of the consideration to the bride could have been before or upon the consummation of the marriage. And it can be understood that it was given in one-shot (the bride had the option of giving part of it back) (Q. 4:4 in 4:1–6).

The Qur'an did not specify how much the consideration for the bride should be; however, I reckon, this consideration (society-dependent variable) in the space-time of the revelation was, for the most part, a considerable amount (it must have also varied depending on the wealth and status of both bride and groom). The consideration given to the bride, aside from serving to provide evidence that a contract existed (it was probably mostly given in the form of cattle in that space-time), was to ensure that the arrangement was not meant only for the short term (it was not an arrangement to take a lover on the side), and to ensure the wife's sustenance in the event of divorce (Q. 2:229, 2:236–237, 4:19–21 and 4:24 in 4:19–24). One is to remember that women in the space-time of revelation were mostly not financially independent: they had little means if any at all to support themselves (inheritance).

Furthermore, the Qur'an legitimized divorce (before or after determining the consideration for the bride and the consummation of the marriage)—if there ever be a need for it. The Qur'an specified a process for divorce; it included specific time provisions, and clarified the wife's rights and the husband's obligations in the process (Q. 2:226–242, 4:19–21 and 4:24 in 4:19–24, 4:35 in 4:32–35, 4:128–129 in 4:127–129, 33:49, 65:1–7).

Islamic law has used the term *mahr* or *sadak* to represent the consideration for the bride in a marriage contract (commonly translated as: marriage portions; dower; marriage gift—though it is consideration for the bride and is not a gift; and even—incorrectly—"dowry"). I will use the term "bride-consideration" to represent the consideration for the bride in a marriage contract—as per my understanding of marriage in the Qur'an—since I find it closest to the Qur'anic terminology.

Side note 6.3 On sexual relations with slave-women: The Qur'an versus Islamic law

Islamic law violated the core of the Qur'anic directives on marriage by making sexual relations outside of marriage between slave-owners and their female slaves permissible. Islamic law made permissible for slave-owners to have sexual relations with the slave-women they owned without being married to them (*tasarri*; concubinage), and it even did not put a limit on the number of slave-women whom a slave-owner could do that with (Kuwait Ministry of Awqaf and Islamic Affairs 1995, 11: 294–301, 23: 45–49).

It is reported about Arabs in pre-Islamic times—for monandric marital arrangements (the wife has only one husband at a time)—that there was no limit to the number of wives a man could have; furthermore, men could have sexual relations with slave-women without marrying them ('Ali 1993, 5: 547–548). In what follows, I present my understanding of the Qur'an's directives on marriage and sexual relations—focus will be given to relations with slaves.

The Qur'an only allowed sexual relations within the framework of marriage (*nikah*), whether we are talking about free-women or slave-women. The maximum number of wives was limited to four (Q. 4:3 in 4:1–6). A bride-consideration (*saduqa, ajr, farida*) was always required to marry a free-woman (Q. 2:236–237, 4:4 in 4:1–6, 4:19–21 and 4:24 in 4:19–28, 5:5, 33:50, 60:10–11): the QMonotheist husband-to-be presents a bride-consideration to the Monotheist bride (the bride-consideration is intended for the bride and not for her parent or guardian). To marry a slave-woman, no bride-consideration was given to the slave-woman; however, in order to marry a slave-woman, the husband-to-be would have to emancipate the slave-woman before he could marry her. Her emancipation represented the bride-consideration. All that has been mentioned so far was regarding financially-capable QMonotheist men who wished to marry Monotheist women (whether free or slave). The Qur'an also prescribed that QMonotheist men who were financially incapable of marrying QMonotheist free-women could marry QMonotheist slave-women, provided the slave-woman's owner approved and the slave-woman was given a bride-consideration (in this case the slave-woman remains to be a slave owned by someone else; this form of marriage was discouraged) (Q. 4:25 in 4:19–28). I will get to the details of marriage to slave-women shortly.

To understand exactly what the Qur'an declared permissible when it came to relations with slave-women, we refer back to the Qur'an where we find four particular instances in which there was mention of this matter: Q. 4:3 in 4:1–6, 4:25 in 4:19–28, 23:5–7 in 23:1–11, and 70:29–31 in 70:19–35. I understand all four instances to refer to relations within the framework of marriage.

In all four instances the verses referenced slave-women using the term "what your (their) right hands own (*ma malakat aymanukum* or its grammatical counterpart *ma malakat aymanuhum*)" (Q. 4:3 in 4:1–6, 4:25 in 4:19–28, 23:6 in 23:1–11, 70:30 in

70:19–35). And in all four cases the verses speak in the plural form addressing or describing a group, and reference is made to the slave-women owned by the group.

There is an important differentiator between these four instances. The first two instances are in the Qur'an's Chapter 4, which is commonly called "the women". They appear within verses where the Qur'an is declaring what was permissible when it came to marriage (the Qur'anic rulings on marriage). These two instances in the Qur'an's Chapter 4 explicitly used the verbal form of *"nikah* (marriage)" (*inkahu, yankih*). The other two instances, appearing in the Qur'an's Chapters 23 and 70, were not part of any direct declaration of what was permissible or prohibited, but rather appeared within verses that described those who abided by God's commandments. These latter two instances had identical wording, word for word, and talked about chastity.

Now for a closer look at these four instances:

■ Q. 4:1–6 starts with the direct address: O people (*ya ayuha al-nas*)
In Q. 4:3 we find the term "what your right hands own (*ma malakat aymanukum*)": in reference to the group "the people."

■ Q. 4:19–28 starts with the direct address: O ye who (have) believed (*ya ayuha al-ladhina amanu*)
In Q. 4:25 we find the phrase "of what your right hands own from among your believing maidens (*min ma malakat aymanukum min fatayatikum al-mu'minat*)": in reference to the group "those who (have) believed."

■ Q. 23:1–11 describes true believers (*al-mu'minun*)
In Q. 23:6 we find the term "what their right hands own (*ma malakat aymanuhum*)": in reference to the group "true believers."

■ Q. 70:19–35 mainly describes those who pray (*al-musalleen*; the observers of prayer)
In Q. 70:30 we find the term "what their right hands own (*ma malakat aymanuhum*)": in reference to the group "those who pray."

From the Qur'an's Chapter 4, the Qur'an's rulings on marriage to slave-women can be deduced from the two verses, Q. 4:3 in 4:1–6 and Q. 4:25 in 4:19–28. From Q. 4:3, in reference to the permissible women to marry (to have sexual relations with), the Qur'an made permissible to marry either free-women or slave-women. In Q. 4:25 it was specified that (only) QMonotheists who were financially incapable of marrying QMonotheist free-women could marry QMonotheist slave-women—in a marriage where the slave-woman remained to be a slave and was not emancipated. This was provided the slave-woman's owner approved; a bride-consideration was required to be given to the slave-woman. I interpreted "believing slave-women" (*fatayatikum al-mu'minat*) appearing in Q. 4:25 as QMonotheist slave-women because at the time of the revelation of this verse, it was not yet permissible for QMonotheists to marry Monotheists from the peoples of previous scriptures. As noted earlier, food and marriage were not prescribed permissible between the Monotheists until the revelation of Q. 5:5. And that was after what is known as the Hudaybiyya truce/treaty that is alluded to at the beginning of the Qur'an's Chapter 5. The historical narrative puts the Hudaybiyya treaty to have occurred in 6 AH / 627 CE. I believe that the Qur'an's Chapter 4, particularly its instruction in connection with matters of marriage, divorce, and inheritance, was revealed shortly after the Prophet's emigration from Mecca to Medina in 1 AH / 622 CE.

In Q. 4:3 of 4:1–6 the Qur'an was addressing a group. It was saying: You (people in the group) could marry free-women—some take one, some take two, some take three, some take four—or slave-women. When interpreted taking into consideration Q. 4:25 of the same chapter, Q. 4:3 would be saying: some could marry free-women, others could marry slave-women. In Q. 4:25 of 4:19–28 the Qur'an specified that it was only those who were financially incapable of marrying free-women who could marry slave-women—in a marriage where the slave-woman remained to be a slave; however, the Qur'an also noted, that it would be better for them to be patient: to abstain until they had the means to marry free-women. From this we understand that to marry a slave-woman—in a marriage where the slave-woman remained to be a slave—was an option to be undertaken only as a last resort by those who were financially incapable of marrying a free-woman. Aside from the fact that such a marriage lacked a lot of what one would expect from marriage, the children resulting from such a marriage would also have become slaves owned by the owner of the slave-woman (Kuwait Ministry of Awqaf and Islamic Affairs 1995, 23: 54). Furthermore, the slave-owner or their heirs could decide to sell the married slave-women, which I believe would have terminated the marriage.

As for the remaining two instances (these two instances have traditionally been used to legitimize concubinage): In Q. 23:5–7 of 23:1–11 and Q. 70:29–31 of 70:19–35—these verses portrayed those who abided by the Qur'an's commands—the Qur'an described male true believers (in the Qur'an's Chapter 23) and male observers of prayers (in the Qur'an's Chapter 70) in that they do not have sexual relations but with their wives or with their slave-women: some have sexual relations with their wives, while others of them have sexual relations with the slave-women owned by the group. It is unthinkable to even imagine the instances of the Qur'an's Chapters 23 and 70 to describe relations outside those prescribed permissible in the Qur'an's Chapter 4. If that were the case, then the Qur'an would be contradicting itself. And how could that even be possible when the instances in the Qur'an's Chapters 23 and 70 were describing the chastity of those the Qur'an called *al-mu'minun* (true believers) and *al-musalleen* (the observers of prayer), respectively?

As for the case when a financially-capable free-person wished to marry a slave-person, I reference Q. 2:221. From Q. 2:221 we understand that belief elevated the social status of a person in the community. Q. 2:221 tells us that belief is what should matter in the spouse-to-be (not social status or tribal lineage). From the wording of Q. 2:221, we understand—when considering marriage in the space-time of the revelation—socially, marriage between a free-person and a slave-person was not something that was held in high regard. On the other hand, that was not the case as far as the Qur'an was concerned. The Qur'an stated that it was not just that it was not permissible to marry an associator; it was even better to marry a believing slave-person than a free-person who was an associator.

In Q. 2:221 the Qur'an declared it prohibited to marry associators (*tankihu*)—unless they became believers—and urged to marry a believing slave-person rather than to marry an associator, even if one admired the associator. It is interesting that Q.

168

2:221 referenced both sexes: the case of a free-man to marry a slave-woman and the case of a free-woman to marry a slave-man. I assume the case of a free-woman to marry a slave-man would have been even less common than a free-man marrying a slave-woman; however, belief made such scenarios possible.

This scenario involving the marriage of a believing free-person to a believing slave-person further shows that the Qur'an encouraged the emancipation of slaves—as to be explained. But how would this scenario transpire? The free-person would have had to emancipate the slave-person, then they would have been able to get married. I interpret this to be the required course of action, since we know, that for the case of QMonotheist free-men who wished to marry QMonotheist slave-women, as explained earlier, we have a constraint spelled out in Q. 4:25 that restricted the marriage of free-men with slave-women—owned by others and who remained to be slaves—to only free-men who were financially incapable of marrying free-women. Note that the case of a free-woman marrying a slave-man was not an option given in Q. 4:25: it would be unimaginable that a free-woman—or her parent/guardian—would accept marriage to a slave-man who was owned by others and who remained to be a slave.

Accordingly, for a financially-capable free-man who wished to marry a slave-woman, he would need to emancipate the slave-woman first (she cannot remain a slave). And in such a case, as mentioned earlier, her emancipation would constitute the bride-consideration. The same would be the case if a free-woman wished to marry a slave-man: she (or her parent/guardian) would need to emancipate the slave-man first. And the bride-consideration in such a case could be anything: it would be a symbolic gesture.

For reference, here is the translation of Q. 2:221 by Pickthall.

> Q. 2:221 (Pickthall):
>
> Wed not idolatresses till they believe; for lo! a believing bondwoman is better than an idolatress though she please you; and give not your daughters in marriage to idolaters till they believe, for lo! a believing slave is better than an idolater though he please you. These invite unto the Fire, and Allah inviteth unto the Garden, and unto forgiveness by His grace, and expoundeth His revelations to mankind that haply they may remember.

Side note 6.4 On the women declared permissible for the Prophet to marry

In the Qur'an's Chapter 33, a great deal of the chapter discussed issues related to the Prophet's person, personal matters, in addition to issues related to the Prophet's households. I believe that the Qur'an's Chapter 33 was revealed around the time of al-Ahzab battle and shortly after. We find verses about this encounter and what followed it in Q. 33:9–27. The historical narrative puts al-Ahzab battle to have occurred in 5 AH / 626 CE.

From the Qur'an's Chapter 33, I find relevant to our discussion about slave-women the Qur'an's talk about the women declared permissible for the Prophet to marry. It should be pointed out that—unlike the QMonotheists—the Qur'an did not place a limit on the number of wives the Prophet could take. From the Qur'an we do not know the number of the wives of the Prophet. We only know they were referenced in the plural form, *nisa' al-nabiy* (women of the Prophet).

On the Qur'an's usage of the term *nisa'* (and its grammatical counterparts; with or without the definite particle *al*, which is the equivalent for the definite article "the"): This term is commonly used to mean "women" (adult females). However, what the term precisely represents could change depending on the context. In the Qur'an, this term is found depending on context to represent: women, females, women members of the family (wives and daughters), wives. Moreover, in some instances it could indicate the free/slave status: it would refer only to free-women (depending on context it could either be unmarried free-women or both married and unmarried free-women). This usage to refer to free-women would be the case particularly in some of the instances where we find other terms in the same verse that explicitly refer to slave-women (Q. 4:3, 24:31, 33:55).

Q. 33:50–52 addressed the Prophet's marriage(s). Q. 33:50–52 tell us, among other things, that it was only permissible for the Prophet to take new wives up until the revelation of these verses. That is, until the first 5 or 6 years from his arrival in Medina. After that, Q. 33:52 tells us that the Prophet could take a wife only after he had divorced a wife (so as to replace a wife), and the new wife—replacing a divorced wife—could only come from the slave-women that he owned. This interpretation opposes the biography of the Prophet and numerous reports (*Hadiths* and otherwise) that claimed that the Prophet married free-women well after 5 or 6 AH.

In Q. 33:50 the Qur'an declared that God had made permissible (in the past tense) for the Prophet marriage with the following:

- Free-women to whom the Prophet had given bride-consideration

- Slave-women bestowed (*afa'*) from God to the Prophet

This idiom "bestowed from God to the Prophet" means that these slaves were not bought by the Prophet. What I translate as "bestow" literally means "shade." It was used as a simile in this context. The verb *afa'* and its noun *fay'* are commonly—incorrectly—used as synonyms for "spoils of war," an interpretation that is connected to legitimizing the enslavement of captives of war.

I would like to draw attention that slave-women were listed amongst the women permissible for the Prophet to marry. Yes, to marry. And not to be taken as concubines as Traditional Islam leads us to believe.

- The Prophet's cousins who migrated to Medina

Four varieties of cousins were listed: daughters of paternal/maternal uncles and aunts. Hence, it was just relatives of the Prophet who migrated whom the Prophet could marry. This category could be differentiated as free-women relatives who migrated and to whom the Prophet had given bride-consideration.

It is to be noted that earlier in the same chapter, the Qur'an's Chapter 33, Q. 33:36–48 addressed the marriage of the Prophet to a woman after the Prophet's adopted son had divorced her. From Q. 33:36–48 we understand that an

170

adopted son is not to be treated like a blood-son when it came to permissibility and prohibition in marriage related issues. The traditional sources reported that the woman in question was a cousin of the Prophet.

■ A QMonotheist free-woman who gave herself to the Prophet, and the Prophet desired to take her in marriage

There was one exception to the bride-consideration required to marry a free-woman and that was given only to the Prophet. The Qur'an prescribed that only the Prophet could marry a QMonotheist free-woman who requested no bride-consideration.

I translated the term "believing woman" (*imra'a mu'mina*) appearing in the verse as QMonotheist free-woman. The reader is to remember that up until the revelation of Q. 5:5 (sometime after the Hudaybiyya treaty in 6 AH), it had not been declared permissible for the Prophet nor the QMonotheists to marry Monotheists from the peoples of previous scriptures.

When considering bride-consideration, the four types of women eligible for the Prophet to marry can be categorized as follows:

■ Those given bride-consideration

(1) Free-women (non-relatives) to whom the Prophet had given bride-consideration

(2) Free-women (relatives who had migrated) to whom the Prophet had given bride-consideration

(3) The Prophet's slave-women who were emancipated (emancipation constituted the bride-consideration)

■ Those not given bride-consideration

(1) A QMonotheist free-woman who gave herself to the Prophet, and the Prophet desired to take her in marriage

Q. 33:51 addressed the Prophet, basically saying, that it was up to him to choose how he was to spend time with his wives. Q. 33:52 directed the Prophet, that after that point in time (the revelation of this verse), he could not take additional wives. And from the wives he had, he could not replace them with other wives (*an tabaddal bihin min azwaj*)—even if he found the others attractive—unless from his slave-women. This also clearly shows that sexual relations with slave-women was based (only) on marriage: replacing a current wife could only be achieved by divorcing her and taking a slave-woman as a wife in her place.

It is to be noted that throughout Muslim history Muslim exegetes have interpreted Q. 33:50–52 in numerous different ways. I assume this was mostly because these verses conflicted with many of the reports (*Hadiths* or otherwise) they had about slave-women, marriage, and especially the Prophet's marriages. They wanted to find a way to give legitimacy to—or even explain—these reports in light of what Q. 33:50–52 was saying. Hence, they tried to interpret the Qur'an in light of these reports that they had.

Here is Pickthall's translation of Q. 33:50–52 as is. I have made three comments that appear in BRACKETS [].

Q. 33:50 (Pickthall):

O Prophet! Lo! We have made lawful unto thee thy wives unto whom thou hast paid their dowries [COMMENT: what I refer to as "bride-considerations"], and those whom thy right hand possesseth [COMMENT: Qur'anic term used to represent slave-women] of those whom Allah hath given thee as spoils of war [COMMENT: the Arabic text says *fay'* from God: *mima afa' allah 'alayk*], and the daughters of thine uncle on the father's side and the daughters of thine aunts on the father's side, and the daughters of thine uncle on the mother's side and the daughters of thine aunts on the mother's side who emigrated with thee, and a believing woman if she give herself unto the Prophet and the Prophet desire to ask her in marriage - a privilege for thee only, not for the (rest of) believers - We are Aware of that which We enjoined upon them concerning their wives and those whom their right hands possess - that thou mayst be free from blame, for Allah is ever Forgiving, Merciful.

Q. 33:51 (Pickthall):

Thou canst defer whom thou wilt of them and receive unto thee whom thou wilt, and whomsoever thou desirest of those whom thou hast set aside (temporarily), it is no sin for thee (to receive her again); that is better; that they may be comforted and not grieve, and may all be pleased with what thou givest them. Allah knoweth what is in your hearts (O men), and Allah is ever Forgiving, Clement.

Q. 33:52 (Pickthall):

It is not allowed thee to take (other) women henceforth, nor that thou shouldst change them for other wives even though their beauty pleased thee, save those whom thy right hand possesseth. And Allah is ever Watcher over all things.

Side note 6.5: Was prostitution explicitly mentioned in the Qur'an?

We find exegetes to claim that the Qur'an in Q. 24:33 prohibited slave-owners from coercing their slave-women to prostitution. If that were the correct interpretation, would prostitution be permissible if there was no coercion? But is that really what the Qur'an was saying? Let us examine the verse in question, Q. 24:33 in 24:27–34.

Q. 24:33 serves as an example in which exegetes interpreted a Qur'anic statement in—what I claim to be—a completely different manner from what the statement originally intended, when taking the context into consideration. How Q. 24:33 has been interpreted over the years serves to demonstrate the consequences of interpreting a single Qur'anic statement in isolation from its paragraph and passage. And that depending on other sources to interpret the Qur'an changes the intended meaning of the verses. In this case, the other sources were what is referred to as the (alleged) *asbab al-nuzul*, what is alleged to be the causes of the revelation—some prefer to call it "the occasion of the revelation." Furthermore, the example demonstrates the importance of understanding the Qur'anic vocabulary from within its usage in the Qur'an, and not from anywhere else.

This is the statement that appears in Q. 24:33 that we will be examining:

172

> And coerce not your slave-women into *bigha'* (exegetes interpreted the word to mean "prostitution") if they want *tahassun* (most exegetes interpreted the word to mean "chastity") in order for you to seek the goods in the present life. And whosoever coerces them, then God, after their coercion, is All-forgiving All-compassionate.

I disagree with the classical interpretation(s) and propose the following interpretation:

> And coerce not your slave-women into *bigha'* (transgression) if they want *tahassun* (monandry marriage: the—only—form of marriage recognized by the Qur'an as permissible) in order for you to seek the goods in the present life. And whosoever coerces them, then God, after their coercion, is All-forgiving All-compassionate.

The key to understand the statement under study depends on understanding what the words *bigha'* and *tahassun* mean. In addition to understanding the meaning generated from their usage within the context of the passage Q. 24:27–34 and the paragraph Q. 24:32–33. The term *tahassun* has already been touched upon. I will also briefly explain its meaning in the subsequent paragraphs.

The term *bigha'* found in Q. 24:33 comes from the word-root *bgha* (*bagha*, a transcription showing short vowels). I understand the word-root *bgha*—in this usage—to mean "transgress (on what is right)." Furthermore, what the term *bigha'* (transgression) precisely represents depends on context: the resulting meaning attained from its usage in the statement depends on context. In the context of Q. 24:32–33, *bigha'* would represent the transgression on monandry marriage (a woman has one husband at a time). In the space-time of the revelation, when it came to marriage, slave-owners would have sought polyandry marriage for their slave-women (a woman has more than one husband at a time): the slave-owners would choose the slave-men that were to mate with the slave-women; thus, polyandry marriage would have better served their needs in producing better fit slaves and more slaves altogether (slave breeding).

In the following discussion I will follow the Qur'an's lead, in that when I refer to marriage, it is always the monandry form of marriage that is referenced unless explicitly stated otherwise.

Now for an in-depth analysis. The passage Q. 24:27–34 addressed issues related to preserving the sanctity of private space and private parts. The paragraph Q. 24:32–33 addressed issues of marriage, and in particular prescribed that slave-owners marry off and facilitate the marriage of the slaves they owned, regardless of the religious affiliation(s) of these slaves.

Before we get to the verse that we seek to understand, Q. 24:33, let us first examine the verse just before it. Q. 24:32 directed QMonotheists to marry off those unmarried of them (free-persons) (*al-ayama minkum*) and (also) the—fit-for-marriage—slave-men and slave-women they owned (*al-saliheen min 'ibadikum wa ima'ikum*). The statement did not specify the religious affiliation of the slaves but was general to all fit-for-marriage slaves.

The Qur'an goes on to elaborate on this commandment in what remains of Q. 24:32 and throughout Q. 24:33. In Q. 24:32 the verse went on to say: And if they (unmarried free-persons) were poor, then that should not be a deterrent. Q. 24:33 continued about the unmarried free-persons in that those who do not find marriage (a match or possibly the means) should be chaste.

In the remainder of Q. 24:33, the Qur'an elaborated on the marriage of slave-men and slave-women. Two issues were addressed. I believe both issues to have been traditionally misinterpreted (*wal-latheen yabtaghun al-kitab* and *wala tukrihu fatayatikum*). I understand Q. 24:33—on both issues—to be referring to the marriage of slaves owned by QMonotheists. It was about the marriage of any slaves who sought monandry marriage, regardless of the slave's religious affiliation.

I interpret the first issue (*wal-latheen yabtaghun al-kitab*) to be talking about how slave-owners were to approve and financially facilitate marriage for their slave-men (to assist financially with what is needed for the bride-consideration). And it was not—as has traditionally been claimed—about writing out a manumission contract with the slave-persons: it has traditionally been interpreted to be about manumission contracts and not marriage contracts.

I interpret the second issue (*wala tukrihu fatayatikum*) to be talking about how slave-owners should not coerce their slave-women into polyandry marriage if the slave-women wanted monandry marriage. And it was not—as has traditionally been claimed—about prohibiting slave-owners from coercing their slave-women to prostitution.

Q. 24:33 concluded with stating that God was forgiving towards those who coerced slave-women. It is necessary to point out that in the Qur'an, God's forgiveness was always contingent upon repenting and amending (making amends) beforehand (Q. 6:54).

Now back to the statement under study in Q. 24:33; it is the statement that discussed the second issue mentioned above:

> And coerce not your slave-women into *bigha'* (transgression) *in aradn tahassun* (if they want marriage) in order for you to seek the goods in the present life. And whosoever coerces them, then God, after their coercion, is All-forgiving All-compassionate.

In this statement, we find the word *tahassun* in the phrase "if they want marriage (*in aradn tahassun*)," that shares the same root *hssn* as in "when they marry (*itha uhssin*)" (Q. 4:25). I would like to clarify my understanding of the Qur'an's usage of the word-root *hssn* in connection with women, men, and relationships (*hassana*, transcription showing short vowels).

> The word-root *hssn* is commonly translated to mean: to be guarded, be inaccessible, be chaste, be strongly fortified, be preserved, be protected (we find *hssn* sometimes spelled *hsn* in English) (Omar 2010, 126). I understand the Qur'an's usage of word-patterns sharing the root *hssn*—in the context of marital relationships between women and men—to mean that the woman is securing her private parts. It refers to the only form of marriage endorsed by the Qur'an: a marriage in which a woman has only one husband at a time.

174

In the Qur'an, apart from *tahssun*, a marriage that is publicly declared and in which a woman has only one husband (monandry marriage), all other relationships involving sexual intercourse were considered unacceptable. Examples of unacceptable relationships are polyandry marriage (*musafihat, musafihin*) and taking lovers (*mutakhithat akhdan, mutakhithin akhdan*) (Q. 4:24–25, 5:5).

I see the statement under study in Q. 24:33 was not at all about prostitution. It was about *tahassun*: a woman has one husband at a time (monandry marriage). The Qur'an was instructing QMonotheists to honor the request for *tahassun* of their slave-women, even if that went against the material gain of the slave-owners.

I understand the paragraph Q. 24:32–33 to be about pushing for monandry marriage and its importance—to maintain chastity—both for free-persons and slave-persons alike. In its instruction about monandry marriage for slave-persons in particular (*ankihu, katibuhum, la tikrihu*), the paragraph recognized the humane right of slave-persons—regardless of religious affiliation—to dignity and marriage.

I find it staggering that Islamic law, though it prohibited prostitution, yet it declared permissible for QMonotheist men to have sexual relations with the slave-women they owned without requiring them to be married to the slave-women: the slave-owners cannot hire the slave-women out to others for sex; however, they themselves could have sexual relations with them without being married to them.

There are specific points related to Q. 24:32–33 that I would further like to comment upon:

■ Traditionally, commentators and jurists have interpreted the Qur'anic terms *al-kitab* and *katibuhum* appearing in Q. 24:33 to be related to drawing up a contract of manumission between a master and a slave, what traditionally is known as *mukataba*. However, my interpretation of *al-kitab* in Q. 24:33 is that it referenced "what God had ordained (among which would be what had been prescribed permissible and prohibited)," which within the context of Q. 24:32–33 in 24:27–34 would refer to marriage. The subsequent verb *katibuhum* in the same verse would be referring to answering the request of the slaves in drawing up a contract of marriage.

■ In the phrase "if they want marriage (*in aradn tahassun*)," the Qur'an used the Arabic term *in* and not *itha* (the English equivalent "if" and not "when"). Linguistically this would indicate possibility and not certainty, i.e. not all slave-women would choose *tahassun*: a woman has one husband at a time (monandry marriage). This tells us that other forms of marriage were common, like what the Qur'an referred to when using the terms *musafihin* and *musafihat*: a woman has multiple husbands at a time (polyandry marriage).

■ I understand the expression in Q. 24:33 that God is "All-forgiving All-compassionate (*ghafur rahim*)" to be directed at the QMonotheist slave-owners who coerced into *bigha'* slave-women who wanted monandry marriage—regardless of the slave's religious affiliation. It is possible that this was to encourage these slave-owners to still do the right thing: it was to motivate the slave-owners in order that they cease to coerce into polyandry marriage the slave-women who wanted monandry marriage. And not as it has commonly been interpreted to be about Monotheist slave-women who had been coerced into *bigha'* in that God would forgive them for what they did.

This paradigm change—in dominant culture—that called for slaves to be treated with dignity, and that slaves too should have the right to marry was something, I believe, the Qur'an recognized would need time to sink in. Aside from regulating sexual relations between free-persons and slave-women, that it should only be within the context of marriage, the Qur'an also made clear that slave-owners were to allow—and even facilitate—for their slaves to marry (other slaves). Even if this went against what slave-owners considered to be in their own best interest when it came to slaves (slave breeding).

When saying God is "All-forgiving All-compassionate (*ghafur rahim*)," we need to realize that the Qur'an in other instances stated that God's mercy embraces all things (Q. 7:156 in 7:155–156). It also stated that God does not forgive that anything should be associated with Him and forgives all sins other than that to whomever He wills (Q. 4:48, 4:116). It is believers who did good to whom God would grant forgiveness (Q. 22:49–51). It is believers who repented and amended (made amends) to whom God would be All-forgiving All-compassionate (Q. 6:54). God is not forgiving towards those who die as disbelievers (Q. 47:34).

Therefore, when the two attributes All-forgiving and All-compassionate appear concatenated together, "All-forgiving All-compassionate (*ghafur rahim*)," we understand that it is believers who are being referenced (Q. 33:72–73). In Q. 24:33 we know from the context of Q. 24:27–34 that the slave-owners were QMonotheists; however, the slave-women were not necessarily believers. We know this for a fact because the verse said about the slave-women "if they want marriage (*in aradn tahassun*)." This means that not all slave-women would seek monandry marriage: only for sure Monotheist slave-women would do so (no other form of marriage was permissible for Monotheists), in addition to possibly some non-Monotheist slave-women but not necessarily all non-Monotheist slave-women. Furthermore, we find the same expression that God is "All-forgiving All-compassionate (*ghafur rahim*)" to have been used in the Qur'an in connection with QMonotheists who did wrong. Without getting into the details of the Qur'an's penal code, examples on QMonotheists who did wrong include QMonotheists who stole, or accused women of having forbidden heterosexual intercourse without bringing forward four witnesses, then repented and amended (made amends) afterwards (Q. 5:39 in 5:38–40, 24:5 in 24:4–5).

It is clear and it goes without saying, that God would be All-forgiving All-compassionate towards Monotheists who under duress had to break His code. In this case that would be the Monotheist slave-women who were coerced into polyandry marriage. We find the same expression that God is "All-forgiving All-compassionate (*ghafur rahim*)" to have been used in the Qur'an in connection with those constrained—while not transgressing and not

176

overstepping the limit—to eat from the prohibited foods (Q. 2:173, 6:145, 16:115).

■ I cite another example from the Qur'an that illustrates that—also—the term *baghiyya*, someone who practices *bigha'*, was not used in the Qur'an to mean "someone who practiced prostitution." Nor was the term *baghiyya* used to mean "someone who practiced polyandry marriage." The example illustrates how context drives meaning for word-patterns based on the same word-root.

We only find two occurrences of the term *baghiyya* (someone who practices *bigha'*) in the Qur'an. It was used in Q. 19:20 and Q. 19:28 in the passage Q. 19:16–40. Both instances involved Mary, the daughter of *'imran* (Q. 3:35–36 in 3:33–63, 66:12), the mother of Prophet Jesus Christ (Q. 19:16–40). The Qur'an described Mary—the only woman mentioned in the Qur'an by name— to be a woman of truth (*siddeeqa*) (Q. 5:75 in 5:72–81).

Before we get to examining both occurrences of the term *baghiyya*, it would be helpful to understand the context in which both occurrences appeared, it was within the passage Q. 19:16–40. Q. 19:16-40 narrate the story of Mary and the miraculous birth of Prophet Jesus Christ. Mary secluded herself, and an angel—or rather, archangel—appeared to give her the news of a pure son. Mary, surprised and questioning how she could have a child as a virgin, was assured that it was God's will. She gave birth to Jesus and faced accusations from her people. Jesus, as an infant, spoke in her defense, declaring himself a servant of God and a prophet. He affirmed his mission, his blessed nature, and his duty to serve God. The passage concludes with a reminder of God's oneness, rejecting the notion of Him having a son, and emphasizing His sovereignty and justice.

I start with the first occurrence of the term *baghiyya*, as it appears in Q. 19:20. In Q. 19:20, Mary was responding to the archangel—who appeared before her in human form—after the archangel had introduced himself saying he was a messenger of God sent to bestow upon her a pure boy (pure from accusation and doubt of illegitimacy). Mary asked, questioning how such an event could transpire: How could I have a boy when no human has touched me—in a sexual manner, i.e. there has been no sexual intercourse—and I was not a *baghiyya* (for sexual intercourse to happen)?

The term *baghiyya* is derived from the word-root *bgha* (*bagha*, a transcription showing short vowels). I understand the word-root *bgha*—in this usage—to mean "transgress (on what is right)." Furthermore, what the term *baghiyya* (someone who transgresses) precisely represents depends on context: the resulting meaning attained from its usage in the statement depends on context. I will get to that, but first, let us see what else can we learn from Mary's question to the archangel.

Mary's question to the archangel about how would it be possible for her to have a boy, while clearly indicating that she never had sexual intercourse (she was a virgin) and that she was not someone who transgresses on marriage (in order to have sexual intercourse), implies that she was not married. Otherwise, if she had been married, there would be no point to question where the boy would come from. Unless of course, she was married and there were infertility issues, and that simply was not the case; otherwise, her question to the archangel would have reflected such a situation.

I refer the reader to the story of Prophet Zechariah (*zakaria*) and his wife, as mentioned in Q. 19:1–15, when Zechariah was informed that he would have a son—John (*yahya*)—his question was, how could he have a son when he was very old and his wife was barren (Q. 19:8). Hence, if that had been the case for Mary, to be married, and she, her husband, or both, had been old, then the question to the archangel would have been different.

In Q. 19:20, *baghiyya* would represent someone who transgresses on marriage. In this case, for Mary, being herself a devout follower of the Jewish faith, and—as has been established—being unmarried, transgression on marriage meant: being sexually active without being married.

Now since Mary was not married, sexual intercourse—resulting in a child—would only have happened if she had transgressed. Hence, her statement "and I was not a *baghiyya*," confirmed that she was not someone who transgresses. Simply put: Mary was not married; thus, sexual intercourse could only have happened if she had had a lover. And with the statement "and I was not a *baghiyya*," she made it known she was not someone who took (secret) lovers.

Mary's response asserted her chastity: she was not married, she was a virgin, and she did not take lovers. Therefore, her surprise and question: How could she have a child? This response by Mary allows us to better understand the Qur'an's calling her *siddeeqa*, a woman of truth, thereby further affirming her purity, as she upheld truthfulness in her beliefs, actions, and character.

For the second occurrence of the word *baghiyya*, which appears in Q. 19:28, we need to understand the context as given in Q. 19:27–28. The verses Q. 19:27–28 describe the situation when Mary returned to her people carrying her newborn child, Prophet Jesus Christ, they were shocked and questioned her, accusing her of bringing dishonor to her family. They reminded her of her pious lineage and expressed their disbelief at her situation. In Q. 19:28, her people addressed her saying: your father was not a bad man, nor, was your mother a *baghiyya*. In this context, in reference to Mary's mother, the wife of *'imran* (Q. 3:35–36 in 3:33–63), the word *baghiyya* would also represent someone who transgresses on marriage. However, in the case of Mary's mother, transgression on marriage would correspond to transgression either before or after marriage (or both before and after marriage): being sexually active before being married and/or committing adultery while being married.

Side note 6.6 There were no men or boys (workers or slaves) in the Prophet's households

The Qur'an addressed issues relating to the Prophet, his wives, and his households separately from when it addressed the QMonotheists and their households. From such instances, we can learn about the Prophet's households and in what they differed from the households of the QMonotheists. A good example would be Q. 24:31 in 24:27–31 and Q. 33:53–55:

■ Q. 24:27–31 talked about matters in relation to the households of the QMonotheists

Within this group of verses, Q. 24:31 directed QMonotheist free-women that they should mind how they dress (decent dressing: non-revealing of charms) in the presence of anyone other than certain men from their immediate family, their womenfolk (*nisa'ihinna*), women-slaves (*ma malakat aymanuhunna*), in addition to (free and slave) followers from men who feel no sexual desire and boys.

Those specified in what I label "certain men from their immediate family" were: their own husbands or fathers or husbands' fathers, or their sons or their husbands' sons, or their brothers or their brothers' sons or sisters' sons.

Q. 24:31 listed those who were treated as people of the household—who QMonotheist free-women would be at ease to appear in their presence—in the following sequence: certain men from their immediate family, their free-women and slave-women, in addition to free and slave male helpers who feel no sexual desires.

■ Q. 33:53–55 talked about matters in connection with the Prophet's households

For the Prophet's wives, in their homes, a screen was required between them and the QMonotheists with certain exceptions. According to Q. 33:55 in 33:53–55, the Prophet's wives could appear freely—a screen was not required—before certain men from their immediate family, their womenfolk (*nisa'ihinna*), and their women-slaves (*ma malakat aymanuhunna*). Aside from those listed, if the Prophet's wives were to be asked for any object it should be from behind a screen.

Those specified in what I label "certain men from their immediate family" were: their fathers, or their sons, or their brothers, or their brothers' sons, or the sons of their sisters.

Q. 33:55 listed those who were treated as people of the household—who the wives of the Prophet would be at ease to appear in their presence—in the following sequence: certain men from their immediate family, their free-women and slave-women.

Based on Q. 24:31 and Q. 33:53–55, and after comparing the people listed in both households, I propose that there were no men or boys (workers or slaves) in the Prophet's households. This proposition exposes many of what I consider to be fabricated *Hadiths*, which we find in most compilations of *Hadith*—even those considered to be the most trusted compilations of *Hadith*—that stated to the contrary or (were) claimed to be reported by male workers in the household(s) of the Prophet. Once again, I reiterate as proposed in Volume 2 of this series: Not a single *Hadith* is certain in its attribution to Prophet Muhammad—when holding the *Hadith* to the requirements of authentication set forth in the Qur'an for the verification of oral evidence. Before I get to the issue of male workers in the household(s) of the Prophet, let's first see how the two sets of verses reported about another issue.

When comparing Q. 33:55 in 33:53–55 with Q. 24:31 in 24:27–31, we notice about Q. 33:55 that the men included in what I refer to as "certain men from their immediate family" were less than those included in Q. 24:31. In Q. 24:31 we find additional men to be included: the husband, husband's father and husband's sons (this would be the mature sons of the husband from another marriage). In Q. 33:55, the verse did not mention the Prophet's father and sons since the Prophet's father was not alive, and the Prophet had no sons. Otherwise, the rest of the men listed in what I label "certain men from their immediate family" in the two verses were identical. From this, we understand that Q. 33:55, the verse addressing the Prophet's households, was adjusted in comparison to Q. 24:31, the verse addressing the households of the QMonotheists, so that it fits the specific case of the Prophet's households. Similar is the case for the next observation in connection with these two verses.

From the comparison between Q. 33:55 and Q. 24:31, we understand that there were no men or boys (workers or slaves) in the Prophet's households. This is evident because we find Q. 24:31 to include reference to male helpers, which is not present in Q. 33:55. In Q. 24:31, as Arberry put it, we find the addition: "or such men as attend them, not having sexual desire, or children who have not yet attained knowledge of women's private parts[.]" From this we understand that if there had been men or boys (workers or slaves) in the Prophet's households, the Qur'an would have addressed that directly in Q. 33:55, and it would have instructed the Prophet's wives accordingly. But that simply was not the case; thus, we conclude that there were no men or boys (workers or slaves) in the Prophet's households.

For reference, here is the translation of Q. 24:31 and Q. 33:53–55 by Pickthall.

Q. 24:31 (Pickthall):

And tell the believing women to lower their gaze and be modest, and to display of their adornment only that which is apparent, and to draw their veils over their bosoms, and not to reveal their adornment save to their own husbands or fathers or husbands' fathers, or their sons or their husbands' sons, or their brothers or their brothers' sons or sisters' sons, or their women, or their slaves, or male attendants who lack vigour, or children who know naught of women's nakedness. And let them not stamp their feet so as to reveal what they hide of their adornment. And turn unto Allah together, O believers, in order that ye may succeed.

Q. 33:53 (Pickthall):

O Ye who believe! Enter not the dwellings of the Prophet for a meal without waiting for the proper time, unless permission be granted you. But if ye are invited, enter, and, when your meal is ended, then disperse. Linger not for conversation. Lo! that would cause annoyance to the Prophet, and he would be shy of (asking) you (to go); but Allah is not shy of the truth. And when ye ask of them (the wives of the Prophet) anything, ask it of them from behind a curtain. That is purer for your hearts and for their hearts. And it is not for you to cause annoyance to the messenger of Allah, nor that ye should ever marry his wives after him. Lo! that in Allah's sight would be an enormity.

Q. 33:54 (Pickthall):

Whether ye divulge a thing or keep it hidden, lo! Allah is ever Knower of all things.

Q. 33:55 (Pickthall):

It is no sin for them (thy wives) (to converse freely) with their fathers, or their sons, or their brothers, or their brothers' sons, or the sons of their sisters or of their own women, or their slaves. O women! Keep your duty to Allah. Lo! Allah is ever Witness over all things.

6.4.2.b Forms of punishment

As stated previously, the study of the penal code of the Qur'an is beyond the scope of this book. However, it is noteworthy that the number of offenses covered in the Qur'anic penal code is way below the number of entries in the Qur'anic moral code. It is only a handful of offenses with their prescribed punishments that constitute the Qur'anic penal code.

The Qur'anic penal code is a penal code that applied solely to those who identified themselves as QMonotheists. Verses of the Qur'an that addressed punishments used forms of punishment that were prevalent in early seventh century CE Arabia, such as exile from the land, flogging, amputation of hands or limbs, execution whether it be fast or slow (as in *slb*—crucifixion) (Q. 4:25 in 4:19–28, 5:33–34 and 5:38–39 in 5:27–40, 24:2–3 and 24:4–5 in 24:1–10) ('Ali 1993, 5: 579–611).

In present time, universally accepted norms regarding human rights are reflected by international human rights bodies and international human rights standards that consider physical punishments as torture or inhumane treatment that violate international human rights law (Brems 2001, 217; Vega 2013, 29).

Forms of punishment cannot be accepted to be constant across space-time. Forms of punishment change and have changed as humanity has evolved. Rejecting physical forms of punishment in current times necessitates considering the injunctions of the Qur'an in connection with such physical forms of punishment as unacceptable. This holds true even in the case of those who reject some or most, yet not all the physical forms of punishment prescribed in the Qur'an. Hence, the claim that such Qur'anic Action-Type II injunctions are eternally applicable is disproved.

Side note 6.7 The Qur'an's corporal punishments for extramarital sex

The term "extramarital sex" encompasses both fornication (sexual relations outside of marriage) and adultery (sexual relations with someone other than one's spouse). In connection with QMonotheists having heterosexual extramarital sex, we find the Qur'an to have addressed this matter. I will outline (only) the physical punishments declared in the Qur'an as they relate to this issue, categorized according to whether the QMonotheist women involved were married or unmarried:

■ For a woman married to a free-man

The case where a married free-woman had sexual intercourse with a man other than her husband is what was specifically referred to in the Qur'an as *zina* (adultery). However, traditionally, the term has taken a more general meaning and has been commonly interpreted to refer to illegal heterosexual intercourse in general.

The Qur'an distinguished between whether the married women involved in sexual intercourse with a man other than her (free) husband were free or slave.

The Qur'an required that the act—in order to be recognized—had to be witnessed by four male witnesses (Q. 24:4 in 24:1–10). When the married woman was a free-person, the man and woman involved were to be flogged 100 lashes each (Q. 24:2–3 in 24:1–10). On the other hand, if the married woman was a QMonotheist slave, then she would receive 50 lashes, half the punishment of a free-woman (Q. 4:25).

■ For unmarried free-women

For QMonotheist unmarried free-women who were caught having forbidden heterosexual intercourse (*fahisha*). This had to be witnessed by four QMonotheist male witnesses. The women involved were to be locked up in their homes until death takes them away or God opens for them a way (they repented and married?) (Q. 4:15 in 4:15–18).

For the QMonotheist men involved, applies to both married and single, who were referred to in the Qur'an with the term *al-lathan* (both), the Qur'an stated in regard to these men, that those who had forbidden heterosexual intercourse (*fahisha*) with unmarried free-women were to be harmed (*athuhuma*). The Qur'an did not specify how they were to be harmed, probably slight bodily injury but not to the level of flogging. And it was to continue until they repented and amended (made amends; to marry the women involved?) (Q. 4:16 in 4:15–18).

I would like to point out that stoning was never declared as a punishment in the Qur'an—for any offense. Furthermore, we do not find the Qur'an to have declared punishment for homosexual intercourse in the space-time of the Prophet, though clearly declared to be *fahisha* (Q. 7:80–81 in 7:80–84).

I understand the Qur'anic term *fahisha* (plural *al-fawahish*; also found as *fahsha'*)—what I would translate as "obscenity," also found translated as: indecency, shameful deed, and many others—to represent what the Qur'an considered to be the forbidden sexual intercourse. It is my understanding that the term *fahisha* in the Qur'an referred to any penetrative sexual intercourse involving human sex organs apart from vaginal intercourse in a monandry marriage. It is important to note that it was only monandry marriage that was recognized permissible in the Qur'an: a heterosexual marriage in which a woman has only one husband at a time.

6.4.2.c Women's rights

From the Qur'an, its Meccan verses in particular, one gets the impression that women's rights were almost non-existent at the time the Qur'an was revealed. Society then had a demeaning look towards women (Q. 16:57–59 and 16:62 in 16:51–62, 43:17 in 43:1–25, 53:19–25). It was a time when some even buried their daughters alive (Q. 16:57–59 in 16:51–62, 81:8–9 in 81:1–14).

In such a space-time, the Qur'an came with a message that did not make a distinction between the sexes when it came to origins, belief, and reward. The Qur'an attested that both sexes were from the same origins (Q. 4:1, 6:98, 7:189, 22:5, 30:20 in 3:20–26, 35:11, 39:6, 40:67, 75:36–40, 76:1–2), and that the only differentiator between people was righteousness (Q. 49:13 in 49:11–13); that both sexes were free in their choice of belief and choice of code (Q. 2:256–257, 6:100–107, 10:99–109, 17:13–15, 18:27–31, 27:91–93, 39:9–18, 42:6, 42:47–48, 88:17–26, 109:1–6), and that both sexes would be rewarded according to true belief and actions (Q. 3:189–195 in 3:186–200, 4:123–126, 16:97, 40:40 in 40:23–52).

Numerous Qur'anic injunctions addressed prevalent social norms and practices that were biased against women. The change brought about by these injunctions was surely progressive for early seventh century CE Arabia and the region; however, what some of these injunctions called for cannot be accepted in modern times. Here are a couple of examples:

■ Testimony

Aside from the Qur'anic instances in which an accepted testimony was clearly stated to be that of men, and the instances in which it was not clearly stated that a woman's testimony would be accepted (Q. 4:6 in 4:1–6, 4:15–18, 5:106–108, 24:4–5 and 24:13 in 24:1–26, 65:2 in 65:1–7), we find two instances in the Qur'an that explicitly called for and actually clearly accepted the testimony of women.

The first case is related to when a husband accuses his wife of adultery (Q. 24:6–9 in 24:1–10). In this instance, we have a husband who accuses his wife of adultery while there are no witnesses but himself. According to the Qur'an, the wife can testify to the contrary and her testimony is accepted and would stand as opposing to his testimony against her. In this case we understand that both testimonies have equal weight.

The second case relates to financial dealings where a woman's testimony, according to the orthodox interpretation, is not considered to be equal to that of a man. We find this instances in the so-called verse of debt, Q. 2:282 in 2:282–283, the longest verse in the Qur'an. In Q. 2:282, the part relevant to this discussion, the interpretation of the meaning of the Arabic text as per Pickthall's translation is as follows: "And call to witness, from among your men, two witnesses. And if two men be not (at hand) then a man and two women, of such as ye approve as witnesses, so that if the one erreth (through forgetfulness) the other [would remind her]."*1

NOTICE: If the instances stated in the Qur'an in regard to testimony tell us anything, they indicate that the Qur'an's requirements for testimony—whether exclusively from men or, in specific cases, from women as well—were customized to the social norms of the space-time of the revelation.

■ Inheritance—Fractional shares of inheritance for male versus female relatives of the deceased

The Qur'an asserted that women had the right to inherit (Q. 4:7 in 4:7–14); however, not in all situations were women's shares of inheritance equal to those of men. For instance, according to the orthodox interpretation of Q. 4:11 in 4:7–14, if the deceased had both male and female children, then out of the children's share, the male child would inherit twice as much as the female child.

NOTICE: It is the view of the present author that the Qur'an's verses on fractional shares of inheritance related only to intestate succession in the space-time of the revelation. The reader is referred to side note 9.1 for more on this topic.

In line with the evolution of social norms, women's rights along with other rights have evolved across nations and over time. In current times, practices that discriminate against women are considered to be in violation of human rights conventions (CEDAW n.d.; Joseph and Najmabadi 2003, 309)—such conventions reflect the globally accepted norms of the current era. This serves to demonstrate that the Qur'anic Action-Type II injunctions that deal with women's rights should be viewed as pertaining to a particular instance in space-time, and surely should not be accepted to be applicable across space-time. Such injunctions can be considered as the absolute minimum that any law from that point forward should have improved upon.

Rejecting discrimination against women in current times necessitates considering the injunctions of the Qur'an on issues related to women's testimony and inheritance as unacceptable. Hence, the claim that such Qur'anic Action-Type II injunctions are eternally applicable is rejected.

NOTE*1: I disagree with the orthodox Islamic law principle (or legal rule) in regard to women's testimony, as derived from Q. 2:282, that the testimony of two women equaled the testimony of a single man. I find it of vital importance to ponder on why the Qur'an stated that if two men were not available, then to have a man and two women as witnesses. The Qur'an elaborated, and I attempt to translate: "that if one of the two women was to go astray, the other will remind her."

It is my view that requiring two women to witness, was taking into account the traditions and customs of the patriarchal tribal peoples of Hijaz at the time: it was a man's world—in every sense of the word. Let me explain. The environment where such contracts/transactions would take place was male predominated, it was a male predominated environment. And as per the culture at the time—taking all possible scenarios into consideration—you cannot just ask a woman to come into that space and witness a contract. It would—only—be appropriate, culturally, to have another woman also present, to make sure that everything was in order, with no sexually inappropriate conduct taking place. In other words, requiring two women to be present and not only one, was for the purpose of ensuring that the situation was really about witnessing a contract (the writing of) and nothing else. And in the event, if someone were to say something to the contrary about a female witness (accuse her of illegal sexual relations), then you would have two female witnesses to provide a counter-witness.

Furthermore, I see the use of the phrase "to go astray" to aid in providing an understanding of potential interpretations. Once again, here is the sentence, "that if one of the two women was to go astray (*an tadill*), the other will remind her."

Going astray in the Qur'anic context implies a loss of spiritual direction or alignment with divine guidance, which may result in spiritual or moral consequences. In the context of Q. 2:282, I understand "to go astray" to represent more than one course that could lead away from the right path, including but not limited to giving false testimony (in the future, at the time of testimony). The phrase "to go astray" could also refer to suggestive remarks, inappropriate behavior, all the way to engaging in illegal sexual relations (in the present, at the time of the witnessing, or in the future, at the time of testimony). Who knows, maybe being a witness would become a job—or even it was already a job at the time. And, otherwise, you would have a man and a woman—in Hijaz in the early seventh century CE—alone, together all day. Thus, having a man and two women as witnesses, aside from securing an adequate witness pool, it would likely help prevent situations that were deemed inappropriate.

From this, one understands that free-women (in this context, and not slave-women) in the space-time of the Qur'anic revelation were not seen—alone—in public that often. And women were primarily confined to domestic roles, with limited participation in broader societal affairs.

Therefore, it is my view about witnesses, that to have two women present was not only about cultural appropriateness but also about protecting the women and their reputation. While ensuring witness availability was crucial to verify the authenticity of the contract, it was equally important to uphold decency and conduct matters in a socially acceptable manner. And it was not that the testimony of two women equaled the testimony of a single man.

I reckon that Muslim jurists were aware of the plausibility of the abovementioned interpretation that I forward; however, they chose to disregard it, because, according to their understanding, the Qur'an's statements were eternal. And if choosing the interpretation I gave—while also assuming the Qur'an's statements to be eternal— this meant they also had to maintain the societal norms of the space-time of the revelation, which they (already knew), even in their own space-time, it was not possible to do so. Thus, what they could control and did control, was to impose that the testimony of two women equaled the testimony of a single man.

From this understanding in regard to societal norms in the space-time of the Qur'anic revelation, we see how societies today, in most parts of the world, have changed when it comes to gender relations and roles. And that social norms are definitely not the same today as they were in the tribal patriarchal society of Medina at the time of the revelation. And imposing space-time specific law (and requirements concerning witnesses) of that space-time on people today does not make sense nor should it be acceptable. And above all, as this book argues, the Qur'an does not oblige us to do so.

Side note 6.8 Child killing: A pre-Islamic practice explicitly prohibited in the Qur'an

From the Qur'an one understands that the killing of children by the child's parent(s) was a practice that was in existence at the time of the revelation (whether it be child homicide, infanticide or neonaticide). The Qur'an prohibited child killing outright in all forms. The Qur'an mentioned that the motivator for some to kill their male or female children was fear of *imlaq* (poverty). The Qur'an added that there were others who killed only their newborn baby girls just because they were female. The reader is to note that abortion is not the same as—nor considered part of—child killing, and it is not covered in the discussion herein.

Once we identify the place of revelation of the Qur'an's verses that addressed child killing, we get the impression that child killing seems to have been more of a Meccan than a Medinan practice. All verses that addressed this practice are believed to have been revealed in Mecca. That is, all except one particular case, Q. 60:12, which is part of the Qur'an's Chapter 60 that was revealed in Medina. However, Q. 60:12 was talking about emigrant Meccan women (see side note 9.6 on the Qur'an's Chapter 60).

The Qur'an prohibited child killing in both Meccan verses, Q. 6:151 in 6:151–153 and Q. 17:31 in 17:22–39. The prohibition used the term *awlad* (children: sons and/or daughters; singular *walad*), which is derived from the root *wld* (*walada*, a transcription showing short vowels) that means to beget; to give birth (Omar 2010, 620–621). Both verses stated that those who killed their children were doing so in fear of poverty. Additionally, there are the Meccan verses of Q. 6:137–140, which stated that the associators' killing of their children was not based on knowledge but rather on folly—the motivator behind why they would want to kill their children was not mentioned (these particular verses could be referring to child sacrifice). These verses were saying (roughly): Those whom they associated with God made it permissible for them to kill their children. In other words, the code they were following allowed such acts. We find a Medinan verse to be talking about how (newly arriving) emigrant female QMonotheists from Mecca were expected to pledge to the Prophet, among other things, that they would not kill their children (Q. 60:12 in 60:10–12). Once again, the motivator behind why they—the emigrant female QMonotheists—would want to kill their children was not given. Most likely the verse was talking about single emigrant mothers (when considering the context of Q. 60:10–12 and Chapter 60 as a whole); in that case, it is likely that the motivator was fear of not being able to provide sustenance for their children.

From the verses mentioned so far, one understands that in the space-time of the revelation—in regard to Meccans in particular—the killing of male or female children by their parents was done in fear of poverty, possibly as sacrifice or for whatever other reason. However, these forms of child killings were different from what other verses also limited to the Mecca era described. We find Meccan verses from which we understand that the burying alive of newborn baby girls had been practiced (*wa'd*) for no other reason than for the baby to have been female (Q. 16:57–59 in 16:51–62, 81:8–9 in 81:1–14).

It is possible that the burying alive of newborn girls was mentioned only in Meccan verses because such an act was prevalent in Mecca and not in Medina. The burying alive of newborn girls reflects social norms that hold a demeaning attitude towards the female sex, norms that would be expected to be prevalent in social systems that were more patrilineal. This observation would agree with Watt's hypothesis that Mecca followed a more patrilineal system, whereas Medina was mostly matrilineal at the time the Qur'an was revealed, as to be discussed in the following side note.

Side note 6.9 The rights of women in early seventh century CE Arabia

In an interview with the late orientalist William Montgomery Watt (d. 2006 CE), during his 90th year in 1999 CE (Maan and McIntosh 2000, 2011), when asked about the attitude of Prophet Muhammad towards women, he answered: "It is true that Islam is still, in many ways, a man's religion. But I think I've found evidence in some of the early sources that seems to show that Muhammad made things better for women. It appears that in some parts of Arabia, notably in Mecca, a matrilineal system was in the process of being replaced by a patrilineal one at the time of Muhammad. Growing prosperity caused by a shifting of trade routes was accompanied by a growth in individualism. Men were amassing considerable personal wealth and wanted to be sure that this would be inherited by their own actual sons, and not simply by an extended family of their sisters' sons. This led to a deterioration in the rights of women. At the time Islam began, the conditions of women were terrible – they had no right to own property, were supposed to be the property of the man, and if the man died everything went to his sons. Muhammad improved things quite a lot. By instituting rights of property ownership, inheritance, education and divorce, he gave women certain basic safeguards. Set in such historical context the Prophet can be seen as a figure who testified on behalf of women's rights." (Maan and McIntosh 2000, 9)

Transitioning to Watt's previous work concerning women in the space-time of the revelation and preceding periods. According to Watt (Watt 1991; Watt and McIntosh 2005), the Qur'an endorsed and regulated the move from a matrilineal system to a patrilineal system. Watt (1991) forwarded a hypothesis, according to which, Mecca followed a more patrilineal system at the time the Qur'an was revealed, whereas Medina and most of Arabia were mostly matrilineal. A matrilineal system of kinship is one where only descent from the mother was significant; however, this did not mean matriarchy or rule by women. The control of the family would be in the hands of a uterine brother of the senior woman, and would pass from him to her son. There were two main forms of marital arrangements associated with this social system: limited and unlimited polyandry, where a woman could have a limited (under ten) or unlimited number of husbands. The "marriage" was uxorilocal, i.e. it took place in the house where the woman lived. The man was said to "visit" her, yet the man could make such visits to several women. On the other hand, a patrilineal system is one in which family membership is traced through the individual's father's lineage. In a patrilineal system, marriage became virilocal rather than uxorilocal, where the woman went to a house provided by the man, hence, a woman would only have one husband, a monandric marital arrangement (161–164).

In endorsing and regulating the move from a matrilineal system to a patrilineal system, Watt described the influence that the Qur'an had on the sphere of marriage and family relations as that effecting profound and far reaching re-organization of the structure of society. Watt summarized this by saying: "In this restructuring of society there were changes in the position of women, some for the better, some perhaps for the worse, though of course we do not really know how women fared in the polyandric system. On the whole, however, it would seem that women benefited from the changes and were given greater security, especially since the change from a communal society to a more individualistic one was inevitable" (Watt 1991, 163–164). Watt, also stated: "Both by European Christian standards

188

and by those of Islam, many of the old practices were immoral, and Muhammad's reorganization was therefore a moral advance." (Watt 1991, 163)

The Qur'anic terms *muhssinin, muhssinat, muhssanat* (Q. 4:24–25, 5:5, 24:33) and *musafihin, musafihat* (Q. 4:24–25, 5:5), which are derived from the roots *hssn* and *sfh* (transcription showing short vowels: *hassana*, also sometimes transliterated as *hasana*; *safaha*) (Omar 2010, 126, 259–260), are integral to the discussion of monandry marriage. Watt presented an interesting interpretation of these terms, shedding light on their significance (Watt 1991; Watt and McIntosh 2005). Watt explains, "[o]ne of the essential changes made by Islam was to insist that a woman should have sexual relations with only one man at a time. Divorce or change of partner was relatively easy, especially for the man, but it was obligatory for a woman, before having another sexual partner, to observe a waiting period (*idda*) to ensure that she was not pregnant. It was not easy, of course, to effect such a sweeping change all at once, and for a time a distinction seems to have been made between women who observed the waiting period and those who did not" (Watt 1991, 162). Watt goes on to say, "[i]t would clearly have been impossible to change within the space of a year or two from the earlier systems of polyandry to one in which all women observed the waiting period. ... *tahassun* is almost certainly a technical term for observing the waiting period; for the men who do so the corresponding participial term is [*muhssinin*] and for the women either [*muhssinat*] or [*muhssanat*], where the latter, being passive, would indicate that they were made to do it. The participial forms for those following the old customs and not observing the waiting-period are *musafihin* and *musafihat*[.]" (Watt 1991, 169–170)

Side note 6.10 Women's right to their own wealth and who to be included in the last will and testament

We find a Medinan verse, Q. 4:19, from which we understand that there were those—at least some—who were inheriting women against their will. I cite Q. 4:19 here because most Qur'anic exegetes have interpreted this verse, in particular the first injunction within it, in a way that allegedly gives insight into (more on) how women were treated in the space-time of the revelation.

The first injunction in Q. 4:19 prohibits QMonotheists from inheriting women against their will: "it is not permissible for you to inherit women against their will." But what does it mean this action/practice that the Qur'an prohibited "to inherit women against their will"?

On Q. 4:19, al-Razi (d. 606 AH / 1209 CE) (al-Razi 1981) comments: There are two viewpoints when it comes to interpreting the first injunction in Q. 4:19, "it is not permissible for you to inherit women against their will (*la yahhil lakum an tarithu al-nisa' karha*)." The first viewpoint considers the injunction to prohibit a pre-Islamic practice that regarded women to be inheritance, as if they were property that could be inherited. An example on the prohibited practice would be that the wives of the deceased would become wives to the beneficiary—without their consent and without him being required to pay *sadaq*, also known as *mahr* (obligatory bridal payment given by the husband to his wife at the time of marriage; what this book refers to as "bride-consideration"—refer to side note 6.2), or he

189

could marry them off to others without their consent and take the *sadaq* from the new marriages for himself. Al-Razi adds, the second viewpoint considers the injunction to relate to the wealth of these (same) women rather than to the women themselves, where it prohibits holding them captive by not allowing them to remarry in order to eventually inherit them (10: 10–11).

I disagree with the abovementioned classical interpretation(s). I understand Q. 4:19–21 to have addressed matters related to women's wealth. There is Q. 4:22 that follows Q. 4:19–21, which explicitly dealt with the matter of men marrying women whom their fathers had previously married. It was forbidden outright. This would include women whom the classical interpretations above alleged would be inherited: the wives of the deceased would become wives to the beneficiary. Thus, it doesn't make sense that the first injunction in Q. 4:19 would also be prohibiting the same practice.

I understand Q. 4:19–21 to assert women's right to their own wealth. Whether that be during their lifetime or after they die. Q. 4:19–21 were basically saying that male QMonotheists should not coerce women to give up their wealth. One exception was given in the case of the wife committing adultery: the husband had the right to claim back some of the bride-consideration.

Q. 4:19–21 addressed QMonotheist men (husbands, fathers, brothers) on how to deal with matters in connection with the wealth of women, whether it be what they leave behind after they die (inheritance) or what these women had in their possession of what their husbands had given them (the bride-consideration).

The presence of the term *karha* (against their will) in the first injunction of Q. 4:19, "it is not permissible for you to inherit women *karha* (against their will)," helps us better understand what is at stake here. It is my viewpoint that this particular injunction in Q. 4:19 was about prohibiting men to interfere with the last will and testament of women. It prohibited, for example, the husband forcing on his wife that he be included in her last will and testament (to be bequeathed upon; to be the heir of), or coercing her to declare him as the sole beneficiary, etc. Moreover, the presence of the term *karha* (against their will) further affirms that it was not marriage to these women that was intended, as suggested by the classical interpretations. As per the classical interpretations, how about if a woman did not object to being inherited (her person) to the son of the man she had been married to. Would it be permissible for the son of her deceased husband to marry her then?

Furthermore, I see this statement to give insight about the last will and testament, in that a person gets to freely choose who to include in the last will and testament in spite that we find Q. 2:180 that guides as to who to include in the last will and testament: one's parents and *al-aqrabin* (those close to one) in a manner that was described to be *bilma'ruf* (honorably).

I find it important to distinguish between blood relations and those close to one. When referring to blood relations, we find the Qur'an in Q. 8:75 and Q. 33:6 to have used the term *ulu al-arham*. It is my understanding that *al-aqrabin* (and its grammatical counterpart *al-aqrabun*) would (potentially) include all those close to one aside from one's parents. They could be male or female, blood related or not. This would include adopted children, and even friends (from one's allies and/or

190

those who one had sworn compact with) (Q. 4:33, 33:5–6 in 33:1–8). Furthermore, the Qur'an specified that bequests be *bilma'ruf* (honorably; in a way that is honest and fair). Specifications were given regarding witnesses to the will and how they were to give their testimony (Q. 5:106–108).

For reference, here is the translation of Q. 4:19–22 by Pickthall:

Q. 4:19 (Pickthall):
O ye who believe! It is not lawful for you forcibly to inherit the women (of your deceased kinsmen), nor (that) ye should put constraint upon them that ye may take away a part of that which ye have given them, unless they be guilty of flagrant lewdness. But consort with them in kindness, for if ye hate them it may happen that ye hate a thing wherein Allah hath placed much good.

Q. 4:20 (Pickthall):
And if ye wish to exchange one wife for another and ye have given unto one of them a sum of money (however great), take nothing from it. Would ye take it by the way of calumny and open wrong?

Q. 4:21 (Pickthall):
How can ye take it (back) after one of you hath gone in unto the other, and they have taken a strong pledge from you?

Q. 4:22 (Pickthall):
"And marry not those women whom your fathers married, except what hath already happened (of that nature) in the past. Lo! it was ever lewdness and abomination, and an evil way."

Side note 6.11 Refuting the proposition that *Shari'a* law is eternal

Rejecting *Shari'a* law's stand on issues such as slavery, physical forms of punishment, and women's rights refutes the proposition that *Shari'a* law is eternal. In order to understand why this rejection affects the argument in such a way, we need to look into the reasoning followed.

Below, I have constructed an argument in the form of reductio ad absurdum to clarify this point. Before going any further, it is best to explain the following terms:

■ Reductio ad absurdum: It is a form of argument that establishes its conclusion by showing that the opposite leads to an absurd, contradictory, morally, or practically unacceptable result.

■ Syllogism: A syllogism is a form of logical argument that employs deductive reasoning to reach a conclusion from two or more propositions considered true. Typically, syllogistic arguments are depicted in a three-line format (Wikipedia 2002a, par. 1–2).

■ Deductive reasoning: It is a type of reasoning in which the truth of the input propositions (the premises) logically guarantees the truth of the output proposition (the conclusion).

The argument spelled out in reductio ad absurdum form is as follows:

Thesis to prove: *Shari'a* law is non-eternal.

The subsequent syllogistic argument is as follows:

- Premise 1 (assume the opposite of what we want to prove): *Shari'a* law is eternal. This would mean that the Qur'anic Action-Type II injunctions are eternally applicable.

- Premise 2: Existence of Qur'anic Action-Type II injunctions that describe "how to deal with slaves" implies the acceptance of "the institution of slavery."

- Conclusion: The acceptance of "slavery" is eternal.

As per the above reasoning, assuming *Shari'a* law to be eternal leads to the conclusion that acceptance of "slavery" is eternal. However, this conclusion is found absurd or morally unacceptable—by most Muslims in modern times—which necessitates that premise 1 is wrong. Therefore, we refute premise 1 and accept the thesis that we set out to prove initially: *Shari'a* law is non-eternal.

The same line of reasoning can be applied to the other mentioned controversial issues found in *Shari'a* law, law derived directly from Qur'anic Action-Type II injunctions (interpretation of), by replacing the "quoted text" in the argument with:

- "crucifixion as a form of punishment"

- "the testimony of two women equaled the testimony of a single man"

6.4.3 Analysis

How the Qur'an approached the social norms of early seventh century CE (west) Arabia and the region can be regarded as progressive or even revolutionary for the space-time of the revelation. Yet the solutions provided cannot be accepted as fixed across space-time.

What is common amongst the examples that were discussed is how the Qur'anic Action-Type II injunctions handled the issues in question. The Qur'anic Action-Type II injunctions managed these issues and dealt with them by providing solutions, that probably, considering the prevalent social norms, could be regarded as best solutions for a particular space-time instance. However, these solutions did not provide in any way an optimal solution for these issues across space-time: better solutions have manifested themselves as space-time changed (by humane ethical standards). Therefore, any laws derived from these Qur'anic Action-Type II injunctions cannot and should not be considered to be eternally applicable.

In current times, *Shari'a* law extracted from the Qur'anic Action-Type II injunctions can no longer be considered to represent the realization of the Qur'anic ethics. Societies' norms and values have evolved to a level that makes societies understand the ethics called for in the Qur'an in a different way than that reflected in the Qur'anic Action-Type II injunctions. Today, as per our understanding of fairness, we recognize that it would be hard to regard the Qur'anic Action-Type II injunctions that address issues like slavery, physical forms of punishment, and women's rights as to represent the realization of the Qur'anic injunctions of ethics that call for fairness. Islamic law's approach was—and still is—to consider Action-Type II injunctions to supersede ethics injunctions on such issues; some even consider Action-Type II verses to abrogate the ethics verses. However, while the Action-Type II injunctions were suitable to be applied in the space-time of the Prophet, as time progressed, followers of the Qur'an should have moved on beyond the laws declared by the Action-Type II injunctions. Followers of the Qur'an should have sought to produce law guided by the ethics of the Qur'an suitable for their respective space-time, rather than to remain constrained by the Action-Type II injunctions. If that had happened, law and social norms would have simultaneously evolved in a direction that reflected an understanding of the ethics of the Qur'an consistent with societies' space-time, and we surely would not be having this discussion to begin with.

6.4.4 Historical perspective

The objective behind citing examples from Muslim history is for those who accept the traditional narrative on these (alleged) historical events to think about what it is they accept.

For the sake of argument, in the discussion to follow, let us follow in the footsteps of most Muslims and accept the following two assumptions:

- To assume the historical reports to be true;

- To assume the orthodox interpretation of the Qur'anic verses in question to be correct (or what is commonly believed to represent such interpretation).

Bearing in mind the above, the to-be-cited historical events will yet illustrate the understanding that the applicability of the Qur'anic Action-Type II injunctions is non-eternal but is rather space-time specific. These historical events involve 'Umar ibn al-Khattab, the second to rule after the Prophet.

The traditional narratives inform us that only a few years after the death of the Prophet, 'Umar ibn al-Khattab was reported to not to have followed the injunctions presented in the Qur'an regarding the following matters:

- Punishment for stealing

During the great famine, 18 AH / 639 CE (al-Tabari 1967, 4: 98 1/2574), it was reported that 'Umar did not cut off the hand of a person who was found guilty of stealing (As-Sallabi 2007, 1: 421–422). To cut off the hand of a thief is the orthodox interpretation of the Qur'anic punishment prescribed for stealing (Kuwait Ministry of Awqaf and Islamic Affairs 1995, 24: 335–336) (Q. 5:38–40). Hence, 'Umar is perceived to have (temporarily) suspended acting upon the Qur'anic punishment for stealing (the orthodox understanding of).

- Distribution of the revenue from *sadaqat* (giving; singular *sadaqa*)

The Qur'an described eight categories as rightful recipients of *sadaqat* (Q. 9:60 in 9:58–60). It was reported that 'Umar ceased distribution of the revenue from *sadaqat* to one of these categories, the category of *al-mu'allafa qulubuhum*; "those whose hearts are reconciled" is the English translation of the orthodox interpretation of this phrase (As-Sallabi 2007, 1: 481–484). The common understanding of "those whose hearts are reconciled" is that they are people who are given from *sadaqat* to reconcile their hearts. However, throughout Muslim history, there has never been consensus on who was actually represented by this category (Kuwait Ministry of Awqaf and Islamic Affairs 1995, 23: 319–320, 36: 12–13; Watt 1956, 348–353). In effect, 'Umar is perceived to have suspended (permanently during his reign) one of the eight rightful recipients of *sadaqat*—as declared in the Qur'an—from the *sadaqat* distribution; thereby, setting a precedent for those after him.*1

If we were to accept the abovementioned two assumptions, then the above examples demonstrate that even around the same space-time of the Prophet, adherence to the Qur'anic Action-Type II injunctions was reconsidered, showing they were not always treated as eternally applicable. If from the early beginnings the understanding of the applicability of these injunctions had been as Traditional Islam prescribes—to be eternally applicable—then one would expect 'Umar ibn al-Khattab to be among the first to understand them as such. If that had been the case, then no one, not even 'Umar, would have had the right to suspend their enforcement either temporarily or permanently.

NOTE*1: In the Qur'an *sadaqat* (giving) took two forms: obligatory giving (the *zakat*; 20% of income) and voluntary giving. This (alleged) historical incident was related to spending the revenue from obligatory giving, i.e. the revenue from the *zakat*.

Obligatory giving in the mentioned space-time—due on Monotheists living in a Monotheist state—could be pictured as modern-day income tax that was due on nationals living in a nation-state—where the nation is defined in terms of religious following, in this case, Monotheism. Accordingly, in modern-day language, this (alleged) historical incident was related to how the state spends its revenue from income tax. The Qur'anic terms *sadaqat* and *zakat* are discussed in Volume 1 of this series.

6.5 The last source: The *Hadith*

In the previous section, we found the Action-Type II injunctions of the Qur'an, the revealed speech of God, not to be eternally applicable across space-time. One might wonder, if the Qur'an itself is a non-eternal source of law, how could it be possible for any other source of law to be eternal? We go the extra step and examine the *Hadith*, since we agreed in Chapter 5, when stating the problem, that we would not challenge Traditional Islam's choice in sources. When it comes to *Shari'a* law, Traditional Islam considers the *Hadith* to be a source for *Shari'a* law. Therefore, we proceed to examine the claim of the eternal applicability of the Action-Type II injunctions of the *Hadith*.

6.5.1 Rationale

At this stage of our study, we look into the *Hadith* as a source for *Shari'a* law. We are concerned with examining Action-Type II *Hadith* that is definitive in both attribution and meaning for eternal applicability.

According to Traditional Islam's classification of the *Hadith* per number of narrators that was introduced in Chapter 2, the *Hadith* is considered to be either definitive or speculative when it comes to its attribution to the Prophet. Therefore, unlike the Qur'an, all of which is considered definitive in its attribution, when studying the *Hadith*, there is an extra layer of study that is required: we need to make sure the *Hadith* in question is certain (definitive) in its attribution to the Prophet. For this reason, we must first examine the *Hadith* from the perspective of its attribution to the Prophet.

I call upon the findings of the study of the *Sunna* and the *Hadith* conducted in Volume 2. In Volume 2, the *Sunna* was dismissed as a source of religious knowledge, yet we resumed our examination of Traditional Islam's sources of religious knowledge. We examined what Traditional Islam claims to represent the *Sunna*, we examined the *Hadith*.

We studied the authenticity of *Hadith* while reconsidering the classical standards used to determine authenticity. Instead of blindly accepting Traditional Islam's standards for the authenticity of *Hadith*, we looked into the Qur'an's method to verify oral evidence, and studied the consequences of applying the Qur'anic authentication standard for oral evidence to the *Hadith*.

The study concluded that not even a single *Hadith* existed that was certain in its attribution to the Prophet. Accordingly, it was concluded that the *Hadith* does not represent the *Sunna*, and therefore should be rejected as a source of religious knowledge. The *Sunna* itself was originally rejected as a source of religious knowledge, hence the *Hadith* should not be accepted as such.

If the *Hadith* does not represent the *Sunna*, and the *Hadith* is not considered a source of religious knowledge, then the *Hadith* should not be considered a source of law, let alone a source of eternal law.

6.5.2 Approach

Assume, for the sake of argument, we disregard the findings of the study of the *Sunna* and the *Hadith* conducted in Volume 2, which concluded that the *Sunna* should not be considered a source of religious knowledge and that the *Hadith* did not represent the *Sunna*. In other words, let us assume, as Traditional Islam does, to accept the *Sunna* as a source of religious knowledge. Let us further assume, also as Traditional Islam does, that the *Hadith* represents the *Sunna*.

At this stage of our study—in relation to *Shari'a* law—our objective is to verify the eternal applicability of *Shari'a* law extracted directly from Action-Type II *Hadith* that is definitive in both attribution and meaning.

According to Traditional Islam's classification of the *Hadith* per number of narrators, only *mutawatir Hadith* is considered certain in its attribution to the Prophet. Needless to say, only a handful of *Hadiths* are of this type—some said none, others said one, while there were those who said the count did not exceed seven (Amin 1969, 218).

Let us momentarily accept Traditional Islam's classification of the *Hadith* per number of narrators as being able to reflect the certainty of attribution to the Prophet. Nonetheless, there is no agreed-upon *mutawatir Hadith* in exact wording from which law could be extracted. In view of that, even by the standards of Traditional Islam, we are unable to find *Hadith* definitive in both attribution and meaning from which law could be extracted—let alone examine it for eternal applicability.

As a result, we conclude that *Shari'a* law extracted directly from the definitive Action-Type II *Hadith* does not exist, simply because definitive Action-Type II *Hadith* does not exist.

NOTE: As explained in Chapter 2, *mutawatir Hadith* is of two types when considering the text (*matn*) of the *Hadith*: reporting the text in meaning; and reporting the text in its exact wording (verbatim). It can be argued that only *Hadith* that is *mutawatir* in its exact wording, and not the type that is *mutawatir* in its meaning could be regarded as definitive in both attribution and meaning. Reporting *Hadith* by meaning is subjective, and many factors could affect the *Hadith* being transmitted.

NOTE: When dealing with *mutawatir*, Muslim scholars did not agree on the quality requirements for the *sanads* of the *khabar al-ahads* involved: they did not all require the *sanad* of each of the *khabar al-ahads* within the group to be sound (*sahih*). Thus, in effect, there were several definitions of what constituted a *mutawatir Hadith*. This, I believe, was the reason behind the discrepancy about the number of *mutawatir Hadiths*. Certain scholars established the minimum number of transmissions required for *tawatur* at five, whereas others placed it at different figures such as 12, 20, 40, 70, or 313, each number being supported by a Qur'anic verse or religious narrative (Hallaq 1999, 79).

Some Muslim scholars, when they searched for *mutawatir Hadiths*, only considered those that are made up of *khabar al-ahads* that were sound (*sahih*). Whereas others did not abide by this requirement in their definition of *mutawatir Hadiths*; they included the *hasan*, that came in varying levels of quality; additionally, they did not agree on which of the *hasan* would be acceptable; some even included those of lesser quality. However, it only makes sense that if *mutawatir* was to be considered certain in its attribution to the Prophet, then the *sanad* of each *khabar al-ahad* within the group needs to be sound (*sahih*). That is, the five requirements for the *sanad* to be *sahih* would need to be satisfied by each *khabar al-ahad* within the group: the

> *sanad* is continuous (uninterrupted) until reaching the Prophet; all narrators listed are trustworthy individuals, where narrators would be trustworthy in both righteousness and accurateness; moreover, the *sanad* is not aberrant nor does it have flaws.

6.5.3 Analysis

As per the study of the *Hadith* in Volume 2, we found no *Hadith* to exist that complied with the consecutive testimony requirements. Thus, when adhering to the Qur'anic authentication standard for oral evidence, no *Hadith* exists that is certain in its attribution to the Prophet.

Hadith that is uncertain in its attribution to the Prophet cannot be regarded as a source of religious knowledge; it is not religiously binding (on any matters of religion). If it is not a source of religious knowledge, it should not be considered a (potential) source of religious law, let alone be considered an eternal source of religious law.

6.5.4 Historical perspective

As in the opening of Section 6.4.4, when presenting a historical perspective relevant to the Qur'an; for the *Hadith*, a similar introductory statement is in order:

> The objective behind citing examples from Muslim history is for those who accept the traditional narrative on these (alleged) historical events to think about what it is they accept.

For the sake of argument, in the discussion to follow, let us accept the following two assumptions:

- ■ To assume the historical reports to be true;

- ■ To assume the *Hadiths* in question to be certain in their attribution to the Prophet. By Traditional Islam standards, it means they are *mutawatir* (though in reality they are not *mutawatir*).

Bearing in mind the above, the to-be-cited historical events will yet illustrate the understanding that the applicability of *Hadith* Action-Type II injunctions is non-eternal but is rather space-time specific. Once again we turn to 'Umar ibn al-Khattab. This time, to gain insight from his stance towards precedent in the *Sunna* dealing with worldly matters.

198

'Umar ibn al-Khattab did not need any compilations of *Hadith* to know the *Sunna*, he had lived it. In spite of knowing the *Sunna*, it was reported that 'Umar did not follow the *Sunna* in the following incidents by:

- Doing what the Prophet did not do

As pointed out in Chapter 2, according to the Sunni traditional sources, it was 'Umar ibn al-Khattab who suggested to Abu Bakr al-Siddiq that the scattered written pieces of the Qur'an should be collected (*jam'*) (As-Sallabi 2007, 1: 150–152).

- Doing different to what the Prophet did

When 'Umar ibn Al-Khattab refused to divide ownership of the captured lands (spoils) amongst the warriors, 'Umar had deviated from the norm that was set by the Prophet in Khaybar (As-Sallabi 2007, 1: 453–459).

If we were to accept the abovementioned two assumptions, these examples demonstrate that even around the same space-time of the Prophet, following the *Sunna* when dealing with worldly matters was not the default practice. 'Umar ibn al-Khattab's choosing not to follow the *Sunna* in the above matters, clearly indicates that 'Umar's regard to the *Sunna* was that he saw it as space-time specific when dealing with worldly matters and not as Traditional Islam's sees it to be eternally applicable.

Side note 6.12 The biography of the Prophet

Most works on the biography of the Prophet (*al-sira al-nabawiyya*) reference the work of Ibn Ishaq (d. 150 AH / 767 CE). Ibn Ishaq's biography of the Prophet is the earliest surviving biography, longest, and most widely cited. The original text was lost; however, reconstructions depended on later works that were based on, or that referenced, Ibn Ishaq's biography, like the works of Ibn Hisham (d. 218 AH / 833 CE) and al-Tabari (d. 310 AH / 923 CE).

In Ibn Ishaq's biography of the Prophet, reports that have a continuous chain of narrators (necessary to verify credibility) are seldom found. Additionally, early Muslim scholars—contemporary or later to Ibn Ishaq—have voiced reservations on the biography, ranging from doubting the credibility of Ibn Ishaq to doubting the credibility of his sources (Amin 1969, 217). Moreover, we find modern scholars of early Islam who have questioned, and others who have contested, events initially documented in the biography, in particular its claims of the fall-out with the Jewish tribes of Hijaz (Arafat 1998; Donner 2010, 73; 2013, 3–4).

6.6 Results & Insights

6.6.1 De-legitimizing Islamic law

The study of *Shari'a* law has led us to examine Traditional Islam's claim of the eternal applicability of the primary sources. The eternal applicability of the primary sources has been disproved and can no longer be used to legitimize Islamic law.

Shari'a law, which is considered by Traditional Islam to be the eternal component of Islamic law, has been found to be non-eternal. Because the applicability of the sources of *Shari'a* law, the applicability of the definitive primary sources, has been proven not to be eternal but rather space-time specific.

We have examined certain definitive primary sources and have found their applicability to be space-time specific—those related to slavery, forms of punishment, and women's rights. This reflects on the primary sources as a whole, proving their applicability to be non-eternal, whether being definitive or not. Accordingly, the claim on which Traditional Islam depends on to justify the existence of *Shari'a* law, or Islamic law for that matter—the eternal applicability of the primary sources—has been disproved and can no longer be used to legitimize Islamic law.

When studying the Qur'an, the assumed proposition that *Shari'a* law is eternal was shown to lead to absurd, inapplicable, or morally unacceptable results. When studying the *Hadith*, the same proposition could not even be examined, since we could not find *Hadith* from which law could be extracted that was certain in its attribution to the Prophet. Therefore, we conclude that the proposition that *Shari'a* law is eternal must be false, and the thesis outlined earlier in this chapter is to be accepted: *Shari'a* law is non-eternal.

6.6.2 Change in social norms

If time has taught us anything at all, it is that all living organisms evolve over time. Man is no exception. The part of human evolution that is of concern to us here is that of the intellect, which affects how man lives his life, and which consequently is reflected in human societies.

Man changes due to the accumulated knowledge that man acquires from his experiences living in this world. To better understand how this affects the topic at hand, we refer back to our three-dimensional space metaphor representing the relationships of man, but this time projecting religion on it rather than Islamic law.

Over time, man changes; therefore, how man manages man-man relationships and affairs changes as well. In addition, man's understanding of the world around him changes. All this is reflected in what I called the man-world plane. Hence, the man-world plane is continuously changing, or rather, man's conception of it is non-constant. On the other hand, when it comes to man's conception of God, God is non-changing—this conception of God has not changed over changes in space-time. As a result, man's relationship with God is non-changing. Accordingly, we have a non-changing vertical plane and a changing horizontal plane. Religion with its beliefs, acts of worship, and ethics is supposed to be non-changing; hence, should lie within the vertical plane. Whereas everything else changes if one believes man to evolve over time, and is a matter for the horizontal plane.

However, religion does play a role in bridging between the spiritual and the worldly realms. This role is provided by the ethics conveyed through religion. Religion in such a configuration, and when it comes to regulating man-world relationships and affairs, would not be the source of law, but rather, a source of ethics.

This metaphor depicting the relationships of man is not just affected by time alone, but is rather affected by both space and time together, since not all cultures and societies evolve in the same way or at the same pace.

The space-time effect on man can be observed in how space-time affects social norms. Law is the gauge that reflects social norms. Traditional Islam claims that Islamic law, in particular *Shari'a* law, is applicable across space-time. This would lead to assume that social norms are non-changing with changes in space-time. On the other hand, the above argument makes the case that social norms do change with space-time as man evolves; accordingly, law should change to adapt to changes in social norms. To test both claims, we have looked into norms regarding slavery, physical forms of punishment, and discrimination against women over a span of fourteen hundred years. We have found that only in the last century or so have social norms changed to an extent that has enabled us to reject the previously accepted laws in their regard. This in turn leads us to reject Traditional Islam's claim of the eternal applicability of the primary sources. We thus conclude that social norms are not fixed, and that law should change to reflect changes in social norms.

Social norms do change; however, it is change that is slow. This could help explain why Muslims accepted the claim made by Traditional Islam about the eternal applicability of the primary sources for such a long time. There was not enough change in social norms to bring about change in law.

It has now been over fourteen hundred years since the revelation of the first verses of the Qur'an, during which a lot has changed, especially in the last century or so, in regard to human rights, the abolition of slavery, and so many other changes. It is these vast changes in the civilization of man that have had a dramatic effect on showing the non-compatibility of the bulk of laws produced by Islamic law to the life of the modern-day Muslim.

It has become customary to reject law that is rigid, or that which is biased to matters that we have no control over, especially since humans do not get to choose their genes, sex, parents, or even which space-time to exist. This has been the basis for contemporary human and civil rights laws that also extend equal rights to other matters that we do have choice over, such as religion and expression, among other things.

Assuming solutions to be fixed, i.e. having eternal law for man-world affairs, is neither fair nor just, and the whole idea behind applying fixed solutions to begin with was the assumption that they were fair and just. In other words, there is no such thing as eternal law for man-world affairs. As Kohler (1914, 676) put it, "there is no eternal law. The law that is suitable for one period is not so for another: we can only strive to provide every culture with its corresponding system of law. What is good for one would mean ruin to another."

Societies have and will continue to change along with change in space-time. Awareness, education, and social norms are now different from what they used to be in Arabia at the time of the Prophet. Man has evolved; thus, law needs to evolve accordingly. Producing and implementing law based on values such as fairness, equality, and freedom has proven to be easier said than done. Nonetheless, as humanity has evolved over the years in all aspects, it has been able to, and I am confident, it will continue to provide better and better solutions—by both ethical and humane standards—for managing and regulating man-world affairs.

6.6.3 Ingredients for change and the forces that affect change

If there is anything we know for sure, it is that change is inevitable. This surely does not exclude change in social norms.

It is proposed that producing change in social norms entails a three-step process. Alternatively, one might describe this process as having three crucial ingredients, akin to a recipe for change:

- Ideas advocating change

- Society to accept change

- The actual implementation of change

The pace at which change in social norms occurs is affected mainly by two opposing factors or forces, each exerting its distinctive impact:

- Inertia

It is mainly inertia that makes the acceptance and the implementation of change in social norms sluggish in any society, regardless of religion. As it seems, human nature tends to resist change, and the clinging on to thoughts, traditions, and customs that advocate eternal validity does not help much in moving any faster towards more suitable solutions for changes in space-time.

- Progress

The progress that man has brought about in his living conditions and standards surely has an effect on the pace of change in social norms. Several factors, such as better health care, better political, educational, and economic environments, among other things, with technology in the lead have led to bring the various sources of knowledge closer to the modern man.

These advancements provide a nourishing environment with tools and means that facilitate generating the initial ingredient for change: the ideas. Additionally, the availability and the faster dissemination of information help expedite the acceptance of change. Implementation of change is facilitated in modern-day social systems through efficient governance and legal systems. The effect of such systems is manifested through introducing and enforcing law that aligns with the new ideas.

The relationship between law and social norms is a two-way street (social norms ⇔ law). In other words, there is a reciprocal relationship between law and social norms, with each influencing and being influenced by the other. More on the relationship between law and social norms is discussed in Chapter 9.

It would be reasonable to assume that in modern times—with the progress achieved in living conditions and standards—it is possible for change in the norms of society to occur at a relatively faster pace than it used to in previous eras. Although one thing for certain, regardless of space-time, that is crucial for instigating change and for societies to accept and implement change, and that is the need for man to always think. This is not to be understood as a call advocating to trust man more than God, but rather, that trust in God leads to trust in man.

7. Islamic law indirectly from the primary sources: *Fiqh*-based law

Rejecting the eternal applicability of *Shari'a* law was enough in itself to establish that any Qur'anic-based interpretation of religion should not have a law component. Why then continue with the study of Islamic law and dedicate a separate chapter to study the other component of Islamic law that we already know to be non-eternal by definition? The short answer is that we do that to learn more about Islamic law; we do that to resume with the sources approach and to learn about the other sources of Islamic law.

In this chapter we examine the second component of Islamic law, what I refer to as *Fiqh*-based law, which comprises the bulk of the body of Islamic law. This will allow the reader to understand how man has influenced and to this day still influences the interpretations of Islam.

To assume that Islamic law—effectively—considers only the Qur'an and the *Hadith* to be the eternal sources of law would be incorrect. This chapter will introduce yet another source of law besides the primary sources that Islamic law has traditionally treated as having the authority to produce eternal law. This source of law is consensus (*ijma'*), the agreement of a group on a point of law.

7.1 *Fiqh*, *Fiqh*-based law, and Islamic law

Islamic law extends beyond *Shari'a* law, which brings us to law based on *Fiqh*. Thus far, I have described *Fiqh*-based law, as it relates to Islamic law, to be law derived indirectly from the primary sources. However, I have not talked much about the word *Fiqh* itself, nor have I talked about the modern perspective of what *Fiqh* represents or has historically represented in terms of the scope it covers. Next, I talk about these points.

7.1.1 *Fiqh*: More about the word

Linguistically, the noun *Fiqh* is derived from the root *fqh* (*faqiha*, a transcription showing short vowels). Word patterns sharing this root cover the semantic field of understanding. *Fiqh*, technically, in the sphere of Islamic law, is a term used to describe both the jurisprudence based on the primary sources and the outcome of this jurisprudence.

Fiqh utilizes *ijtihad* to produce law. *Ijtihad* is exerting one's reasoning faculty in determining a point of law. Reasoning though, in the case of *Fiqh*, is constrained to be within the scope of the spirit and principles of the primary sources. *Ijtihad* is used to produce law for matters discussed in the primary sources but were not definitive in both attribution and meaning (*laysat qat'iyyat al-thubut wa al-dalala*), in addition to produce law for matters not discussed in the primary sources (al-Bardisi 198-?, 459–472; Madkur 1996, 292–295).

Fiqh is considered to be the dynamic component of Islamic law. In the study of Islamic law, *Fiqh* is considered fallible since it depends on the attempts of man to infer, deduce, and apply the principles of the primary sources, unlike *Shari'a* law that is considered infallible.

Scholars who work in *Fiqh* are called *fuqaha'* (jurists; singular *faqih*). Hence, *Fiqh*-based law can be seen to refer to the bodies of law produced by the rulings (*fatawa*, singular *fatwa*) of the *fuqaha'*.

7.1.2 *Fiqh*: Historically (in terms of scope)

What the term *Fiqh* represents in terms of the scope it covers has changed over the years. As Dasuqi and Jabir (1999) point out, three periods can be identified:

■ The first period [ended probably around the mid-second century AH]

The term *Fiqh* described all injunctions declared in the Qur'an and the *Hadith* (and their interpretation), which covers the injunctions of belief, virtue, and the action injunctions—synonym for religion. As the study of religion grew, specialization was needed. This brings us to the second period.

■ The second period [around mid-second to mid-fourth century AH; covering the establishment and development of the schools of jurisprudence]

The term *Fiqh* became known to describe exclusively the action injunctions developed through jurisprudence based on the primary sources. In this period *Fiqh* excluded the definitive primary sources.

■ The third period [started around the mid-fourth century AH and gained momentum towards the end of the Abbasid era—lasting till now]

The term *Fiqh* was used to describe all action injunctions, whether those extracted directly from the definitive primary sources or those developed through jurisprudence based on the primary sources (52–55).

Nowadays, in most circles, it has become customary for the Arabic term *Shari'a* to be used to describe the same thing that the term *Fiqh* covered in the third period. Yet the third period's understanding of the scope of *Fiqh* is what the English term Islamic law in Chapter 5 was defined to encompass.

At present time, in universities of the Muslim world, a school that teaches *Fiqh*, as defined by the third period, is called "school of *Shari'a* (*kuliyyat al-shari'a*)," a trend that started in Egypt and spread to other Muslim countries (dar-alifta.org 2011, sec. 2, par. 3). Terminology as such causes confusion. This was the reason that led me to distinguish between the terms Islamic law and *Shari'a* law when discussing *Shari'a* law in Chapter 6.

7.1.3 Terminology recap: Islamic law and its two components

To summarize, here are the terms introduced thus far—the adopted terminology:

■ Islamic law
The term Islamic law refers to the body of laws derived directly and indirectly from the primary sources (*al-ahkam al-'amaliyya*), i.e. a term that encompasses all religious law.

■ *Shari'a* law
The term *Shari'a* law is used to describe law extracted directly from primary sources that are definitive in both attribution and meaning (*qat'iyyat al-thubut wa al-dalala*).

■ *Fiqh*-based law
The remainder of Islamic law, its bulk, constitutes *Fiqh* or what I refer to by the term *Fiqh*-based law (*Fiqh*-based law = Islamic law – *Shari'a* law).

Depicting *Fiqh*-based law in this manner is in accordance with understanding it to be law produced by *ijtihad*. Furthermore, it is in line with what *Fiqh* represented in the second period: action injunctions developed through jurisprudence based on the primary sources. It is an understanding that excludes from *Fiqh* the definitive primary sources that are addressed by *Shari'a* law.

7.2 Islamic law from classical to contemporary: An overview

The interpretations of Islamic law today encompass law beyond that of the classical schools of jurisprudence. For the Muslim of the present era, Islamic law can be regarded to be composed of two components. The first component is law produced by the schools of jurisprudence. The second component is the Islamic law of the fairly recent era, which I will refer to as "modern Islamic law."

The classical schools of jurisprudence produced both *Shari'a* law and *Fiqh*-based law. When it comes to studying the development and history of *Fiqh*-based law, it is not that straightforward to attempt to study *Fiqh*-based law separately from *Shari'a* law, nor does doing so serve the purpose of this book in any special way. Therefore, this section explores the development and history of Islamic law as a whole, encompassing both *Shari'a* law and *Fiqh*-based law.

7.2.1 The different interpretations of Islamic law

Up to the mid-fourth century AH (second half of the tenth century CE), works of prominent Muslim scholars brought us the schools of law or jurisprudence (*madhahib fiqhiyya*, singular *madhhab fiqhi*). Scholars incorporated their understanding of the Qur'an and the *Hadith*, along with their personal viewpoints, conclusions and judgments, and molded them into legal interpretations. This led to the birth of what became known as *madhahib fiqhiyya* (schools of law or jurisprudence), which were later called *madhahib* for short—also found in English as *madhhabs*. The *madhahib* were an indigenous Islamic phenomena that was not borrowed from any cultural predecessor: the concept of such doctrinal schools is not found in earlier civilizations (Hallaq 2005a, 164–165).

The interpretations of Islamic law are diverse, and have been so ever since the establishment of the schools of jurisprudence. The differences amongst the schools of jurisprudence in their interpretations of Islamic law are basically due to two factors:

■ The primary sources (identification of)

The schools of jurisprudence differed in identifying which injunctions of the primary sources were considered non-abrogated; they also differed in identifying which were considered definitive. This affected the size of the pool of injunctions that was considered a source for each of the two components of Islamic law, *Shari'a* law and *Fiqh*-based law. Moreover, the schools differed amongst each other in the extent to which each school depended on the *Hadith* and what each school recognized as accepted *Hadith*.*1

■ Approaches to *ijtihad*

The schools of jurisprudence differed in the adopted *ijtihad* approaches to reach a point of law.

Modern Islamic law started only a hundred-fifty or so years back. It describes the efforts of Muslim jurists—from that time onwards—to find solutions for contemporary issues and the bodies of law produced by such efforts. In modern Islamic law, there has been to some extent reinterpretation of some points of law in the light of modern social circumstances, where reinterpretations have been formed that renounce the classical interpretations (Coulson 1999, sec. 5 Shari'ah law in contemporary Islam). However, it would be safe to say that modern Islamic law, with few exceptions, does not try to revise the solutions already put forward by the schools of jurisprudence, which are generally over a thousand years old. The vast bulk of modern Islamic law does not revisit the old corpora of Islamic law in fear of going against the early jurists, or more specifically in fear of going against consensus of the early jurists (*ijma'*).

In the contemporary era, when it comes to determining the content of a codified body of law to adopt—whether it be by a state, group, or individual—we find the most prevalent approach is that of pick-and-choose. For example, most contemporary liberal interpretations of Islamic law adopt laws from the more liberal corpora of Islamic law (picking and choosing laws from both the classical and modern bodies of Islamic law—not adhering to the body of law of a particular doctrinal school). On the other hand, most conservative interpretations of Islamic law tend to go to the other extreme when choosing from the available bodies of Islamic law and tend to select laws from the more conservative alternatives. Additionally, when it comes to the *Hadith*, the conservative readings consider *khabar al-ahad* to be a source of law.

In recent years, there have been increasing calls to reform Islamic law, but there is disagreement about the extent and scope of these reforms. Some argue for partial changes, while others advocate for comprehensive reform. Additionally, there are varying trends among reformists (al-Nuwayhi 2010, 99–181; Neusner 2003, 176–178).

NOTE*1: If we were to assume there had been (unanimous) agreement on which injunctions of the primary sources were considered definitive, for some of these injunctions—particularly the ones involving punishments—if we were to further assume there was a clear understanding on what these injunctions were saying, we still find that they were interpreted differently by the various schools of jurisprudence: we find that the schools of jurisprudence differed in how such injunctions were to be applied (application conditions, implementation details, etc.).

Side note 7.1 The relationship between the terms *madhhab* and *Fiqh*

In the context of this book, linguistically speaking, the Arabic word *madhhab* essentially means "interpretation of."

When it comes to the study of religion, a *madhhab* can be thought of as an interpretation of *Fiqh*, a school of thought in *Fiqh*. Originally, when the scope of *Fiqh* covered all aspects of religious thought (religion)—the first period (as discussed in Section 7.1)—a *madhhab* was a school of religious thought that covered schools of both theology and law (*madhhab dini*, interpretation of religion). When *Fiqh* was later restricted to cover the study of action injunctions (or part of) (*al-ahkam al-'amaliyya*)—the second and third periods—a *madhhab* became to represent a school of religious law or jurisprudence (*madhhab fiqhi*, interpretation of religious law).

7.2.2 Islamic law from a historical standpoint (a life-cycle perspective)

7.2.2.a The establishment and development

The establishment and development of the schools of jurisprudence extended over a period that lasted up to the mid-fourth century AH (second half of the tenth century CE). It was a process that brought about the doctrinal schools of jurisprudence.

As a consequence of the first civil war (35–40 AH / 656–661 CE), political factions had come to establish independent interpretations of religion. Once the era of recording (*asr al-tadwin*) had started, probably around the mid-second century AH, and with the increase in the corpus of religious material, specialization was needed. Each of the main disciplines categorized under religion started to have its own areas of study—including but not limited to Islamic law. By the mid-fourth century AH, we find the development of Islamic law to have matured and to have produced the doctrinal schools of law. Out of the thirteen leading schools of jurisprudence that had developed in this period, six are now obsolete (Dasuqi and Jabir 1999, 155–189, 193–195).

In discussing the nature of legal authority in Islam, Hallaq (2005a) emphasized the significance of doctrinal *madhhabs*, stating: "[I]n Islam it was the doctrinal *madhhab* that produced law and afforded its axis of authority; in other words, legal authority resided in the collective, juristic doctrinal enterprise of the school, not in the body politic or in the doctrine of a single jurist" (167). Each school commanded loyalty to its own collective, cumulative, accretive, and self-contained body of legal doctrine (Hallaq 2005a, 150–177). In essence, from the jurists affiliated with each of the doctrinal schools, it was loyalty to the doctrinal school's legal methodology and principles of positive law that was commanded (Hallaq 2005a, 194–206).

7.2.2.b The state and its laws

For the Umayyad era, 41–132 AH / 661–750 CE, it is regarded that laws enacted in the Qur'an were generally followed, in addition to some earlier practices from the time of the first four to rule after the Prophet. Nevertheless, elements and institutions of Roman-Byzantine and Persian-Sasanian law were absorbed into the Umayyad legal practice (Coulson 1999, sec. 3 Historical development of Shari'ah law; Schacht 1950, 190–213).

Legislation started to take on a religious characteristic with the start of the Abbasid era, 132–656 AH / 750–1258 CE, marking the Islamization of law, where religion was considered the source of law. The early Abbasid era was when most of the schools of jurisprudence were established and when they developed. However, the Abbasids' stance towards Islamic law was more political than religious. As Dasuqi and Jabir (1999) describe, the Abbasids' seizing of power was claimed to be in the name of religion. After seizing power from the Umayyads, in order to ascertain to the masses that they were true to their claim, they needed to portray that their rule was of a religious character. Thus, the Abbasids backed the jurists and brought them closer to the ruling circles so that the jurists would become advocates for the Abbasid rulers amongst the people. The Abbasids encouraged jurists to legislate in matters of concern to the state, particularly financial affairs, yet at the same time, the Abbasids did not tolerate political opposition from jurists (134–135).

The law that we are talking about, Islamic law, was never the type of law that we find today, that of the modern state. There was no such thing as the legal codes that we find today. Within each doctrinal school's body of law, we find pluralist views on almost every point of law (non-codified body of law).

Furthermore, it can safely be said, that at least until the end of the Abassid era (656 AH / 1258 CE), the making of law was not within the realm of the state; it was independent from the state. Societies adhering to the legal and cultural norms of the pre-modern *Shari'a* portrayed a form of decentralized governance; they were largely self-governing, with self-rule serving as a distinct indicator of the absence of the state—a situation deemed almost inconceivable in the present day (Hallaq 2005b, 159).*1

NOTE*1: Hallaq (2005a, 193) comments on the principle of the rule of law in the pre-modern Islamic culture: "On balance, if there was any pre-modern legal and political culture that maintained the principle of the rule of law so well, it was the culture of Islam." Hallaq (2005a) argues that, basically, there was a fine balance that characterized the relationship between the ruling elite and the legists who constituted the linkage between the ruling elite and the masses. The success or failure of a doctrinal school had much to do with the material and political support that the ruling elite elected to give or withhold. At the same time, the dire need of the ruling elite for political control and legitimacy imposed on them the imperative of compliance with the law (178–193).

Side note 7.2 The Islamization of law: The beginnings

Islamization of law at the state level was politically induced by the Abbasids (132–656 AH / 750–1258 CE) who wanted to distinguish their rule from their predecessors, the Umayyads (41–132 AH / 661–750 CE). It was during the Abbasid era when Islamic law developed and matured.

The Umayyads (*banu Umayya*, sons of *Umayya*) belonged to the same tribe of the Prophet, Quraysh. However, the Abbasids belonged not just to the same tribe of the Prophet but also to the same clan, *banu Hashim* (sons of *Hashim*, also transliterated as *Hashem* in English). Therefore, as a way to legitimize their rule, the Abbasids claimed that they were more worthy to rule as they were immediate relatives of the Prophet—thereby claiming the right to rule as if it were an inheritance right. This, however, goes against the Qur'an that only distinguished the Prophet as being a messenger of God (Q. 3:144), and did not distinguish him based on ethnicity or ancestry. The Qur'an also indicated that the Prophet did not have any male descendants (Q. 33:40)—paternal lineage was how ancestry was determined according to Arab custom, Meccan in particular.

The Abbasids manipulated their (blood) relation to the Prophet to position themselves as more wary and prudent when it came to abide by and uphold the teachings of the Qur'an (the understanding of). Islamization was their tactic, although power was their purpose. The Abbasids, who were descendants of the youngest paternal uncle of the Prophet, al-Abbas, even fought their own kin, the Alids, descendants of 'Ali ibn Abi Talib, when the Alids challenged their authority.

7.2.2.c The decline and its stages

Most modern scholars of Islamic legal history describe a period of decline of Islamic law, spanning from the mid-tenth to around mid-nineteenth century CE. This period started after what is commonly known as "closing the door (gate) of *ijtihad* (the abandonment of independent reasoning in search of a legal opinion)" and with *ijtihad* being replaced with *taqlid*. In Islamic law, *taqlid* is commonly understood to be the unquestioned acceptance of the legal decisions of one's school and its leading jurists without necessarily knowing the basis of those decisions. According to this view, by the mid-fourth century AH (second half of the tenth century CE), Muslim scholars started calling to bring *ijtihad* to a close, and Islamic law was to be confined to the accumulated heritage of the schools of jurisprudence up to that time.*1

We find modern scholars to have approached the alleged closing of the door of *ijtihad* in different manners depending on the subject of discussion. Some attributed the closure to have been a means to maintain the immunity of Islamic law from the influence of government, others used it to illustrate the problem of the decadence of Islamic institutions and culture, along with many other viewpoints (Hallaq 1984).

According to Madkur (1996, 94–98)—whom I cite here as a representative of a prevalent view—in the eyes of the Muslim scholars who called to bring *ijtihad* to a close, the schools of jurisprudence had matured enough, and the closing of the door of *ijtihad* was to preserve Islamic law from chaos due to the weakening of the state. Madkur remarked that the Abbasid rule at that time had weakened to an extent that it was no longer in control of the vast territories it had once reigned over. The state was no longer able to assign posts in the fields of the judiciary in the different lands.*2

Madkur (1996, 94–98) further stated that:

The bringing of *ijtihad* to a close was gradual. A limited form of *ijtihad* existed from around the mid-fourth to the mid-seventh century AH—while *taqlid* (within the boundaries of a particular school) became more dominant. During this transitional period, *ijtihad* took the form of *ijtihad madhhabi*, where the principle rulings of a particular school of jurisprudence were treated as if they constituted a source of law for the jurists of that particular school, even if opposing the primary sources. To these jurists, in such instances, the primary sources must have been abrogated or should be interpreted in a different way. This form of *ijtihad* resulted in works focused on refining and organizing the bodies of law of the established schools of jurisprudence. And it ended with the end of the Abbasid era itself in 656 AH / 1258 CE, with the fall of Baghdad to the Mongols. From then onwards, marking the start of the second era of *taqlid*, for each of the established schools of jurisprudence, *ijtihad* was replaced more or less with *taqlid*.

Jurists in the second era of *taqlid* undertook the task of distinguishing between strong and weak opinions, and those opinions that make up established doctrine (*dhahir al-riwaya*) from those legal opinions that are considered fringe (*nawadir*). This era generated extensive collections of legal compendia representing the doctrines of various schools. These compilations presented the established legal doctrines while excluding opinions deemed weak. Commentaries, glosses, and compilations of *fatawi* (religious legal rulings) were also evident.

This state of affairs led to the rigidity of Islamic law, making Islamic law distant from the everyday reality and the needs of Muslims. With few exceptions, *taqlid* remained to be the general trend, probably up until the last hundred-fifty or so years (mid-nineteenth century CE).

Some even say *taqlid* remains to be the state of Islamic law to this day (Dasuqi and Jabir 1999, 195). On the other hand, we find those who argue that there is no evidence that the closing of the door of *ijtihad* ever occurred, and that there has never been consensus to that effect (Hallaq 1984; Rabb 2016).

In regard to *ijtihad* for Shi'a Muslims, Rabb (2016) holds that Shi'a generally deem *ijtihad* to be an ongoing process (with the

214

exception of Zaidi Shi'a); hence, discussions about closing the door of *ijtihad* never arose.

It can be seen that the formulation of the schools of jurisprudence organized the legal system and better served justice. To ensure the survival of these schools, *taqlid* was a necessary requirement by the affiliated jurists. Hence, *taqlid* can be understood to be a consequence of the establishment of the schools of jurisprudence and a necessity for their existence.

NOTE*1: If assuming the closing of the door of *ijtihad* to reference *ijtihad* in its absolute and independent sense, then this would be referring to prohibiting the establishment of new schools of Jurisprudence. The last of the known jurists who practiced *ijtihad* in its absolute and independent sense—to deduce from the primary sources without being restricted by rulings of previous jurists—was al-Tabari (d. 310 AH / 923 CE) (Madkur 1996, 85). Al-Tabari was the founder of one of the—now obsolete—schools of jurisprudence.

NOTE*2: To clarify, Madkur (1996, 94–98) remarked that, at that time, the state was no longer able to assign posts in the fields of both the judiciary and *ifta'* in the different lands—*ifta'* is the act of issuing a legal opinion by an authoritative specialist in matters of law. However, Hallaq (2003, 249) stated, that until the era of the Ottomans (698–1340 AH / 1299–1922 CE), the judges (*qadis*) were the only legal functionaries who were appointed, paid, and dismissed by government agencies. I am inclined to agree with Hallaq's account, as it better aligns with what is known about the dynamics of lawmaking in the Abbasid era. Therefore, contrary to Madkur's assertion regarding *ifta'*, it seems more accurate to say that during the Abbasid era (132–656 AH / 750–1258 CE), only judges were appointed by the state, not *muftis* (assuming job specialization, particularly after the mid-fourth century AH). This agrees with what has been mentioned earlier about the Abbasid era in regard to the independence of lawmaking from the political apparatus.

NOTE: The practice of *talfiq* was unheard of in earlier times. In Islamic law, *talfiq* refers to the practice of combining rulings or legal opinions from different schools of jurisprudence to create a customized or hybrid legal opinion. This practice involves selecting rulings from multiple *madhhabs* based on convenience or personal preference rather than strictly adhering to the principles and methodologies of a single school.

Traditional Islamic legal theory emphasizes adherence to a single school (*taqlid*), whereas *talfiq* involves picking and choosing rulings from different schools. The practice of *talfiq* was unheard of not only in the making of law but also among judges. For example, it was not until 1915 CE that judges in Egypt were permitted to base judgments on laws from schools of jurisprudence other than the ones they followed (al-Nuwayhi 2010, 129).

7.2.3 Islamic law: A deeper look

The topics discussed in this section are not directly related to the main arguments of this book. Nonetheless, I have included them in order to give the reader a better overall understanding of Islamic law, particularly the Islamic law of the pre-modern era.

7.2.3.a Islamic law as a system of law: Is it case law or civil law?

As a system of law, how can we understand Islamic law with respect to today's common systems, case law (in the form of published judicial opinions) and civil law systems (which rely on codified statutes)? In terms of classification, Islamic law does not neatly fit into the categories of case law or civil law as understood in Western legal systems. Instead, it can be seen as having elements of both, yet constituting a unique legal system in its own right.

The *Shari'a* law component of Islamic law could be regarded as its civil law element. For the provisions in this element, their authority is derived from divine revelation, rather than legislative enactment.

As for the *Fiqh*-based component of Islamic law, we can't really say that it is case law per se since the judges never had a real role in the making of Islamic law. It was the jurists (*fuqaha'*, sing. *faqih*) of the doctrinal schools, whether author-jurists or juriconsults (*muftis*), and not the judges (*qadis*) who were directly involved in the making of Islamic law.

Islamic law is not based on judiciary case law, "the collection of past legal decisions written by courts and similar tribunals in the course of deciding cases, in which the law was analyzed using these cases to resolve ambiguities for deciding current cases" (Wikipedia 2003b, par. 1). In the Islamic law system, a judge's rulings were non-binding for the other judges who were affiliated with the same school of jurisprudence (in his or different space-time), and naturally were non-binding for judges of the other schools of jurisprudence. Though this system did not allow judges to make law, yet it provided the judge with a wide array of opinions to choose from. It allowed for the consideration of the custom of the locality in a judge's decision. This explains the mechanism to how Islamic law reigned supreme across different cultures and customs (Hallaq 2010, 181). Relatively speaking, Islamic law accommodated for change and exhibited some flexibility compared to codified law.

7.2.3.b The jurists: Juriconsults and author-jurists

The body of law of a particular school of jurisprudence (school-affiliated Islamic law) is the collection of past rulings made by its jurists (*fuqaha'*, sing. *faqih*), both juriconsults (*muftis*) and author-jurists alike.

I use the term "jurists" here to represent *mujtahids*, those who qualified to practice *ijtihad*. And I assume job specialization of the two types of jurists in order to better explain the terms and their functions.

Now to the difference between these two types of jurists:

■ The Juriconsults

A juriconsult or *mufti* was a jurist who was qualified to give *fatwas* in response to inquiries addressing real and not hypothetical situations. A *fatwa* (singular; *fatawa* plural) is a non-binding legal opinion on a point of Islamic law given by a qualified jurist in response to a question posed by a private individual, judge or government (Wikipedia 2001a, par. 1). Over time, *muftis* were more into *taqlid* than *ijtihad*.*1*2

■ The author jurists

Author jurists were jurists who were devoted to teaching, writing treaties, and who, for the most part, did not act as *muftis*.

The previous rulings of a school's jurists acted as precedent. Within the context of school-affiliated Islamic law, previous rulings made by jurists of a particular school served as the basis for analyzing and resolving any uncertainties or ambiguities that arose when deciding contemporary issues and cases.

NOTE*1: Adherents of the dominant Twelver branch of Shi'i Islam have in modern times been expected to designate a high-ranking *mujtahid*—function similar to that of the sunni *mufti*—as their *marja' al-taqlid* (source of emulation) in religious matters. Unlike the *fatwas* of other jurists, those of the designated *marja'* are binding for his followers (Böwering, Crone, and Mirza 2013, 174).

NOTE*2: In most of the pre-modern Islamic world, though highly recommended, judges were not required by any political authority to consult *muftis*; however, in Andalusia (Muslim Spain) this practice was mandatory to the extent that a judicial decision was considered invalid if it did not have prior approval by a *mufti* (Hallaq 2010, 159, 172).

NOTE: In English it is common to use the term *fatwas*—it is not an Arabic term, as it adds the suffix "s" to the singular term—to represent the plural of *fatwa*, rather than to use the proper Arabic plural *fatawa*. The same pluralization technique is used with *mujtahid*—an individual who is qualified to exercise *ijtihad* in the evaluation of Islamic law; *mufti*; *Hadith*; and so on.

7.2.3.c The use and abuse of *fatwa* in the contemporary world

Historically, the judge was a civil servant of the state whereas the *mufti* was not an appointed official. This tells us that in such times, in theory at least, matters of religion (including law) were decided independently from the state.

Under the Ottomans, the *muftis* were part of the state apparatus (Berger 2014, par. 6). This setup is still found in modern times where in most Muslim-majority states we find a state-appointed body that issues *fatwas*. This has served to articulate and promote—in each Muslim-majority state—a national vision of Islam that is compatible with state law (Wikipedia 2004b, sec. 4.1, par. 1–2).

In the past, for Muslims living in the regions under Muslim rule, a *fatwa* played an important role in the courts. It was a time when the courts were all religious courts, and the law that applied on Muslims was Islamic law. Moreover, Islamic law then was not codified: the body of law of each doctrinal school had pluralist views on almost every point of law. In that era, a *fatwa* served to advise courts on difficult points of Islamic law and to elaborate substantive law.*1

On the other hand, in most of the Muslim-majority states of today, a *fatwa* neither has authority nor added value in the courts of these modern states. Today, most, if not all, Muslim-majority states have codified laws for all the categories of law, and in the courts of these states, a *fatwa* has no role or impact whatsoever.*2

Today, *fatwas* are mostly given on matters of religious ritual practice, ethics and social issues. They are sought even beyond a Muslim's locality with the availability of modern-day media and communication channels particularly the internet, radio and satellite TV. Nevertheless, today, we do find non-state affiliated persons who give *fatwas* on more diverse issues.

Furthermore, many militant and reform movements have disseminated *fatwas* issued by individuals who do not possess the qualifications traditionally required of a *mufti*. The impact of some such *fatwas*, particularly those issued by radicals on political issues, has been drastic to both Muslims and non-Muslims alike, and has brought nothing but havoc and destruction.*3

218

The vast number of *fatwas* produced in the modern world attests to the importance of religious authenticity to many Muslims. However, it is unknown to what extent Muslims acknowledge the authority of *fatwas* and actually heed to them in real life (Berger 2014, sec. 1, par. 9).

NOTE*1: Historically, privately issued *fatwas* served to educate Muslim communities about Islam, provide guidance to courts on intricate aspects of Islamic law, and elaborate on substantive legal matters. In later times, public and political *fatwas* emerged to address doctrinal disputes, endorse government policies, or express the grievances of the populace. During the era of European colonialism, *fatwas* also contributed to mobilizing resistance against foreign domination (Wikipedia 2001a, par. 2).

Messick (1995) stated that aside from answering queries in regard to the areas of law governed by the courts, a *mufti* would also answer queries regarding any matter covered by Islamic law whether of the private or public realm such as social matters, politics, ethics, and ritual practices. It even extended to other areas of religion besides Islamic law, though some early theorists argued that a *mufti* should not respond to questions on theology and Qur'anic exegesis. In Ottoman times, we even find *fatwas* on issues regulated by state secular law (2: 11–12).

NOTE*2: As of today, the world consists of 195 countries. Among them, 193 are member countries of the United Nations, while 2 are non-member observer countries: the Holy See and the State of Palestine [also known as the Occupied Palestinian Territory] (Worldometers.info 2017). As of 2010, there are 49 countries where Muslims constitute over 50% of the population (Pew Research Center. and Pew Forum on Religion & Public Life. 2011, 26). Out of the 49 Muslim-majority states, there are few states that have all-secular or all-religious legal systems with all-secular or all-religious legal codes in place, respectively. However, the bulk of Muslim-majority states have mixed legal codes: the legal codes are comprised of law from both secular and religious sources.

In the Muslim-majority states that have mixed legal codes, the Islamic law that is found in their legal codes is codified, and is mostly reserved for personal status (marriage, divorce, child custody, adoption, and inheritance) and communal endowment issues. It is applied solely on the Muslim citizens of the state and in some states where a non-Muslim party agrees or chooses for it to be applied to their case.

Out of the Muslim-majority states with mixed legal codes there are some that do not have religious courts as separate entities: they have a unified system of national courts. Other Muslim-majority states with mixed legal codes have both civil courts and religious courts. In these states, the civil courts decide cases on the basis of secular law and adjudicate all civil and criminal cases not expressly reserved to the religious courts; the religious courts decide relevant cases on the basis of codified religious law among their respective communities.

NOTE*3: Disregarding classical jurisprudence has led to the emergence of notorious *fatwas* by militant extremists, who, misinterpreting the Qur'an and *Hadith*, justify acts such as suicide bombings, the indiscriminate killing of bystanders, and the declaration of self-professed Muslims as unbelievers (*takfir*) (Wikipedia 2001a, sec. 4.3).

7.2.3.d The metamorphosis of Islamic law

In contemporary Muslim-majority countries, we find Islamic law existing, for the most part, solely in codified form and mainly restricted to certain aspects of law; it is state-made law. Additionally, we find Islamic law issued in the form of *fatwas*—aside from the state apparatus responsible for issuing *fatwas*—by certain groups, movements, and even individuals who do not necessarily qualify, according to the classical standards, to be issuing *fatwas*. In both cases—whether it is law codified by the state or issued in the form of *fatwas*—the law itself, in most instances, is not affiliated with (it does not follow the precedent of) just one, or even any, doctrinal school of jurisprudence.

In the general scheme of things, precedent following within each of the doctrinal schools of jurisprudence, what is traditionally known as *taqlid*, was what had kept Islamic law alive across vast geographical areas and over the centuries. Moreover, the separation between the state and the making of law, between those with political power and the jurists, was what mainly helped in keeping Islamic law independent from the whims and desires of the ruling elite (the politicization of law). However, with the absence of both of these significant characteristics that distinguished Islamic law during the pre-modern era, we find ourselves today in front of something new that we attribute to it the name Islamic law. But in reality, this so-called Islamic law of the present era has not much to do with the classical understanding of Islamic law and its role as a system of law.

7.3 Sources to deduce and establish *Fiqh*-based law

There have existed Muslim scholars, like the Mu'tazilite Ibrahim al-Nazzam (d. 231 AH / 845 CE), who hardly recognized any other sources besides the Qur'an and reason as valid sources of Islamic law (Amin 1964, 3: 126). The Akhbari Twelver Shi'a school, a minority within Twelver Shi'a Islam, reject *ijtihad* as a source of law. Instead, the Akhbaris base their legal interpretations solely on the Qur'an, the

Sunna of the Prophet, and the dictums or teachings of the (twelve) imams (*qawl al-a'imma*).

Nonetheless, pertaining to the field of legal methodology (*usul al-Fiqh*; the field of the principles of jurisprudence), most Muslim jurists agreed upon specific sources (*masadir al-tashri'*) to be used to deduce and establish *Fiqh*-based law. However, there have been and continue to be variations and differences among jurists regarding the interpretation and application of these sources.

Fiqh has the primary sources as inputs, but adds to them secondary sources (al-Bardisi 198-?, 169–302; Dasuqi and Jabir 1999, 259–262). The sources to deduce and establish *Fiqh*-based law are:*1

NOTICE: To my understanding, the sole source of *Fiqh*-based law is *ijtihad*. One can consider the traditional categorization of the sources of *Fiqh*-based law below as a means to express both the inputs and the tools of *ijtihad*. These inputs and tools were utilized to varying degrees by different schools of jurisprudence, where the inputs of *ijtihad* are denoted as primary sources of *Fiqh*-based law, and the tools of *ijtihad* are denoted as secondary sources.

The objective of categorizing the sources of *Fiqh*-based law in this manner is likely to assert that reasoning through *ijtihad* is constrained within the scope of the spirit and principles of the primary sources.

i. Primary sources of *Fiqh*

The primary sources of *Fiqh* are:

- The Qur'an

- The *Sunna*—what is accepted to represent the *Sunna*

The primary sources constitute the inputs of *ijtihad*; hence, they are considered to be primary sources of *Fiqh*. Reasoning through *ijtihad* is constrained to be within the scope of the spirit and principles of the primary sources.

ii. Secondary sources of *Fiqh* (mostly agreed-upon)

Ijtihad is used to produce law for matters discussed in the primary sources but were not definitive in both attribution and meaning, in addition to produce law for matters not discussed in the primary sources.

Ijtihad can be achieved through:

■ Collective reasoning—consensus (*ijma'*)

Consensus is agreement of a group on a point of law. In effect, consensus gives a ruling (*fatwa*) authority on par with that of the primary sources.*2

Now let's explore how each of the contemporary predominant interpretations based on Traditional Islam regards consensus:

► Sunni consensus

For the Sunnis, who constitute the majority of Muslims, consensus is understood as agreement among Muslim scholars engaged in *ijtihad* during a specific era; some argue that it involves all scholars, while others suggest it involves the majority (al-Bardisi 198-?, 216–229). The majority view asserted that consensus necessitates a foundation or reference (*sanad al-ijma'*) for its validity and emphasized the importance of the primary sources in this regard (al-Bardisi 198-?, 222–225).

While the bases for consensus are speculative primary sources—otherwise there would be no need for consensus—consensus renders the ruling on the matter definitive. Once consensus is reached on a particular issue, it becomes a source of law for jurists, which should not be opposed, and the matter is no longer subject to *ijtihad* (Madkur 1996, 221–223). In effect, scholarly consensus elevates a speculative ruling to assume divine sanction (position of).

It is worth noting that while the primary sources were indeed accepted as a basis for consensus, there were some scholars who argued to consider other sources, such as *qiyas* (analogical reasoning) or *maslahah mursalah* (consideration of public interest), in instances where no reference from the primary sources was available (al-Bardisi 198-?, 222–225; Madkur 1996, 222–223).

► Shi'a Twelvers consensus

For the Twelvers, who constitute the majority of Shi'a Muslims, consensus operates differently. Although it involves the agreement of a group on a point of law, the presence of an infallible figure—as recognized by Twelver Shi'a—is necessary within the group, or it must be certain that what reached the group was from the infallible. Therefore, consensus holds significance only when it can definitively reflect the *Sunna* of an infallible (Muzaffar 1990, 2: 85–103).

■ Individual reasoning is used to produce law in matters for which there was no consensus (*ijma'*).

▶ Analogical reasoning—*qiyas*

This source is recognized by most Sunni scholars and some Shi'a scholars (al-Bardisi 198-?, 243–255). *Qiyas* is only for matters not discussed in the first three sources and that can be applied to reason. *Qiyas* is reasoning by analogical deduction from the first three sources. Some confuse *ijtihad* with *qiyas*; all *qiyas* is *ijtihad* but not all *ijtihad* is *qiyas* (al-Bardisi 198-?, 461–462).

Besides *qiyas*, Sunni schools of law adopt other methods of legal reasoning; however, among these methods, Sunni schools of law differ in what each recognizes as a valid approach to *ijtihad* (Kamali 2003). The other methods of reasoning include *istihsan* (juristic preference), *maslahah mursalah* (consideration of public interest), *'urf* (social norms or customs within a particular society or community), *istishab* (presumption of continuity or the presumption of the existing state of affairs), *sadd al-dhara'i* (blocking the means), among others.

▶ Intellect (human reason)—*'aql*

Most Shi'a scholars consider intellect the source to be referenced in situations when a ruling on a worldly matter cannot be found in the first three sources. Intellect is counted as a source, since good (*hasan*) and evil (*qubh*, ugliness) are considered inherent features of matters that intellect can differentiate between and recognize.

The Shi'a Ja'fari school of jurisprudence, named after the sixth Shi'a *imam*, Ja'far al-Sadiq, recognizes human reason as the fourth source of Islamic law. Human reason is deemed capable of deducing categorical judgments from both pure and practical reasoning, and what is deemed necessary by reason is also considered necessary by revelation (Esposito 2003, 154).*3

NOTE*1: When referring to the primary sources of Islamic law, which constitute the sources of *shari'a* law and are primary sources of *Fiqh*-based law, traditionally, they are usually stated to be the Qur'an and the *Sunna*. However, it is effectively only the action injunctions of the Qur'an and the *Hadith*—what is accepted from the compilations of *Hadith*—that constitute the primary sources of Islamic law.

NOTE*2: Regarding the matter of consensus, I would like to highlight a subject previously touched upon: the concept of infallibility. I reference the same source. Hasan (1972) discussed the concept of infallibility in Islam, highlighting its evolution in response to the absence of divine revelation after the Prophet's death. He argued that with the progression of Islamic society beyond the context of seventh century CE Arabia, a challenge emerged: how to ensure correct decisions without divine guidance. This led to the development of the concept of infallibility, encompassing the Prophet, other prophets, the Muslim community, and for Shi'a Muslims, the *imams*. Hasan suggested that infallibility served as a substitute for divine revelation in guiding decisions (2).

NOTE*3: According to Esposito (2003), the Shi'a Ja'fari school of jurisprudence, named after *imam* Ja'far al-Sadiq, recognizes four sources of Islamic law: the Qur'an, the *Sunna* (including traditions reported by the Prophet and the *imams*), consensus (which must include the opinion of the Prophet or an infallible *imam* to establish validity), and human reason (154).

The Ja'fari school of jurisprudence serves as the common foundation for both Usuli and Akhbari schools of law within Twelver Shi'a Islam. Usulis and Akhbaris diverge in their approaches to legal reasoning and interpretation. The Twelvers' Usuli school of law accepts the use of *ijtihad* and is known for having the largest number of followers among the Shi'a. On the other hand, the Akhbari school, rejects *ijtihad* as a source of law and emphasizes reliance on narrated traditions (*akhbar*) from the *imams*.

7.4 Analysis & Results

In this section the objective is to examine the applicability of *Fiqh*-based law, law derived through *ijtihad*, beyond the space-time of the revelation. In order to do that, we look into the body of law produced by *ijtihad*, which is of two types:

NOTICE: In the following discussion, the reader is asked to distinguish between two distinct uses of the term "primary sources." As a reminder, when talking about Islamic law's sources and components, the referencing of the categories of injunctions is according to the traditional Q.I. classification. In this classification, the term "primary sources" would denote an Action-Type II category of injunctions that includes the ethics injunctions. On the other hand, when referring to this work's findings and approach, the referencing of the categories of injunctions is according to the proposed Q.I.

224

classification. In this proposed classification, the term "primary sources" denotes an Action-Type II category of injunctions that does not include the ethics injunctions.

(1) Law that is based on the speculative primary sources

There is no *ijtihad* in matters discussed by the definitive primary sources, where the injunctions are (considered) definitive in both meaning and attribution (the realm of *Shari'a* law).

The practice of *ijtihad* is utilized to derive legal rulings from the speculative primary sources. The speculative primary sources include the following types:

▶ Speculative in meaning and definitive in attribution (*zanni al-dalala wa qat'iy al-thubut*)—found in both the Qur'an and the *Hadith*.

▶ Speculative in both meaning and attribution (*zanni al-dalala wa al-thubut*)—found only in the *Hadith*.

▶ Definitive in meaning and speculative in attribution (*qat'iy al-dalala wa zanni al-thubut*)—found only in the *Hadith*.

(2) Law that deals with matters that there was no precedent for in the primary sources

Law of this type would not be directly extracted from the primary sources since the primary sources did not directly discuss the matters involved. However, law of this type would consider the primary sources to be the basis and standard to be followed. Furthermore, when producing this type of law, it is required of the jurist who is qualified to exercise *ijtihad* (*mujtahid*) to be aware of previous consensuses in the field so as not to oppose them in his *ijtihad*.

To examine the applicability of *Fiqh*-based law beyond the space-time of the revelation, let us examine both its components, one at a time, for applicability beyond the space-time of the revelation:

■ The applicability of *Fiqh*-based law derived from the speculative primary sources

I call upon the conclusion that we arrived at during the study of *Shari'a* law. When studying *Shari'a* law, we found the applicability of the primary sources to be space-time specific. Accordingly, the primary sources were found to be non-viable sources to establish eternal law. These findings were a result of examining definitive primary sources that were used as sources for *Shari'a* law.

Now, since we were able to find instances where the applicability of primary sources was found to be space-time specific, this reflects on the primary sources as a whole proving their applicability to be non-eternal. In view of that, to have sources of specific space-time applicability as primary sources of law, and to extract law from them—whether directly as in *Shari'a* law or indirectly through *ijtihad* as in *Fiqh*-based law—would result in bodies of law not suitable for all space-time, but rather only suitable for a specific space-time, that of the sources themselves.

■ The applicability of *Fiqh*-based law produced for matters that there was no precedent for in the primary sources

It is imperative to recognize that law produced by *ijtihad* is a best efforts endeavor that is space-time dependent. According to Islamic law, law produced by *ijtihad* should be within the realm of the primary sources, and should not oppose them, as these sources are considered applicable across space-time. Moreover, law produced by *ijtihad* should align with established consensus. Notably, the unanimously accepted bases for consensus are derived from the primary sources.

Therefore, although we are talking about *Fiqh*-based law produced for matters that there was no precedent for in the primary sources, yet we are still restricted by the primary sources. However, we have already established the primary sources to be non-viable sources for producing eternal law, as their applicability was found to be space-time specific.

It follows, then, that this type of *Fiqh*-based law, inherently space-time dependent and potentially constructed not to oppose sources of specific space-time applicability, may not necessarily be the best option for law: it may not necessarily be applicable beyond the space-time of the revelation or the space-time of its formulation.

By definition, *Fiqh*-based law is not eternal (Dasuqi and Jabir 1999, 54–55); nevertheless, many Muslims seem to think it is. A good number of Muslim-majority countries still implement, to some extent,

226

Fiqh-based law within their legal systems. Most merely copy or imitate the law of the schools of jurisprudence. In other words, they copy or imitate space-time dependent laws originally produced for specific spaces and times.

From the analysis of *Fiqh*, we found that *Fiqh*-based law would potentially be constrained by the primary sources. Given that *Fiqh*-based law produces laws that best suit a particular space-time, then to produce space-time dependent law today, there surely exist better alternatives to *Fiqh*-based law that would not be constrained by sources of space-time specific applicability.

Therefore, we should reject the unquestionable applicability of *Fiqh*-based law beyond the space-time of the revelation, as we previously rejected the eternal applicability of *Shari'a* law, and we should look elsewhere for more suitable solutions for managing and regulating man-world affairs.

7.5 The influence of space-time dependent factors on *Fiqh*-based law

In order to get a feel of what it means that *Fiqh*-based law is space-time dependent law originally produced for specific spaces and times, and why *Fiqh*-based law should not be accepted in current space-time, we look into the influence of two space-time dependent factors on *Fiqh*-based law:

- Customs, traditions, and common ways of thinking
- Power—The state

7.5.1 Customs, traditions, and common ways of thinking

The schools of jurisprudence were definitely genuine and surely valuable to their times in producing law that was based on interpreting the Qur'an, the *Hadith*, and the world. However, to consider *Fiqh* of the schools of jurisprudence to be a—or the—source of law in current times is unacceptable. The times have changed; with that, so have the social norms of societies. Moreover, science has evolved. Consequently, our understanding of the world around us has also changed. Hence, our thinking related to matters that concern and govern man-world affairs should also be changing and not fixed.

The schools of jurisprudence produced law that was surely influenced by the customs, traditions, and common ways of thinking that were prevalent in the space-time of the early scholars who started these schools, and were further influenced by these same factors in the space-time of those who followed in their steps. Dasuqi and Jabir (1999) point out that the social environment and norms of the particular locality where a school of jurisprudence first emerged affected its approach towards *ijtihad*. While the *Hadith* schools of jurisprudence were influenced by the Hijaz norms (west Arabia), the schools of *al-ra'y* (the schools of jurisprudence that relied mostly on reasoning to arrive at legal decisions), which relied less on the *Hadith*, were influenced by the Iraq norms. Even al-Shafi'i (d. 204 AH / 820 CE), who is attributed to establishing the principles of jurisprudence (*usul al-Fiqh*), when he moved to Egypt renounced some of the rulings he had made while he was living in Iraq (152).

Knowledge, awareness, and the science of those days also had its effect on the common ways of thinking of the peoples of those times. Needless to say, science has progressed a lot since then. I find *Fiqh* rulings in regard to the minimum and maximum lengths of pregnancy to provide a good example on how *Fiqh* rulings are nothing more than products of their times. And that they surely should not be accepted across space-time.

The classical Muslim jurists considered that the length of pregnancy would fall between a minimum and a maximum (in maintenance, paternity, or inheritance claims). Looking up what *Fiqh* considers to be the maximum length of pregnancy for a woman (maximum period of gestation); it says depending on the school of jurisprudence consulted, that pregnancy could last up to one, two, four, or five years (al-Fawzan 2005, 2: 315; Anderson 1959, 71; Kuwait Ministry of Awqaf and Islamic Affairs 1995, 18: 144–145, 40: 239–240; Mughniyya 2021, sec. 4). And according to some *Fiqh* scholars, it could last even longer (al-Qurtubi 1935, 9: 287–288). They considered the minimum length of pregnancy to be six lunar months (Kuwait Ministry of Awqaf and Islamic Affairs 1995, 18:143–144, 40: 239).

These *Fiqh* rulings on the minimum and maximum lengths of pregnancy, aside from contradicting what we know today about pregnancy from modern science, also contradict the Qur'an itself. They contradict—how I understand—the essence of the Qur'an's rulings on the waiting period divorced women and widows must observe before remarrying, the 'idda. This topic may possibly be discussed in a future book.

228

7.5.2 Power—The state

Power—by which I mean "the ruling power," namely the state—has surely had a hand in *Fiqh*, and still has to some extent, as evidenced by the codification of Islamic law and the teaching of religion in schools, as discussed in Section 5.5.2.d.

The effect of power on *Fiqh*-based law can be appreciated when considering the following *Fiqh*-shapers that involved power:

■ Succession of power

Amin (1964) described, that right from the very beginnings, and in the first half of the first century AH, four out of the five early major Muslim religious groups (*firaq*)—the Umayyads, Shi'a, Khawarej, and Murji'a, excluding the Mu'tazila—originated out of Muslims' disagreement on issues that related to power succession: a matter of purely political nature. It was the sort of disagreement that led Muslims to take up arms against each other (those who later became known as the factions of the Umayyads, Shi'a, and Khawarej), and which eventually led each of the fighting parties to later identify as a distinct religious group modeling its religious convictions after its political convictions (3: 4–7).*1

Amin (1969) maintained, that as time went by, when it came for Muslims to choose which religious group to follow, Muslims' preferences were influenced by their cultural and ethnic backgrounds. For example, Arabs were more Khawarej and Murji'a, while non-Arabs were more Shi'a and Mu'tazila. At the same time, cultural, ethnic, and prior religious backgrounds also had their effect, to some extent, on shaping these Muslim religious groups—since each had more Muslims who came from one particular background than from another—which, as a result, reflected back and affected the perception of Islam of that particular religious group (252–303). This schism, owing to power or politics—whatever you choose to call it—also affected the *Hadith*, where each faction distrusted the other even in the *Hadiths* it reported (Madkur 1996, 80–82). All this reflected upon the *Fiqh* each faction followed.

Such diverse backgrounds also facilitated for the early major religious groups to branch off and subdivide. Amin (1964) stated that the Mu'tazila subdivided into around thirteen subgroups, the Khawarej into around twenty, the Shi'a into around thirty, and the Murji'a into around seven. There were also numerous other religious groups that held independent views from the major ones mentioned (3: 348–352).

■ Adoption by power

The state had a role in how a particular school of law (or theology—see note below) was positively or negatively perceived, and consequently followed or abandoned by the masses.*2

Over Muslim history, we find Muslim states (early caliphates and sultanates) to have appointed jurists of a particular school of jurisprudence as judges. This, in effect, represented the state's adopting a particular school's teachings as the official law of the state, which consequently led to the said school becoming more prevalent in the geographic locations under the reign of the state (Dasuqi and Jabir 1999, 157–158).

The Ottomans (1299–1922 CE), for example, adopted the Hanafi school of jurisprudence as the official school of jurisprudence. At present, laws of the Hanafi school of jurisprudence are still adopted in the laws of the (non-secular) Muslim-majority countries that were previously under Ottoman rule—in the religiously influenced parts of their laws. Similarly, is the case for the Maliki school of jurisprudence, which was adopted by the Umayyad remnants in the Muslim west, and which currently prevails throughout northern and western Africa. The Maliki school of jurisprudence was also previously found in the parts of Europe under Muslim rule, particularly Sicily and the Iberian Peninsula.

■ Support of power

During the Abbasid rule, the *Hadith* was compiled and *Fiqh* evolved. No wonder then that we find *Fiqh* rulings ever since those times that directed Muslims not to rebel against their rulers (al-Fawzan 2005, 2: 632–633; Hanifa 1368/1949, 44).

It seems likely that some of these rulings came from a standpoint that wanted to preserve the unity of the Muslims. While on the other hand, flimsy exegesis of the text of Qur'an and the *Hadith*, not to mention fabricated *Hadith*s, also brought about politicized *Fiqh* rulings in order to give legitimacy to the rulers of those times (religious stamp). Such politicized *Fiqh* rulings are still common in current times.

NOTE*1: Followers of the Qur'an fought each other after the murder of the third to rule after the Prophet, 'Uthman ibn 'Affan, in the first civil war (35–40 AH / 656–661 CE)—a war that originated from dispute over political leadership: the disagreement on who should rule after 'Uthman. It was basically believer fighting fellow believer; the companions of the Prophet fought and killed each other. It was not until the first civil war that we start to learn about the political factions of the Umayyads (supporters of Mu'awiya ibn Abi Sufyan), Shi'a (supporters of 'Ali ibn Abi Talib), Khawarej (opposed both Mu'awiya and 'Ali), and Murji'a (who were neutral and did not support either Mu'awiya or 'Ali). Within the Umayyad era, 41–132 AH / 661–750 CE, there were other religious groups that were also established, like that of the Mu'tazila, an early school of Islamic theology based on reason and rational thought, which—according to the traditional account—did not emerge out of a political faction.

NOTE*2: On how the state affected the perception towards a particular school of theology, the notorious controversy over the createdness of the Qur'an discussed in Chapter 5 comes to mind. Though the controversy was over a theological issue and not *Fiqh*, I find it to be more about power than anything else: the state (rulers of) attempting to control and impose a particular understanding of religion over the masses.

In the early Abbasid era, Amin (1964) described that three successive Abbasid rulers adopted the Mu'tazila school's stance on the createdness of the Qur'an as the official state doctrine. An inquisition was instigated where prominent religious scholars and employees of the government were questioned on "the createdness of the Qur'an"—those who opposed the official state doctrine were persecuted during what became known as the *mihna* (ordeal or inquisition) in the years 218–234 AH / 833–849 CE. This reflected negatively on the Mu'tazila thought in general and led to it becoming unpopular, and for the Mu'tazila to eventually die off as a religious group (3: 21–207). In reaction (against the inquisition), the majority of Muslims adopted the viewpoint of the opponents of the Mu'tazila, that of the uncreatedness of the Qur'an, which eventually became the orthodox Sunni view.

8. Findings on Islamic law

In order to justify that the interpretation of religion associated with the proposed Q.I. classification should not have a law component, we needed to verify that the proposed Q.I. classification's Action-Type II category of injunctions did not have eternal applicability. This was accomplished through the study of Islamic law.

The study of Islamic law in Chapters 5 through 7 explained and clarified the intricacies of Islamic law. I hope in these chapters I have been able to demonstrate that eternal religious law is but an illusion put forward by men who claim religion to be the source of law.

8.1 What it is not

The attribute of eternal validity that is extended to Islamic law (or part of) has been examined. To produce eternal law, law would need to be established from sources that are eternal. All sources of both *Shari'a* law and *Fiqh*-based law have been shown not to be eternal but rather space-time dependent. As a result, bodies of law produced by the different interpretations of Islamic law are not in any way eternal.

8.2 What it is

Islamic law is an interpretation of law put forward by men who consider religion to be the source of law. Islamic law is a man-made attempt to eternalize space-time dependent law originally produced for specific spaces and times.

The significance of Islamic law lies in its historical value, which depicts how law evolved and developed in line with how Muslim communities and societies themselves evolved and developed over the years. If any such law is still prevalent today, it should be appropriately identified as residue from custom and tradition rather than as obligatory by religion.

8.3 What next?

The notion of the existence of eternal religious law was a result of Traditional Islam's claim of the eternal applicability of all injunctions of the various injunction categories of the Qur'an. We have studied all sources of Islamic law, and it has been shown that none of its sources is viable to be considered a source of eternal law. Thus, there is no convincing argument to compel Muslims to follow Islamic law besides custom and tradition. From a religious perspective, it is therefore important for Muslim communities, societies, and individuals alike to realize that they do have a choice in the law they follow—through differentiating between custom, tradition, and religion. It is important to understand that eternal religious law is just a myth in the heads of those who advocate and endorse the existence of such law. Hence, Muslims should not allow a few to dictate law in the name of archaic interpretations of Islam.

As I see it, the only way for law to be able to provide acceptable solutions for man-world affairs in changing space-time is for law to be separated from religion: law needs to be secular. Religion is supposed to deal with the non-changing: the matters of belief, ethics, and acts of worship. On the other hand, worldly matters change with space-time, or rather, man's understanding of them changes. Accordingly, law changes too, since law regulates man's relationship with the world. The changing can never be considered non-changing; thus, we need to separate the changing from the non-changing: to separate the regulation of worldly matters from religion. This can only be achieved by secular law.

With this understanding, Muslims would be liberated from being taken advantage of by those who use religion as an excuse to gain or to maintain power. Religion would also be liberated from being used as a means to manipulate the masses. Muslims living in Muslim-majority countries would thus be better equipped to select and to establish political, economic, and legal systems that reflect their modern-day needs and aspirations. Muslims residing in non-Muslim-majority countries would, as a result, potentially become more politically active and more accepting to abide by the law within the countries in which they live. This is especially true if these countries are governed by secular-based political systems that adhere to the principles of secularism, where the state is officially neutral in matters of religion, and people of different religions and beliefs are equal before the law.

I find it important to always remember that all humanity is very much alike despite our differences in language and color: both men and women share the same humble origins, and we all have the same basic needs and aspirations (Q. 30:20–26). When it comes to law, followers of the Qur'an need to adopt law that is guided by the ethics of the Qur'an, which call for fairness (Q. 4:58, 4:135, 5:8, 6:152, 7:29 in 7:26–30, 16:90, 17:34–35 in 17:22–39, 42:15 in 42:13–16, 60:7–

11 in 60:1–13) and freedom in choice of belief and choice of code (Q. 2:256–257, 5:103–105, 6:100–107, 10:99–109, 17:13–15, 18:27–31, 27:91–93, 39:9–18, 109:1–6). They need to adopt law that is suitable for their current space-time; that is founded on secular law, covering all matters and affairs without exception; and that evolves as man evolves over time.

9. Religious reform beyond religious law reform

The term religious reform when used with the religion of Islam has mainly been associated with religious law reform. There have been scores of Muslims, particularly in the last century or so, who have written about religious reform through religious law reform. However, that is not the reform that is sought for in this book.

This work does not consider Traditional Islam to be an acceptable representation of the Qur'anic revelation; hence, it is a comprehensive religious reform that is being called for and that which is proposed. As for religious law reform, the proposed interpretation of the Qur'anic revelation sees that any acceptable interpretation of religion that is based on revealed scripture should have no law component. It does not consider religion to be the source of law; quite the contrary, it rejects religious law altogether and calls for the implementation of secular law. In consequence, the proposed interpretation of the Qur'anic revelation would be redefining the role of religion and its domain of operation.

For Islam, there are limitations to any attempt at religious law reform simply because none of the sources of Islamic law are eternal. To understand the implications of accepting the legitimacy of religious law and the limitations of any attempt at religious law reform, I cite an example from recent history. This example also serves to demonstrate the interaction between culture and change, and how change in culture is always possible.

The cited example has to do with what has been called "the Arab spring," where the above objectives are addressed in the context of discussing how the different interpretations of Islamic law could be seen to have influenced the aftermath of the Arab spring.

Before getting to that, there are two important concepts covered in the following two sections that are necessary to understand.

9.1 The struggle for power and the different interpretations of Islamic law

Power struggles in the name of religion amongst the Muslims themselves and with others can be attributed to the different interpretations of Islamic law. When considering interpretations of Islam, people seem to always stress on the theological differences as what sets apart the numerous interpretations of Islam. However, there is another factor that leads to variation in the interpretations of Islam, and that is the differences in the interpretation of Islamic law. With this in mind, the struggle for power in the name of Islam could theoretically be due to two factors: theology and Islamic law (interpretations of). Nonetheless, the sole component of any interpretation of Islam that actually calls for action and possibly for political domination is not belief but is rather Islamic law.

As we are about to discuss the aftermath of the Arab Spring, it is important to note that political unrest in Arab countries, historically, has been primarily caused by power struggles to rule and to run the state. No matter which interpretation of theology or Islamic law is followed, it is Islamic law that always brings religion into this struggle. Once it is realized that religion should not be the source of law: there is no legitimacy to religious law, then it would be clear that religion has no place in the power struggles of the state, or in any power struggle for that matter, and the problem is reduced to a non-religious issue.

9.2 The modern concept of citizenship

In the modern state, citizenship is a legal status that is associated with equality before the law. Many think that citizenship expresses one's national identity; furthermore, that it frequently becomes an integral part of an individual's personal identity.

Citizenship in the modern concept of citizenship is a legal status that gives uniform rights and duties upon all members of the state. For citizens living in the modern state, the boundaries of identity and belonging have expanded way beyond the boundaries of the clan or tribe; they have expanded even beyond boundaries based on racial, ethnic, and religious bases to something more inclusive. The sense of identity and belonging that is important for social cohesion and integration has expanded to embrace all citizens of the state.

For people living in today's world, to look back at the seventh century CE and to consider the social norms and (assumed) systems in place by the followers of the Qur'an in that era as the ideal for all space-time is absurd. The modern state and the concept of citizenship of the present era did not exist at that time. Religion is no longer the common factor that unites people within societies, especially when considering the different interpretations of any religion.

NOTE: Humanity has taken giant steps at all levels since the seventh century CE. Today, when it comes to establishing an environment the core of which respects and protects human dignity, freedoms and rights, which would allow diverse groups to co-exist and prosper, humanity has found alternative solutions (systems) suitable for the scale and complexity of the modern state that are better suited for current times—and that better align with the modern understanding of the Qur'anic ethics—than those proposed by Islamic law, in all fields, whether it be political, legal, economic, etc.

NOTE: Today it would seem absurd that any state would discriminate against its citizens based on ethnicity, religion, country of origin, language, or any other base for discrimination. Yet unfortunately states like that still do exist. Let me use the term "nation-state" to explain. Today we find nation-states in which the nation is recognized based on a certain metric, whether it be ethnicity, religion, country of origin, or whatever else. In these states, some and not all citizens are—officially or unofficially—regarded as nationals (part of the nation), those who are trusted in their allegiance to the state, whilst others are not. All nationals are citizens, but not vice versa. All citizens pay income tax; however, it is only nationals who are required or selected to participate in the military. And nationals are given privileges when it comes to education, employment, housing, among others.

9.3 The Arab Spring: A religion-based perspective

The Arab Spring started initially in Tunisia in late 2010 CE and spread throughout most Arab countries (all Arab countries are Muslim-majority countries). The wave of initial revolutions and protests had already faded by mid-2012 CE. "By the end of February 2012 [CE], rulers had been forced from power in Tunisia, Egypt, Libya, and Yemen; civil uprisings had erupted in Bahrain and Syria; major protests had broken out in Algeria, Iraq, Jordan, Kuwait, Morocco, and Sudan; and minor protests had occurred in Mauritania, Oman, Saudi Arabia, Djibouti, Western Sahara, and Palestine [also known as the Occupied Palestinian Territory]" (Wikipedia 2011, par. 2). As of this writing, political unrest can still describe the state of affairs in Libya, Yemen, Iraq, and Syria.

Only in a single Arab country that encountered power changes, which is Tunisia, did the revolution materialize in power changes that did not involve bloodshed or in militant Islamists taking over. However, mainstream Islamists did enter the political scene of Tunisia; nevertheless, the Tunisians have been able to maintain Tunisia's progressive secular political and legal systems.

NOTE: As of January 1, 2007, there are 22 countries in the Arab league (League of Arab States), all of which are Muslim-majority countries (Wikipedia 2007). The combined population of Muslims in these countries forms about 20% of the global Muslim population.

9.3.1 Why did Tunisia turn out differently?

To answer the question as to why the outcome of the revolution in Tunisia turned out differently, one must realize that the answer surely has many facets—all of which contribute in one way or another to the end result. In the following discussion, I focus on one particular facet: the perspective of religion, aiming to provide insights from this angle.

From the perspective of religion, in my analysis, the answer lies in that the Muslims of Tunisia adopt a different interpretation of Islam than the rest of the Arab countries. This interpretation of Islam made the Muslims of Tunisia rather immune to violent and non-violent radical Islamist movements that seek power in the name of religion.

The core of the interpretation of Islam followed in Tunisia is Traditional Islam, which is the same core interpretation followed across all Arab countries and even by all Muslims for that matter. When it comes to the theological component of the adopted interpretation, most Tunisian Muslims share the same beliefs as most Muslims in other Arab countries, the Sunni theology. However, most Tunisian Muslims adopt a more liberal reading of Islamic law compared to the commonplace interpretations of Islamic law (the classical Sunni schools of jurisprudence); thus, resulting in a different interpretation of Islam altogether. It is therefore important for us to learn more about this liberal interpretation of Islamic law and how it came to exist.*1

NOTE*1: When referring to an interpretation of Islamic law as being liberal, one can think of its (*Fiqh*-based law) rulings as leaning more towards the ethics injunctions rather than the Action-Type II injunctions of the Qur'an and the *Hadith*. On the other hand, the rulings of a conservative interpretation would not just lean towards the Action-Type II injunctions of the Qur'an and the *Hadith*, but would also use more *Hadith* in deriving its rulings than would the hypothetical uniform interpretation of Islamic law.

9.3.2 Tunisia and its interpretation of Islamic law

Tunisia gained its independence from French colonial rule in 1956 CE. The Tunisian society in the 1950s CE was a relatively conservative society, whose culture was heavily based on religion and traditions. Upon independence, the political authority saw that change in social norms was necessary for Tunisia's development as a modern state. Recognizing the need for modernization while preserving cultural identity, the first Tunisian government introduced new secular laws alongside efforts to maintain a delicate balance with religious and traditional values.

The story of Tunisia and its liberal interpretation of Islamic law goes back to the early days of the modern Tunisian state, the year 1956 CE. What happened in that year was the introduction of a relatively secular family law—progressive for its time and the region—the Code of Personal Status (CPS). This was followed in later years by amendments to the CPS and the introduction of successive secular laws in other fields.

Besides the CPS, the early Tunisian social reforms included giving women the right to vote and to stand for elections (1957 CE) (Mili 2009, 138; Wikipedia 2008a, sec. 5), and the legalization of regulated abortion (only for women with more than five children in 1965 CE, and extended for all women in 1973 CE) (Dabash and Roudi-Fahimi 2008, 5). Since 1956 CE, the political authority in Tunisia has reiterated on numerous occasions that the CPS and subsequent laws were not in opposition to Islam, but rather part of a broader societal reform within Islam (Wikipedia 2008a, sec. 7).

The modern Tunisian state can be characterized by giving its people secular freedoms (Mili 2009, 131–147). The founding of the modern Tunisian state and its secularization efforts, depicted in the CPS and successive laws along with the unification of the judicial system, allowed the Muslims of Tunisia and Tunisians of other religions to taste the fruits of secularism early on. These efforts had a vital role in strengthening the population's conviction in the modern concept of citizenship.

I find it important to emphasize specific aspects of the modern Tunisian state's efforts towards secularization, with further commentary on certain items:

- Tunisia stands out as the only Arab country with a relatively secular family law. This distinction was evident in 1956 CE and remains relevant today.

I say relatively secular because, after all, it was an Islamic-law-inspired national personal status code; however, it included radical reforms compared to codes based on the commonplace interpretations of Islamic law. From its promulgation on August 13, 1956 CE, there was a firm belief that this code needed to be deeply rooted in Islamic law, unlike the Turkish code, which was modeled after European principles. This decision aimed to accommodate the predominantly conservative Muslim sentiment (Anderson 1958, 264).

The mention of Turkey is relevant because, among Muslim-majority countries, Turkey played a significant role as a non-Arab Muslim-majority country in advancing secularization efforts. In 1926 CE, Turkey adopted the Swiss civil code with minimal modifications, forming the basis of its own civil code (Anderson 1959, 87–89; Ochsenbein 2017).*1

However, from the perspective of the commonplace interpretations of Islamic law, it could be argued that the CPS was a secular code, since it introduced family law that had radical departures from the commonplace interpretations of Islamic law. If taking the ban on polygamy as a measure of the extent to which secular family law was incorporated into it, then we find the CPS of Tunisia to be the only personal status code of all Arab countries in which polygamy was unconditionally banned.

■ One of the modern Tunisian state's main objectives was to unify the judicial system—to have unified national (secular) courts enforcing statute law that applied to all citizens and to abolish all other courts (instead of having separate religious and civil courts, as was the case before Tunisia's independence) (Anderson 1958). This objective was achieved within the first year the CPS came into effect.

Initially, the CPS only applied to Muslim Tunisians when it first came into effect on January 1, 1957 CE, while Christian and Jewish Tunisians followed different family laws (Sfeir 1957). However, within the same year, the CPS was extended to cover all Tunisians (Anderson 1959, 34, 98; Mayer 1995, 4).*2

■ The introduction of secular laws that addressed gender disparities, along with the enforcement of these laws in unified national courts, shaped the Tunisians' perception of citizenship in alignment with the modern concept of citizenship, which advocates for equal rights for all citizens.

Equality of rights is something that is impossible to actualize under Islamic law, where the rights of non-Muslims and Muslim women are never considered equal to the rights of Muslim men.

The commonplace interpretations of Islamic law, not to mention the conservative interpretations, do not accept the principle of total equality under the law, which is a fundamental aspect of citizenship in modern states. Therefore, Islamic law is at odds with the notion of citizenship as held by the modern state.

The principle of equality is fundamental to human dignity, and its formal recognition in law reinforces its importance. While Tunisia has taken significant steps towards gender equality through initiatives such as the CPS and other secular reforms, disparities persist. Nonetheless, the taste of equal rights that Tunisian citizens have begun to savor since the implementation of these reforms has become deeply ingrained in their expectations. This newfound experience of equality represents a marked improvement over previous conditions, despite remaining disparities. Those who have tasted these rights are unlikely to relinquish them, especially in the face of opposition from those who seek power but do not embrace the principle of equal rights.

NOTE*1: The secularization efforts in Turkey, initiated by Mustafa Kemal Ataturk following the collapse of the Ottoman Empire, were characterized by the deliberate separation of religion and state. These efforts aimed to modernize Turkish society and establish a secular state based on Western principles of governance and secularism.

It is important to note that while Turkey's secularization efforts under Ataturk were significant, they built upon earlier initiatives during the late Ottoman period. The Ottoman Empire, particularly during the Tanzimat period (1839-1876), was the first Muslim-majority entity to undergo significant secularization reforms. These reforms, which encompassed administrative, legal, and educational changes, laid the groundwork for Turkey's subsequent secularization efforts. However, the success and extent of secularization varied over time and across different regions within the empire.

NOTE*2: Shortly after Tunisia achieved independence on March 20, 1956 CE, a legislative and judicial reform swept across the country. Anderson (1958) gives a detailed account. A summary of the major highlights he provides is as follows:

The CPS was promulgated on August 13, 1956 CE. With the CPS, the law of personal status had been reduced to the form of a code: a codification of family law had been achieved, which could be understood and applied by judges of the national (secular) courts who did not have to be specialists in the texts of Islamic law—or the texts of law of other religions.

By October 1, 1956 CE, the civil courts and the Muslim religious courts (including both the Maliki and Hanafi *shari'a* courts) had been unified—dissolving the *shari'a* courts in the process—thereby taking away jurisdiction over Muslim Tunisians

241

from Hanafi and Maliki judges (*qadis*) of *shari'a* courts and centralizing it exclusively in unified national courts. Personal status matters for Jewish Tunisians remained subject to the Rabbinical tribunal; personal status matters for Tunisians who were neither Muslim nor Jewish were governed by French law as applied by the Tunisian courts; litigation concerning foreign nationals was outside the jurisdiction of these courts altogether.

On July 1, 1957 CE, an agreement was forged with the French, granting Tunisian courts sole jurisdiction over all residents in the country. Shortly thereafter, on September 27, a law was enacted stipulating the dissolution of the Rabbinical tribunal, effective from October of that year (262–266).

9.3.3 What makes the Tunisian example so significant?

The importance of the Tunisian example to our analysis lies in that it represents an example of change in the systems of society that was able to affect culture. The patriarchal norms that had been prevalent in the Tunisian Muslim society were challenged, and steps towards changing them had been established and implemented.

The CPS and successive secular laws can be regarded as the vehicle that was able to change the interpretation of Islamic law that was followed by the Tunisian Muslim society. These changes in law were able to change social norms, and eventually influence the position of the Tunisian society towards secularism—as can be seen today in post-revolution times with Tunisians calling for more secular reforms.

As a result, and in relation to the Arab spring, it is then no surprise that Tunisia was the sole Arab country where the population was rather immune to Islamists calling for the adoption of more conservative interpretations of religious law.

9.3.4 The Tunisian Code of Personal Status (CPS)

In order to best realize the relationship between law and social norms as exemplified by the Tunisian example, we need first to learn more about the Tunisian CPS.

Charrad (2014) describes the CPS as a series of progressive Tunisian laws aiming to institute equality between women and men in a number of areas. The CPS helped reduce gender inequality before the law, but it did not eliminate it. The CPS when it was first introduced came with laws that abolished polygamy, altered regulations on marriage, divorce, alimony, custody, and guardianship; however, the CPS left Islamic law of inheritance almost intact.

Subsequent amendments increased women's guardianship rights, and dropped the clause present in the original 1956 CE text that required a wife to obey her husband. Moreover, law that allowed women to transfer citizenship to their children was also passed in the amendments (1–10).*1

In its approach towards family law reform, the political authority in order to instigate change had to convince the Muslim population that it was not going against religion. The political authority asserted that the CPS was *ijtihad* (religious legal reasoning) within the traditional interpretation of Islam. Thus, the CPS can be considered as a somewhat secular attempt at family law reform that came under the umbrella of a liberal reading of Islamic law (Wikipedia 2008a, sec. 7).

> NOTE*1: The CPS only had minor changes introduced to the commonplace interpretation(s) of inheritance law—by prioritizing spouses and female descendants over male cousins in certain kinship configurations (Charrad 2004, par. 4).

9.3.5 The change in the social norms of the Tunisian Muslim society

We look further into the Tunisian example, focusing particularly on the CPS, to learn more about the steps that made it possible for law to change culture. In the following section, we examine the primary obstacle to any change, including changes in social norms, and explore the limitations to the adopted approach by the political authority in Tunisia.

Charrad states: "The reforms of the CPS can be seen as an effort to reshape kinship in Tunisian society in the aftermath of independence from colonial rule. The CPS replaced the vision of the family as an extended kinship group built on strong ties crisscrossing a community of male relatives [i.e. a clan or tribe] with the vision of a conjugal unit in which ties between spouses and between parents and children are prominent. The elite in power in the 1950s treated family law reform as part of the transformation of society necessary for the development of a modern state." (Charrad 2004, par. 6)

We analyze the relationship between the CPS and change in the social norms of Tunisian Muslim society. In this analysis, we consider the three essential ingredients outlined in Section 6.6.3 that I propose to be a recipe for change, the "change recipe." This framework suggests that for social norms to change, three elements are crucial:

the promotion of ideas advocating change, societal acceptance of these ideas, and the effective implementation of change.

The story of how the CPS fits in with all this is as follows:

■ The first ingredient—Idea

The political authority recognized the need for certain changes in social norms deemed unsuitable for the time. The sought-after changes (new ideas) were incorporated into the CPS.

From the perspective of the commonplace interpretations of Islam, the CPS was seen as a secular family law. However, in my opinion, a more appropriate description of the CPS would be that it was a step towards secular family law. The CPS was publicized as representing an alternative reading of Islamic law—largely based on an interpretation of Islamic law that aligned with the values held by the political authority of Tunisia at the time.

■ The second ingredient—Acceptance

Reason was used to convince the Tunisian population that the CPS dealt with family issues based on a liberal reading of Islamic law. And that it did not oppose the Qur'an. The Muslims of Tunisia accepted the CPS since they saw it as not to oppose the Qur'an.

■ The third ingredient—Implementation

Once the CPS came into effect and became the law of the land, its implementation worked on reforming old customs and traditions that were deemed inappropriate for the time. The CPS brought about noticeable changes in the mindset and behavior of many Muslims in Tunisia regarding family-related matters and gender dynamics.

9.3.6 The resistance to change

It is usually inertia that hinders change in social norms, hindering both the acceptance of change and the implementation of change; however, gradual changes in laws over long periods of time lead to successfully change norms. Even if most of the Muslims of Tunisia did not fully appreciate the new secular laws to begin with, over time, adherence to the law made the actual change in social norms possible. Changing social norms takes time; it is like an attempt to break an old habit, but at the society level.

The political authority of Tunisia promoted its social reforms as reflecting a liberal reading of Islamic law. It did so through raising awareness, reforming religious education, and tightly administering religious institutions. Over time, the Muslims of Tunisia—or at least a significant number of them—became believers in the reforms, in both theory and practice. Amendments of a more secular nature were introduced, with no further religious justification provided for these changes. This indicates that over time, the Muslims of Tunisia became more accepting of secular law, as long as—in their minds—it could be labeled as being in accordance with Islamic law (an interpretation of). In the eyes of the Tunisian Muslims, they were not going against their religion of which Islamic law constituted a component.

The Muslims of Tunisia needed to accept the changes incorporated in the new laws for change in culture to occur. The social reforms would not have been accepted by the Muslims of Tunisia had they not been convinced to begin with that such changes did not oppose the Qur'an. The Muslims of Tunisia accepted the proposed changes when they were presented as reflecting a liberal reading of Islamic law rather than as being secular changes. This explains why major changes to inheritance law were not suggested by the CPS. When it comes to inheritance in Islamic law, the language of the Qur'an used in the injunctions related to inheritance is definitive in meaning (Q. 4:11–12 in 4:7–14, 4:176), and assuming the eternal applicability of these injunctions leaves little room, if any at all, for alternate readings.*1

The Tunisian example goes to show that Muslim societies are open to change, and can accept change in social norms as long as the proposed change does not oppose the Qur'an (an interpretation of). The Tunisian approach to secularization has its limitations though, as can be experienced in any attempt to overcome Islamic law of inheritance. At best, liberal or rationalistic readings of Islamic law can be considered as workaround approaches—with limitations—to deal with the discrepancies between Islamic law and modern-day norms.

NOTE*1: Given the fact that the Qur'anic verses on inheritance are considered definitive in meaning, it is not to be understood that all interpretations of Islamic law when it comes to matters of inheritance are identical—that is not at all the case. This serves as an example where we have Qur'anic verses that are definitive in meaning, yet we have different interpretations in Islamic law. This is due to the fact that other sources besides the Qur'an are used to interpret the Qur'an; furthermore, Islamic law is derived from other sources apart from the Qur'an.

There are considerable differences between the Sunni versus Shi'a approaches to inheritance law (Anderson 1959, 59–80; Coulson 1999, sec. 4.4 Law of succession); moreover, we also find differences in inheritance law to exist amongst the schools of jurisprudence of each of these two branches of Islam.

NOTE: The attempts of the post-independence Tunisian leadership to bring change to the Tunisian society were not limited civil matters. The Tunisian leadership attempted to bring change to Muslim religious ritual. In 1960 CE, J.A.C. Brown (2014) reports that the Tunisian president, Habib Bourguiba, argued that fasting in Ramadan hampered economic productivity and called on Tunisian Muslim workers not to fast the month of Ramadan. Bourguiba assumed that prominent Tunisian Muslim scholars would support his view. However, the leading Tunisian Muslim scholars of the time, the senior Hanafi Mufti and the renowned Maliki scholar Muhammad al-Tahir ibn 'Ashur (d. 1973 CE) publicly opposed the president's views. The scholars were soon dismissed from their posts. And the Tunisian Muslims did not buy into the president's rhetoric (279–280). It is noteworthy that Tahir bin 'Ashur is recognized for generally supporting the provisions of the CPS (Anderson 1958, 276; Wikimedia 2016).

Side note 9.1 On succession rules in the Qur'an versus Islamic law

With respect to succession rules in the Qur'an, we find a clear distinction between testate succession (a will exists) and intestate succession (no will exists). There is a lot to say about this topic; however, herein, I limit the discussion to the essentials.

Islamic law placed restrictions on the last will and testament that we do not find any mention of in the Qur'an. According to Islamic law, the last will and testament should not cover more than one-third of the estate and that no (recognized) heirs should be assigned as beneficiaries in the will. These limitations placed on the will were based on two *Hadiths*, "a bequest may not exceed one-third of the estate (*al-wasiyya fi al-thulth*)" and "no bequest to an heir (*la wasiyya li-warith*)" (Powers 1982). Hence, according to Islamic law, even if a will existed, after executing the will, there would always be inheritance left (at least two-thirds of the estate) that should be distributed between the heirs according to forced shares as specified by the particular interpretation of Islamic law followed by either the family or, depending on the context, the state at the time.

In contrast to common practice, if depending solely on the Qur'an to interpret the verses commonly understood to be related to succession (Q. 2:180–182, 2:240 in 2:240–242, 4:7–14, 4:33 in 4:29–35, 4:176, 5:106–108, 8:75 in 8:72–75, 33:5–6 in 33:1–8), we find the situation to be much simpler. We find a scenario for succession that is similar to how inheritance is dealt with in most secular countries around the world today: There is no restriction on how much of the testator's estate can be included in the will. And fractional shares of inheritance (forced shares) would apply in the case of intestate succession, covering situations when there was no will and situations when something was left after the will. Furthermore, it is to be noted

246

that forced shares in intestate succession differ between countries and have differed over time.

This work sees that the fixed shares specified in the Qur'an (injunctions categorized under the Action-Type II category)—applicable only for intestate succession as to be explained shortly—were customized (optimized) for the space-time of the revelation: they were space-time specific. These figures should not be considered constant across space-time.

The following outlines the succession rules prescribed in the Qur'an, encompassing both testate and intestate succession scenarios:

■ Testate succession

The Qur'an ordained that the QMonotheists have a will (Q. 2:180 in 2:180–182). The wording used was *kutiba 'alaykum* "prescribed for you." We find this exact same wording to have been used in other occasions, such as to ordain the rite of fasting (Q. 2:183 in 2:183–187) and regarding other matters (Q. 2:178, 2:216).

In spite of this wording, it is interesting to note that throughout Muslim history there have been those who have claimed the abrogation of the bequest verses, Q. 2:180 and 2:240, with what is commonly known as the inheritance verses, Q. 4:11–12 (Powers 1982).

The Qur'an did not clearly specify details regarding testate succession other than it be to one's parents and *al-aqrabin* (the closest to one) (Q. 2:180). It is my understanding that *al-aqrabin* (or its grammatical counterpart *al-aqrabun*—together in total appearing six times in the Qur'an—found in Q. 2:180, 2:215, 4:7, 4:33, 4:135) would potentially include all those close to one aside from one's parents. They could be male or female, blood related or not. This would include spouses, adopted children, and others (like those whom one considers partners and/or those who one had sworn compact with) (Q. 2:240, 4:33, 33:5–6). Furthermore, the Qur'an specified that testate succession be *bilma'ruf* (honorably; in a way that is honest and fair) (Q. 2:180). Specifications were given regarding witnesses to the will and how they were to give their testimony (Q. 5:106–108).

■ Intestate succession

In what is commonly referred to as the inheritance verses, Q. 4:11–12 in 4:7–14 and Q. 4:176, the Qur'an specified forced shares of inheritance (it is principally Q. 4:11–12; Q. 4:176 adds to a case in Q. 4:11–12). In these verses, the Qur'an declared the categories of benefactors and specified the shares they inherit.

What tells us that Q. 4:11–12 clearly addressed intestate succession is that each time the shares within a category were specified, the Qur'an repeatedly declared that the specified shares should be distributed only after the fulfillment of the will and paying off the debt of the deceased. The statement, as per Pickthall's translation, "after any legacy he may have bequeathed, or debt (hath been paid)," or variations of it, appeared in total four times in Q. 4:11–12.

According to Powers (1982), Islamic law of inheritance gives forced shares more weight, since it considers the Qur'anic verses on bequests to have been abrogated. Powers (1982, 292) states: "The following statement by the commentator al-Qurtubi [d. 671 AH / 1273 CE], made with reference to the prophetic dictum «no bequest to an heir», is especially noteworthy:

> «If it had not been for that *Hadith*, then it would have been possible to have both of these verses (Q. 2:180, 4:11), so that they (the heirs) would either take property from the testator in accordance with a last will and testament, or by inheritance if he did not leave a will or if something remained after the will. However this possibility is prevented by the *Hadith* and *ijma'*»."

Powers goes on to say, "the legal maxim «no bequest to an heir» was put in the form of a prophetic dictum at the beginning of the ninth century [CE / fourth century AH] in order to provide an authoritative indicator of abrogation; the doctrine of consensus was invoked, beginning in the ninth century [CE / fourth century AH], first in order to compensate for the fact that the *sanad* of the earliest versions of the *Hadith* was interrupted, and subsequently in order to overcome the status of the improved *Hadith* as an isolated report. Thus, from the standpoint of the historian, the *Hadith* and *ijma'* do not necessarily preclude the possibility alluded to by Qurtubi." (Powers 1982, 293)

The Qur'an did not explicitly declare whether the beneficiaries in testate and intestate succession were required to be Monotheists; however, from what I understand, a beneficiary could be from any religious following. That said, we find the Qur'an to have given exceptions—on political and non-religious grounds. Thus, if considering the political situation of the space-time of the revelation, in that time, the beneficiary could have been from any religious following as long as the beneficiary was not from a people who were at war with the QMonotheists. Moreover, when there was an armistice treaty in place, the beneficiary should not be of those who had been enemy fighters fighting against the QMonotheists (or partner, ally, and/or supporter of—or aided in the expulsion of). This can be deduced from verses that addressed QMonotheists relations with non-Monotheists such as Q. 4:92–93, 9:23–24 in 9:1–37, and Q. 60:8–9 in 60:1–9.

9.4 The vulnerability and limitations of Traditional Islam

Most mainstream Muslims who follow interpretations of religion based on Traditional Islam are generally concerned with only the private aspects of the various interpretations of Islamic law. However, Traditional Islam leaves room for calls to implement both public and private categories of Islamic law.

The Arab Spring example demonstrates the potential political ramifications of some interpretations of religion that are based on Traditional Islam. It depicts how religion can be—and was—used for political purposes through manipulating the public side of some interpretations of Islamic law. The Arab Spring example shows how the Islamic law component in the contemporary interpretations of Islam could be manipulated to make it possible for some Muslims to become radicalized and to adopt violent tendencies towards others, Muslims and non-Muslims alike. Furthermore, it shows how some radical readings of Islamic law could potentially set off Islamist ideologies that are fueled by supply chains of global fanatics and extremists who champion armed resistance.

The Tunisian example will have hopefully helped the reader gain perspective on the need for religious reform beyond that of religious law reform. As I see it, the real issue Muslims, not just those in Tunisia, need to address is religious reform through the outright rejection of religious law. The approach adopted in Tunisia through the CPS and successive laws was religious law reform (both in presentation by the authorities and perception by the general public). However, any attempt to reform Islamic law will always have its limitations.

In the earlier chapters, we found that the call for religion to be the source of law was but a man-made attempt to impose law that was originally not meant to be applied across space-time. As a result, application of any of the interpretations of Islamic law today would contradict with the calls of the Qur'an for fairness—as per our present-day understanding of this term. On the other hand, secularism and its calls to implement space-time dependent secular law that adheres to the modern-day understanding of fairness would be in line with the calls of the Qur'an. To have secular law rather than Islamic law agrees with the proposed interpretation of the Qur'anic revelation, since it sees that any acceptable interpretation of religion that is based on revealed scripture should not have a law component.

10. Findings: Volumes 1–3

This book along with the first two volumes in this series presented an attempt to understand the Qur'anic revelation. The findings of these three volumes regarding the Qur'anic revelation are summarized in the following three sections covering:

- What it is not

The religion of Islam is an unacceptable representation of the Qur'anic revelation.

- What it is

The proposed interpretation of the Qur'anic revelation, according to the present author, not only offers a more precise portrayal and understanding of the Qur'an and its message but also constitutes a more accurate representation thereof.

- What next

The ways in which the proposed interpretation of the Qur'anic revelation could potentially affect all followers of the revealed scriptures.

10.1 Traditional Islam is an unacceptable representation of the Qur'anic revelation

The objective of any Qur'anic-based interpretation of religion should be to reflect and explain the revelation from God to Prophet Muhammad. As any Qur'anic-based interpretation of religion, Traditional Islam is entitled to have its own perspective regarding the Qur'anic revelation. Traditional Islam holds particular standpoints on various matters that other Qur'anic-based interpretations of religion could disagree with or even regard as controversial. However, if an interpretation's standpoints on major issues were found not to reflect the position of the Qur'an on the same issues, then the interpretation in question should be rejected as an acceptable representation of the Qur'anic revelation.

In this book and in the first two volumes of this series, we have analyzed the standpoints of Traditional Islam on three major issues: inclusiveness, the sources of religious knowledge, and composition. The standpoints of Traditional Islam on these issues have been found to oppose the position of the Qur'an on the same issues. Therefore, Traditional Islam along with all interpretations based on Traditional

Islam should not be accepted as interpretations that represent the Qur'anic revelation.

The following sums up the arguments raised in relation to Traditional Islam's standpoints on inclusiveness, the sources of religious knowledge, and composition:

■ Inclusiveness

Historically, the term "Islam" has been associated with the religion of those who identify themselves as followers of the teachings of the Qur'an. Traditional Islam considers Islam to be followed exclusively by followers of the Qur'an. However, it has been argued that the Qur'an and particularly its vocabulary tell us otherwise.

In the Qur'an, Islam is not the name of a religion; it is the name of God's code of ethics and worship. Furthermore, according to the Qur'an, in the time of the revelation, there were followers of the earlier revealed scriptures who accepted the Qur'anic revelation while at the same time maintained their religious identities as followers of the earlier scriptures: they did not convert as Traditional Islam leads us to believe.

■ The sources of religious knowledge

Traditional Islam considers the *Sunna* to be a source of religious knowledge. However, the Qur'an commanded to take divine instruction only from God. And the Qur'an did not mention the revelation to the Prophet to have been in any form other than the Qur'an.

It has been established that not even a single *Hadith* can be attributed to the Prophet with certainty. Therefore, the *Hadith* should not be regarded to represent the *Sunna*, let alone be considered a source of religious knowledge.

■ Composition

It has been argued that the claim about the eternal applicability of the Qur'an's Action-Type II injunctions was a claim made by Traditional Islam, and that the Qur'an never declared its Action-Type II injunctions to have eternal applicability.

Examining Islamic law has led us to reject the claim made by Traditional Islam that the primary sources that elaborate on regulating worldly matters are of eternal applicability. To derive law from sources that are space-time specific would not result in law that is appropriate to be used across space-time. And doing so would go against one of the main pillars of the Qur'an: the pillar of justice. Thus, the legitimacy that Traditional Islam gives to Islamic law is rebutted.

Religion deals with the non-changing, the eternal. The components of religion should reflect this understanding about religion. Therefore, law, which changes with space-time and is not constant (if we want it to be just), should not constitute a component in any acceptable Qur'anic-based interpretation of religion.

10.2 The alternative: A new interpretation of the Qur'anic revelation

An interpretation of the Qur'anic revelation has been proposed. It is an interpretation that understands the Qur'anic message to be a call to all people to believe in the one and only God, to fulfill His code of ethics and worship, and not to be divided. Furthermore, as an interpretation of religion, the proposed interpretation forwards a different perspective than that of Traditional Islam on three key issues: inclusiveness, the sources of religious knowledge, and composition.

Outlined here are the standpoints of the proposed interpretation of the Qur'anic revelation regarding inclusiveness, the sources of religious knowledge, and composition:

■ Inclusiveness

The proposed interpretation understands inclusiveness in the Qur'anic context to involve the encompassing of all Monotheists regardless of the revealed scripture they follow. It is an interpretation that promotes inclusiveness within Monotheism.

■ The sources of religious knowledge

The proposed interpretation acknowledges the Qur'an to be the sole source of religious knowledge. It does not recognize the *Sunna* to be a source of religious knowledge. Moreover, it does not accept any alleged *Hadith* to be attributed to the Prophet, since when applying the Qur'anic authentication standard for oral evidence to verify the authenticity of *Hadith*, there is not a single *Hadith* that can be attributed with certainty to the Prophet.

■ Composition

The proposed interpretation is comprised solely of components on belief, ethics, and worship; it has no law component. It confines the scope of religion solely to spiritual and ethical aspects.

The proposed interpretation calls for the separation of law from religion, while at the same time maintains that this does not oppose the Qur'an. It considers the role of religion in worldly affairs to be limited to that religion be a source of ethics and not the source of law.

It is the present author's viewpoint that these shifts in thinking about the Qur'anic revelation constitute a paradigm shift, making it even clearer the esteemed standing that is worthy of both the Qur'an and the legacy of the last of the prophets.

10.3 Beyond interpretation

The impact of the proposed interpretation of the Qur'anic revelation extends to all followers of the revealed scriptures. For it is an interpretation that emphasizes that the Qur'anic message came with a call to unite all true followers of the revealed scriptures, and that it considered these followers all equal on the same path to God regardless of the revealed scripture they followed. Once followers of the revealed scriptures realize how they ought to relate to one another; that it was the Code that God commanded them to obey and uphold, yet not to coerce the Code on others; and that religion was not meant to be the source of law, they would feel more at peace with themselves, with others, and with their surroundings.

There is so much in common amongst the followers of the revealed scriptures, much more than most care to admit. The way of Prophet Abraham was the path the Qur'an prescribed for Prophet Muhammad to follow. It is the path of those who fulfill God's code of ethics and worship and who are not divided. The ethics prescribed in the various revealed scriptures are one of the main sources of values for many societies all around the world. These ethics, no matter what scripture, stress the sacredness and value of human life, every human life. They stress that doing and saying good, being just, and helping out one's fellow man should be amongst the deeds of those who seek an afterlife in Paradise. The Qur'an also teaches that man is free to choose what to believe, and that it is only for God to judge one's choice of belief. These are the core of the teachings of the Qur'an, and upholding them should be of the highest priority to all true believers.

Reflecting upon the potential changes the proposed interpretation of the Qur'anic revelation could bring about for Muslims in particular. The role and scope of religion would no longer be a source of dilemmas. Muslims would be able to clearly identify what falls within the realm of religion and what falls within the realm of man. And Muslims would no longer be held back by superstitions and illusions, and would be able to live their lives up to their full potentials.

If Muslims were to accept the proposed interpretation, this would have consequences that touch every single aspect of Muslims' lives, whether they live in Muslim-majority countries or elsewhere. Muslims living in non-Muslim-majority countries would recognize that the societies they live in are much more in harmony with the teachings of the Qur'an than they had previously reckoned. This understanding would lead them to seek a more active role in their societies. As for Muslims living in the so-called Muslim-majority countries, the effect goes beyond the level of the individual to the state. At the state level, primarily, this would lead to a transition towards secularism. Political systems that endorse religious law would be replaced by secular political systems that endorse secular law. The adoption of secularism at the state level, coupled with the conviction that secularism does not oppose religion at the level of the Muslim individual would consequently have its mark on society. Cultures would undergo change from a mindset that is crippled by the limitations of religious law to one that is open to the possibilities that secularism has to offer. However, the move towards secularism will not succeed, unless both culture and state undergo the shift towards secularism side by side.

REFERENCES

'Ali, Jawad. 1993. *al-Mufassal fi Tarikh al-'Arab Qabl al-Islam*. 2nd ed. 10 vols. Baghdad: Jami'at Baghdad.

'Ashmawi, Muhammad Sa'id. 1995. *al-Riba wa al-Fa'ida fi al-Islam*. 2nd ed. Cairo: Maktabat Madbuli al-Saghir.

---. 1996. *Jawhar al-Islam*. 4th ed. Cairo: Maktabat Madbuli al-Saghir.

'Ashur, Muhammad al-Tahir ibn. 1984. *Tafsir al-Tahrir wa-al-Tanwir*. 30 vols. Tunis: al-Dar al-Tunisia lil-Nasher.

Abu-Zayd, Nasr. 2003. "The Dilemma of the Literary Approach to the Qur'an." *Alif: Journal of Comparative Poetics* (23): 8–47. https://doi.org/10.2307/1350075. https://www.jstor.org/stable/1350075.

al-Bardisi, Muhammad Zakariya. 198-? *Usul al-Fiqh*. Cairo: Dar al-Thaqafa.

al-Barri, Zakariya. 1974. *Usul al-Fiqh al-Islami*. 3rd ed. Cairo: Dar al-Nahda 'Arabiyya.

al-Dimashqi, Muhammad Jamal al-Din al-Qasimi. 1961. *Qawa'id al-Tahdith min Funun Mustalah al-Hadith*. Edited by Muhammad Bahjat al-Bitar. 2nd ed. Cairo: Dar Ihya' al-Kutub al-'Arabiyya, 'Isa al-Babi al-Halabi.

al-Fawzan, Salih. 2005. *A Summary of Islamic Jurisprudence*. Translated by al-Arabia for Information Technology. 2 vols. Riyadh: al-Maiman Publishing House.

al-Ghazali, Muhammad. 2003. *Turathuna al-Fikri fi Mizan al-Shar'a wa al-'Aql*. 5th ed. Cairo: Dar al-Shuruq.

al-Jabri, Mohammed Abed. 2006. *Madkhal Ila al-Qur'an al-Karim: al-Ta'rif bi-l-Qur'an*. Beirut: Markaz Dirasat al-Wahda al-'Arabiyya.

---. 2008–9. *Fahm al-Qur'an al-Hakim: al-Tafsir al-Wadih Hasab Tartib al-Nuzul*. First ed. 3 vols. Casablanca: Dar al-Nashr al-Maghribiyya.

al-Jawziyya, Muhammad ibn Abi Bakr ibn Qayyim. 1432 [2010 or 2011]. *Ighathat al-lahfan fi Masayid al-Shaytan*. Edited by Muhammad 'Aziz Shams. Mecca: Dar 'Alam al-Fawa'id lil-Nashr wa al-Tawzi'.

al-Kattani, Muhammad ibn Ja'far. 19--? *Nazm al-Mutanathir fi al-Hadith al-Mutawatir*. 2nd ed. Egypt: Dar al-Kutub al-Salafiyya.

al-Maghluth, Sami ibn 'Abdulla ibn Ahmad. 2007. *Atlas al-Adyan*. Maktabat al-'Ubaykan.

al-Nuwayhi, Muhammad. 2010. *Nahwa Thawra fi al-Fikr al-Dini*. Cairo: Rou'ya lil-Nashr wa al-Tawzi'. Beirut: Dar al-Adab, 1983.

al-Qurtubi, Muhammad ibn Ahmad. 1935. *al-Jami' li Ahkam al-Qur'an*. 2nd ed. 20 vols. Cairo: Dar al-Kutub al-Misriyya.

al-Razi, Fakhr al-Din. 1981. *Mafatih al-Ghayb (Tafsir al-Razi)*. 1st ed. 32 vols. Beirut: Dar al-Fikr.

al-Shanqiti, 'Abdulla Muhammad al-Amin. 19--? *al-Ayat al-Mansukha fi al-Qur'an al-Karim*. Cairo: Maktabit ibn Taymiyya.

al-Tabari, Muhammad ibn Jarir. 1967. *Ta'rikh al-Rusul wa l-Muluk*. Edited by Muhammad Abu al-Fadl Ibrahim. 2nd ed. 11 vols. Egypt: Dar al-Ma'arif.

---. 2001. *Tafsir al-Tabari: Jami' al-Bayan 'an Ta'wil Ay al-Qur'an*. Edited by 'Abdulla ibn 'Abd al-Muhsin al-Turki. First ed. 26 vols. Cairo: Dar Hajr.

al-Zamakhshari, Abi al-Qasim Muhamud ibn 'Umar. 2009. *Tafsir al-Kashshaf 'an Haqa'iq al-Tanzil wa 'Uyun al-Aqawil fi Wujuh al-Ta'wil*. 3rd ed. 30 vols. Beirut: Dar al-Ma'rifa.

al-Zurqani, Muhammad 'Abd al-'Azim. 1995. *Manahil al-'Irfan fi 'Ulum al-Qur'an*. 2 vols., edited by Fawwaz Ahmad Zamarli. Beirut: Dar al-Kitab al-'Arabi.

Ali, A.K.M Ayyub. 1963. "Ash'arism." In *A history of Muslim philosophy. With short accounts of other disciplines and the modern renaissance in Muslim lands*, edited by Mian Mohammad Sharif, 1:259–274. Wiesbaden: Harrassowitz.

Altikulac, Tayyar, and Halit Eren. 2009. *al-Mushaf al-Sharif Attributed to Uthman bin Affan (The copy at al-Mashhad al-Husayni in Cairo)*. First ed. Vol. 1.*Critical editions series; 4*. Istanbul: Organisation of the Islamic Conference, Research Centre for Islamic History, Art and Culture (IRCICA).

Altikulac, Tayyar, Halit Eren, and Ekmeleddin Ihsanoglu. 2007. *al-Mushaf al-Sharif al-Mansub ila 'Uthman ibn 'Affan: Nuskhat Mat-haf Topkapi Sarayi*. Translated by Salih S'adawi. First ed.*Silsilat Nusus Muhaqqaqa; 2*, edited by Ekmeleddin İhsanoğlu and Research Centre for Islamic History Art and Culture. Istanbul: Munazzamat al-Mu'tamar al-Islami, Markaz al-Abhath lil-Tarikh wa-al-Funun wa al-Thaqafa al-Islamiyya bi-Istanbul.

Amin, Ahmad. 1964. *Duha al-Islam*. 7th ed. 3 vols. Cairo: Matba'at Lajnat al-Ta'lif wa al-Tarjama wa al-Nashr. 1933.

---. 1969. *Fajr al-Islam*. 10th ed. Beirut: Dar al-Kitab al-'Arabi. Cairo: Matba'at al-'Itimad, 1929.

Anderson, J. N. D. 1958. "The Tunisian Law of Personal Status." *The International and Comparative Law Quarterly* 7 (2): 262–279. https://www.jstor.org/stable/755498.

---. 1959. *Islamic law in the modern world*. New York: New York University Press.

---. 1966. "CODIFICATION IN THE MUSLIM WORLD: Some Reflections." *Rabels Zeitschrift für ausländisches und internationales Privatrecht / The Rabel Journal of Comparative and International Private Law* 30 (2): 241–253. https://www.jstor.org/stable/27874784.

Arafat, W. N. 1998. "New light on the story of Banu Qurayza and the Jews of Medina (internet version)." Accessed November 19, 2015. archived at the Wayback Machine https://web.archive.org/web/20151025131609/http://www.haqq.com.au/~salam/misc/qurayza.html.

Arberry, A.J. 1996. *The Koran Interpreted*. reprint ed.: Simon & Schuster. 1955.

As-Sallabi, 'Ali Muhammad. 2007. *'Umar ibn al-Khattab: His Life and Times*. Translated by Nasiruddin al-Khattab. 2 vols.: International Islamic Publishing House.

Asad, Muhammad. 2008. *The message of the Qur'an : the full account of the revealed Arabic text accompanied by parallel transliteration*. Bristol, England: The Book Foundation.

Bell, Richard, and W. Montgomery Watt. 1970. *Bell's introduction to the Qur'an*. New ed. Vol. 8*Islamic surveys*. Edinburgh: Edinburgh University Press.

Berger, Maurits S. 2014. "Fatwa." The Oxford Encyclopedia of Islam and Politics. Oxford Islamic Studies Online. Accessed November 24, 2020.

https://www.oxfordreference.com/display/10.1093/acref:oiso
/9780199739356.001.0001/acref-9780199739356-e-0003.

Black, Henry Campbell, Joseph R. Nolan, Michael J. Connolly, and
West Publishing Company. 1979. *Black's law dictionary :
definitions of the terms and phrases of American and English
jurisprudence, ancient and modern.* 5th ed. St. Paul: West
Pub. Co.

Bloom, Jonathan. 2001. *Paper before print : the history and impact
of paper in the Islamic world.* New Haven: Yale University
Press.

Böwering, Gerhard, Patricia Crone, and Mahan Mirza. 2013. *The
Princeton encyclopedia of Islamic political thought.*
Princeton, N.J.: Princeton University Press.

Brems, Eva. 2001. *Human Rights: Universality and Diversity.* Vol.
66*International studies in human rights.* The Hague ; Boston:
Kluwer Law International.

Brockett, Adrian. 1988. "The Value of the Hafs And Warsh
Transmissions for the Textual History of the Qur'an." In
Approaches to the history of the interpretation of the Qur'an,
edited by Andrew Rippin, 31–45. Oxford: Clarendon Press.

Brown, Daniel W. 1999. *Rethinking Tradition in Modern Islamic
Thought.* First paperback ed. Cambridge: Cambridge
University Press. 1996.

Brown, J.A.C. 2014. *Misquoting Muhammad: The Challenge and
Choices of Interpreting the Prophet's Legacy.* Oneworld
Publications.

Campanini, Massimo. 2007. *The Qur'an: the basics.* Translated by
Oliver Leaman. London ; New York: Routledge.

CEDAW. n.d. "Convention on the Elimination of All Forms of
Discrimination against Women." The United Nations. United
Nations Entity for Gender Equality and the Empowerment of
Women. Accessed February 5, 2015.
https://www.un.org/womenwatch/daw/cedaw, archived at the
Wayback Machine
https://web.archive.org/web/20150204201613/https://www.u
n.org/womenwatch/daw/cedaw/.

Chande, Abdin. 2004. "Symbolism and allegory in the Qur'an:
Muhammad Asad's modernist translation." *Islam and*

Christian–Muslim Relations 15 (1): 79-89. https://doi.org/10.1080/0959641031001631830.

Charrad, Mounira M. 2004. "Tunisia: Personal Status Code." Encyclopedia of the Modern Middle East and North Africa. Accessed October 14, 2015. https://www.encyclopedia.com/doc/1G2-3424602734.html, archived at the Wayback Machine https://web.archive.org/web/20160421083612/http://www.encyclopedia.com/doc/1G2-3424602734.html.

---. 2014. Family law reforms in the Arab world: Tunisia and Morocco. https://www.un.org/esa/socdev/family/docs/egm12/PAPER-CHARRAD.pdf.

Coulson, Noel James. 1978. *A History of Islamic Law*. First paperback ed. Edinburgh: Edinburgh University Press. 1964.

---. 1992. *Fi Tarikh al-Tashri' al-Islami – A History of Islamic law*. Translated by Muhammad Ahmad Sraj. Beirut: al-Mu'asasa al-Jami'yya lil-nashr wa al-Tawzi'.

---. 1999. "Shari'ah." Encyclopædia Britannica. Accessed November 28, 2018. https://www.britannica.com/topic/Shariah.

Dabash, Rasha, and Farzaneh Roudi-Fahimi. 2008. Abortion in the Middle East and North Africa. Accessed December 12, 2018. https://assets.prb.org/pdf08/MENAabortion.pdf.

Daftary, Farhad. 2007. *The Isma'ilis : their history and doctrines*. 2nd ed. Cambridge ; New York: Cambridge University Press.

dar-alifta.org. 2011. "al-Shar' wa al-Shari'a." Dar al-Ifta' al-Masriyya. Accessed October 6, 2015. archived at the Wayback Machine https://web.archive.org/web/20170906104552/https://www.dar-alifta.org/AR/ViewFatawaConcept.aspx?ID=%2046.

Dasuqi, Muhammad al-Sayyid, and Aminah Muhammad ibn Yusuf Jabir. 1999. *Muqaddima fi Dirasat al-Fiqh al-Islami*. 2nd ed. Doha: Dar al-Thaqafa.

Di Cesare, Michelina, Avinoam Shalem, Heather Coffey, and Alberto Saviello. 2013. *Constructing the image of Muhammad in Europe*. Edited by Avinoam Shalem. text. De Gruyter.

Donner, Fred M. 2010. *Muhammad and the Believers : at the origins of Islam*. Cambridge, Mass.: The Belknap Press of Harvard University Press.

---. 2013. Thoughts on David Nirenberg, Chapter 4, "Jewish Enmity in Islam," in Anti-Judaism. (March 28, 2018). https://voices.uchicago.edu/religionculture/2013/10/25/to-every-prophet-an-adversary-jewish-enmity-in-islam/, archived at the Wayback Machine https://web.archive.org/web/20180328173857/https://divinity.uchicago.edu/sites/default/files/imce/pdfs/webforum/102013/Donner%20Response%20to%20Nirenberg%20Final.pdf.

---. 2015. The Study of Islam's Origins since W. Montgomery Watt's Publications. Accessed March 18, 2016. https://www.ed.ac.uk/literatures-languages-cultures/alwaleed/resources/public/watt-anniversary, archived at the Wayback Machine (video transcription) https://web.archive.org/web/20170329085455/http://www.ed.ac.uk/files/atoms/files/professor_fred_donner.pdf.

Esposito, John L. 2003. *The Oxford dictionary of Islam*. New York: Oxford University Press.

Fedele, Valentina. 2019. "Fatima." In *Encyclopedia of women in world religions : faith and culture across history*, edited by Susan J. De Gaia, 2: 56. Santa Barbara, California: ABC-CLIO, an imprint of ABC-CLIO, LLC.

Fernando, Jason. 2020. "Usury Rate: Meaning, Assessment, Example." Investopedia. Accessed February 1, 2023. https://www.investopedia.com/terms/u/usury-rate.asp, archived at the Wayback Machine https://web.archive.org/web/20230201105734/https://www.investopedia.com/terms/u/usury-rate.asp.

Gacek, A. 2001. *The Arabic Manuscript Tradition: A Glossary of Technical Terms and Bibliography*. Brill.

Goldziher, Ignác. 1981. *Introduction to Islamic theology and law*. Translated by Andras and Ruth Hamori. Edited by Charles Issawi and Bernard Lewis.*Modern classics in Near Eastern studies*. Princeton, N.J.: Princeton University Press.

Greifenhagen, F. Volker. 2017. "Why did Luther want the Qur'an to be published?". Luther College University of Regina. Accessed June 17, 2020. https://www.luthercollege.edu/university/academics/impetus/winterspring-2017/table-talks/why-did-luther-want-the-quran-to-be-published/, archived at the Wayback Machine https://web.archive.org/web/20200807180837/https://www.l uthercollege.edu/university/academics/impetus/winterspring-2017/table-talks/why-did-luther-want-the-quran-to-be-published/.

Gu, Sharron 2014. *A Cultural History of the Arabic Language*. McFarland, Incorporated Publishers.

Hallaq, Wael B. 1984. "Was the Gate of Ijtihad Closed?" *International Journal of Middle East Studies* 16 (1): 3–41. https://www.jstor.org/stable/162939.

---. 1999. "The Authenticity of Prophetic Ḥadith: A Pseudo-Problem." *Studia Islamica* (89): 75-90. https://doi.org/10.2307/1596086. https://www.jstor.org/stable/1596086.

---. 2003. "Juristic Authority vs. State Power: The Legal Crises of Modern Islam." *Journal of Law and Religion* 19 (2): 243–258. https://doi.org/10.2307/3649176. https://www.jstor.org/stable/3649176.

---. 2005a. *The origins and evolution of Islamic law*. Vol. 1 *Themes in Islamic law*. Cambridge, UK ; New York: Cambridge University Press.

---. 2005b. "What is Shari'a?" *Yearbook of Islamic and Middle Eastern Law Online* 12 (1): 151–180. https://doi.org/10.1163/22112987-91000130. https://brill.com/view/journals/yimo/12/1/article-p151_11.xml.

---. 2010. "Islamic law: history and transformation." In *The New Cambridge History of Islam*, edited by Michael Cook and Robert Irwin, 4:142–183. Cambridge ; New York: Cambridge University Press.

Hanifa, Abu Muti' al-Balkhi 'an Abu. 1368/1949. "al-Fiqh al-Absat." In *al-'Alim wa-l-Muta'allim*, edited by Muhammad Zahid al-Kawthari, 39–60. Cairo: Maktabat al-Khangi.

Hasan, Ahmad. 1972. "The Concept of Infallibility in Islam." *Islamic Studies* 11 (1): 1-11. https://www.jstor.org/stable/20833049.

Hazm, 'Ali ibn Ahmad ibn. 1983. *al-Ahkam fi Usul al-Ahkam*. Edited by Ahmad Muhammad Shakir. 2nd ed. 8 vols. Beirut: Dar al-Afaq al-Jadida.

Hunke, Sigrid. 1993. *Shams al-'Arab Tasta' 'ala al-Gharb: Athar al-Hadara al-'Arabiyya fi Urubba – Allahs Sonne über dem*

Abendland. Unser arabisches Erbe. Translated by Faruq Baydun & Kamal Dasuqi. 8th ed. Beirut: Dar al-Jeel & Dar al-Afaq al-Jadida.

Hye, M. Abdul. 1963. "Ash'arism." In *A history of Muslim philosophy. With short accounts of other disciplines and the modern renaissance in Muslim lands*, edited by Mian Mohammad Sharif, 1:220–243. Wiesbaden: Harrassowitz.

Ibn al-Athir. 1987. *al-Kamil fi al-Tarikh*. Edited by Abi al-Fida' 'Abdulla al-Qadi. 11 vols. Beirut: Dar al-Kutub al-'Ilmiyya.

Ibn Khaldun, 'Abd al-Rahman ibn Mohammad. 1858. *Prolégomènes d'Ebn-Khaldoun, texte Arabe*. 3 vols. Paris: Imprimerie Impériale.

---. 1980. *The Muqaddimah : An Introduction to History*. Translated by Franz Rosenthal. Second printing of 2nd ed. 3 vols.*Bollingen Series 43*. Princeton, N.J.: Princeton University Press.

---. 2000. *Tarikh ibn Khaldun – Kitab al-'ibar wa-diwan al-mubtada' wa-l-khabar fi ayyam al-'Arab wa-l-'ajam wa-l-Barbar wa-man 'asarahum min dhawi l-sultan al-akbar, "The book of examples and archive of early and subsequent history, dealing with the political events concerning the Arabs, non-Arabs and Berbers and the supreme rulers who were contemporary with them"*. Edited by Khalil Shahadeh and Suhail Zakar. 8 vols. Beirut: Dar al-Fikr.

islamic-awareness.org. 2008. "Concise list of Arabic manuscripts of the Qur'an attributable to the first century Hijra." Islamic Awareness. Accessed June 1, 2018. https://www.islamic-awareness.org/quran/text/mss/hijazi.html, archived at the Wayback Machine https://web.archive.org/web/20190214233430/https://www.islamic-awareness.org/quran/text/mss/hijazi.

Joseph, Suad, and Afsaneh Najmabadi, eds. 2003. *Family law and Politics*. 6 vols. Vol. 2, *Encyclopedia of Women & Islamic Cultures*. Leiden ; Boston, Mass.: Brill.

Kamali, Mohammad Hashim. 2003. *Principles of Islamic jurisprudence*. 3rd rev. and enl. ed. Cambridge, UK: Islamic Texts Society.

KFGQPC. 2016. "Table of the abrogating and abrogated verses." King Fahd Complex for Printing of the Holy Qur'an.

Accessed January 18, 2016. archived at the Wayback Machine https://web.archive.org/web/20170327083848/http://quranco mplex.gov.sa/Display.asp?section=1&l=arb&f=nwasekh158 &trans.

Khallaf, 'Abd al-Wahhab. 1968? *'Ilm Usul al-Fiqh*. Kuwait: Dar al-Qalam. Reprint, Maktabat al-Da'wa al-Islamiyya Shabab al-Azhar. 1942.

---. 1971. *Khulasat Tarikh al-Tashri' al-Islami*. Kuwait: Dar al-Qalam.

Khan, Israr Ahmad. 2010. *Authentication of Hadith: Redefining the Criteria*. London: International Institute of Islamic Thought.

Khatib, Ammar, and Nazir Khan. 2019. "The Origins of the Variant Readings of the Qur'an." Yaqeen Institute for Islamic Research. Accessed January 7, 2020. https://yaqeeninstitute.org/nazir-khan/the-origins-of-the-variant-readings-of-the-quran/, archived at the Wayback Machine https://web.archive.org/web/20191220064519/https://yaqeen institute.org/nazir-khan/the-origins-of-the-variant-readings-of-the-quran/.

Kohler, Josef. 1914. "Philosophy of law." In *Readings in Jurisprudence and Legal Philosophy*, edited by Morris Raphael Cohen and Felix S. Cohen, 2:674–678. Washington D.C.: Beard Books. Reprint, 2002. Original edition, 1951.

Kuran, Timur. 2011. *The Long Divergence: How Islamic Law Held Back the Middle East*. Princeton ; Oxford: Princeton University Press.

Kuwait Ministry of Awqaf and Islamic Affairs. 1995. *al-Mawsu'a al-Fiqhiyya*. First ed. 45 vols.*al-Mawsu'a al-Fiqhiyya*. Cairo: Dar al-Safwa lil-Tiba'a wa al-Nashr wa al-Tawzi'.

Lamarti, Samuel Hosain. 2002. "The Development of Apostasy and Punishment Law in Islam." PhD. thesis, Glasgow University. https://theses.gla.ac.uk/id/eprint/991.

Lewis, Bernard, Victor L. Ménage, Charles Pellat, and Joseph Schacht, eds. 1986. *The Encyclopaedia of Islam*. New ed. Vol. 3 (H-Iram): E. J. BRILL, LUZAC & CO. Original edition, 1971.

Lowry, Joseph E. 2007. *Early Islamic legal theory : the Risala of Muḥammad ibn Idris al-Shafi'i*. Vol. 30*Studies in Islamic law and society,*. Leiden ; Boston: Brill.

Maan, Bashir, and Alastair McIntosh. 2000. "An interview with "the Last Orientalist" - the Rev Prof William Montgomery Watt: "The whole house of Islam, and we Christians with them…"." *The Coracle* Summer 2000 (3:51): 8–11.

---. 2011. "Interview with Prof William Montgomery Watt (internet version): "The whole house of Islam, and we Christians with them…"." Alastair McIntosh. Accessed November 28, 2015. https://www.alastairmcintosh.com/articles/2000_watt.htm, archived at the Wayback Machine https://web.archive.org/web/20150905162225/https://www.alastairmcintosh.com/articles/2000_watt.htm.

Madkur, Muhammad Sallam. 1996. *al-Madkhal lil-Fiqh al-Islami*. 2nd ed. Cairo: Dar al-Kitab al-Hadith.

Martin, Richard C. 2004. *Encyclopedia of Islam and the Muslim world*. 2 vols. New York: Macmillan Reference USA : Thomson/Gale.

Mayer, Ann Elizabeth. 1995. "Reform of Personal Status Laws in North Africa: A Problem of Islamic or Mediterranean Laws?" *Middle East Journal* 49 (3): 432–446. https://www.jstor.org/stable/4328833.

Messick, Brinkley. 1995. Fatwa: Process and Function. In *The Oxford Encyclopedia of the Modern Islamic World*, edited by John L. Esposito. New York: Oxford University Press.

Mez, Adam. 19--? *al-Hadara al-Islamiyya fi al-Qarn al-Rabi' al-Hijri aw 'Asr al-Nahda fi al-Islam*. Translated by Muhammad Abd al-Hadi Abu Rida. 5th ed. 2 vols. Beirut: Dar al-Kitab al-'Arabi. 1922 (German).

Mili, Amel. 2009. "Exploring the relation between gender politics and representative government in the Maghreb: Analytical and Empirical Observations." PhD. thesis, Rutgers University. https://doi.org/doi:10.7282/T3445MP1.

Mughniyya, Muhammad Jawad. 2021. "Lineage (Al-Nasab)." al-islam.org. Accessed October 20, 2021. https://www.al-islam.org/marriage-according-five-schools-islamic-law-muhammad-jawad-mughniyya/lineage-al-nasab, archived at the Wayback Machine https://web.archive.org/web/20211020132114/https://www.al-islam.org/marriage-according-five-schools-islamic-law-muhammad-jawad-mughniyya/lineage-al-nasab.

Musa, Aisha Y. 2007. "Al-Shafi'i, the Hadith, and the Concept of the Duality of Revelation." *Islamic Studies* 46 (2): 163-197. https://www.jstor.org/stable/20839066.

Muzaffar, Muhammad Ridha. 1990. *Usul al-Fiqh*. 2 ed. 2 vols. Beirut: Mu'asasat al-'Alami lil-Matbu'at.

Neusner, Jacob. 2003. *God's rule : the politics of world religions*. Washington, D.C.: Georgetown University Press.

Neuwirth, Angelika. 2009 "The "Late Antique Qur'an"." Institute for Advanced Study. Accessed May 23, 2016. https://youtu.be/qHCeYSvazY4.

Ochsenbein, Gaby. 2017. "Turkey's civil code is based on a Swiss model." swissinfo.ch. Accessed December 12, 2018. https://www.swissinfo.ch/eng/1926-to-2017_turkey-s-civil-code-is-based-on-a-swiss-model/43064508, archived at the Wayback Machine https://web.archive.org/web/20190105184935/https://www.swissinfo.ch/eng/1926-to-2017_turkey-s-civil-code-is-based-on-a-swiss-model/43064508.

Omar, 'Abdul Mannan. 2010. *The dictionary of the Holy Qur'an : Arabic words, English meanings (with notes) : classical Arabic dictionaries combined*. 2nd edition reprint ed. 1 vols. Hockessin, DE USA: NOOR Foundation-International Inc. 2003.

Packer, George. 2006. "The Moderate Martyr: A radically peaceful vision of Islam." The New Yorker. Accessed September 22, 2015. https://www.newyorker.com/magazine/2006/09/11/the-moderate-martyr.

Pew Research Center., and Pew Forum on Religion & Public Life. 2011. The future of the global Muslim population: projections for 2010–2030. *Pew-Templeton global religious futures project*. https://www.pewforum.org/wp-content/uploads/sites/7/2011/01/FutureGlobalMuslimPopulation-WebPDF-Feb10.pdf.

---. 2013. The World's Muslims: Religion, Politics and Society. https://www.pewforum.org/wp-content/uploads/sites/7/2013/04/worlds-muslims-religion-politics-society-full-report.pdf.

Pickthall, Marmaduke William. 1930. *The meaning of the glorious Koran : an explanatory translation*. London: A.A. Knopf.

Powers, David S. 1982. "On the Abrogation of the Bequest Verses." Arabica 29 (3). BRILL: 246–95. Accessed January 17, 2016.

Rabb, Intisar A. 2016. "Ijtihad." The Oxford Encyclopedia of the Islamic World. Oxford Islamic Studies Online. Accessed September 28, 2016. https://www.oxfordreference.com/display/10.1093/acref/978 0195305135.001.0001/acref-9780195305135-e-0473.

Ringgren, Helmer, and Nicolai Sinai. 2019. "Qur'an." Encyclopædia Britannica. Accessed January 5, 2020. https://www.britannica.com/topic/Quran.

Robinson, Neal. 1998. "Ash'ariyya and Mu'tazila." In *Routledge encyclopedia of philosophy*, edited by Edward Craig and Routledge (Firm), 1:519–523. London ; New York: Routledge.

Sadeghi, Behnam, and Mohsen Goudarzi. 2012. "San'a' 1 and the Origins of the Qur'an." *Der Islam* Volume 87, Issue 1–2, Pages 1–129, ISSN (Online) 1613-0928, ISSN (Print) 0021-1818 (March). https://doi.org/10.1515/islam-2011-0025.

Schacht, Joseph. 1950. *The origins of Muhammadan jurisprudence*. Oxford: Clarendon Press.

Sfeir, George N. 1957. "The Tunisian Code of Personal Status (Majallat Al-Ahw Al Al-Shakhsiy Ah)." *Middle East Journal* 11 (3): 309–318. https://www.jstor.org/stable/4322925.

Shah, Mustafa. 2020. "Introduction." In *The Oxford Handbook of Qur'anic Studies*, edited by Mustafa Shah and Muhammad Abdel Haleem. Oxford University Press.

Shaker, Ahmad Muhammad. 1983. *al-Ba'ith al-Hathith Sharh Ikhtisar 'Ulum al-Hadith Lil-Hafith ibn Kathir*. Beirut: Dar al-Kutub al-'Ilmiyya.

Shoufani, Elias. 1973. *Al-Riddah and the Muslim conquest of Arabia*. Toronto: University of Toronto Press.

---. 1995. *Hurub al-Ridda*. Beirut: Dar al-Kunuz al-Adabiyya.

Shuhba, Muhammad ibn Muhammad Abu. 1983. *al-Wasit fi 'Ulum wa Mustalah al-Hadith*. Jeddah: 'Alam al-Ma'rifa.

Sinai, Nicolai. 2017. *The Qur'an : a historical-critical introduction.* text. *The New Edinburgh Islamic surveys.*

---. 2018. "The Qur'an." In *Routledge handbook on early Islam,* edited by Herbert Berg, 9–24. New York: Routledge.

Small, Keith E. 2011. *Textual Criticism and Qur'an Manuscripts.* Lexington Books.

Smith, Henry Preserved. 1923. "Luther and Islam." *The American Journal of Semitic Languages and Literatures* 39 (3): 218–220. https://www.jstor.org/stable/528632.

Taymiyah, Ahmad ibn 'Abd al-Halim Ibn. 2004. *Majmu' fatawa Shaykh al-Islam Ahmad ibn Taymiyah.* Edited by 'Abd al-Rahman ibn Muhammad Ibn Qasim and Muhammad ibn 'Abd al-Rahmaan Ibn Qasim. 37 vols. al-Madinah al-Munawwarah: Mujamma' al-Malik Fahd li-Tiba'at al-Mushaf al-Sharif.

Thomas, D., and J.A. Chesworth. 2019. *Christian-Muslim Relations. A Bibliographical History Volume 13 Western Europe (1700–1800).* Brill.

UNCHR. n.d. "The Universal Declaration of Human Rights." The United Nations. Accessed February 5, 2015. https://www.un.org/en/documents/udhr/, archived at the Wayback Machine https://web.archive.org/web/20150205175837/https://www.un.org/en/documents/udhr/.

UNSD. 2015. "The World's Women reports." United Nations Statistics Division – Demographic and Social Statistics. Accessed August 19, 2015. https://unstats.un.org/unsd/demographic/products/Worldswomen/WWreports.htm, archived at the Wayback Machine https://web.archive.org/web/20150511031205/http://unstats.un.org/unsd/demographic/products/Worldswomen/WWreports.htm.

Vega, Connie de la. 2013. *Dictionary of International Human Rights Law.* text. Edward Elgar Publishing.

Watt, William Montgomery. 1956. *Muhammad at Medina.* Oxford University Press.

---. 1985. *Islamic Philosophy and Theology: An Extended Survey.* Edinburgh: Edinburgh University Press. Reprint, 2nd. 1962.

---. 1991. "Women in the Earliest Islam." *Studia Missionalia* 40 (1991): 162–173.

Watt, William Montgomery, and Alastair McIntosh. 2005. "Women in the Earliest Islam (internet version)." Alastair McIntosh. Accessed February 5, 2016. https://www.alastairmcintosh.com/general/2005-montgomery-watt.htm, archived at the Wayback Machine https://web.archive.org/web/20150414150640/https://www.alastairmcintosh.com/general/2005-montgomery-watt.htm.

Wikimedia, contributors. 2016. "File:BourguibaMestiriTaharBenAchour.jpg." Wikimedia Commons. Accessed 25 March 2022. https://commons.wikimedia.org/w/index.php?title=File:BourguibaMestiriTaharBenAchour.jpg&oldid=830780259.

Wikipedia, contributors. 2001a. "Fatwa." Wikipedia, The Free Encyclopedia. Accessed May 27, 2021. https://en.wikipedia.org/w/index.php?title=Fatwa&oldid=1020157066.

---. 2001b. "Shia Islam." Wikipedia, The Free Encyclopedia. Accessed September 28, 2016. https://en.wikipedia.org/w/index.php?title=Shia_Islam&oldid=740682551.

---. 2002a. "Syllogism." Wikipedia, The Free Encyclopedia. Accessed September 28, 2016. https://en.wikipedia.org/w/index.php?title=Syllogism&oldid=740179340.

---. 2002b. "Textual criticism." Wikipedia, The Free Encyclopedia. Accessed January 8, 2019. https://en.wikipedia.org/w/index.php?title=Textual_criticism&oldid=872214116.

---. 2003a. "Bible translations." Wikipedia, The Free Encyclopedia. Accessed August 10, 2020. https://en.wikipedia.org/w/index.php?title=Bible_translations&oldid=969643767.

---. 2003b. "Case law." Wikipedia, The Free Encyclopedia. Accessed November 19, 2020. https://en.wikipedia.org/w/index.php?title=Case_law&oldid=988459591.

---. 2003c. "Quran translations." Wikipedia, The Free Encyclopedia. Accessed May 12, 2020.

https://en.wikipedia.org/w/index.php?title=Quran_translation s&oldid=951900667.

---. 2003d. "Sacred language." Wikipedia, The Free Encyclopedia. Accessed August 10, 2020. https://en.wikipedia.org/w/index.php?title=Sacred_language &oldid=970794894.

---. 2004a. "Aga Khan IV." Wikipedia, The Free Encyclopedia. Accessed September 28, 2016. https://en.wikipedia.org/w/index.php?title=Aga_Khan_IV&o ldid=741498778.

---. 2004b. "Mufti." Wikipedia, The Free Encyclopedia. Accessed November 24, 2020. https://en.wikipedia.org/w/index.php?title=Mufti&oldid=987 807987#Modern_institutions.

---. 2005. "Umama bint Abi al-As." Wikipedia, The Free Encyclopedia. Accessed January 12 2023. https://en.wikipedia.org/w/index.php?title=Umama_bint_Abi _al-As&oldid=1126112044.

---. 2006. "List of translations of the Quran." Wikipedia, The Free Encyclopedia. Accessed June 17, 2020. https://en.wikipedia.org/w/index.php?title=List_of_translatio ns_of_the_Quran&oldid=962481567.

---. 2007. "Demographics of the Arab world." Wikipedia, The Free Encyclopedia. Accessed March 15, 2017. https://en.wikipedia.org/w/index.php?title=Demographics_of _the_Arab_world&oldid=768893612.

---. 2008a. "Code of Personal Status (Tunisia)." Wikipedia, The Free Encyclopedia. Accessed August 27, 2015. https://en.wikipedia.org/w/index.php?title=Code_of_Persona l_Status_in_Tunisia&oldid=675316955.

---. 2008b. "Slavery in Iran: Slavery in Sassanid Iran (c. 224–642 AD)." Wikipedia, The Free Encyclopedia. Accessed December 7, 2021. https://en.wikipedia.org/w/index.php?title=Slavery_in_Iran& oldid=1058888684.

---. 2009. "Reductio ad absurdum." Wikipedia, The Free Encyclopedia. Accessed May 22, 2015. https://en.wikipedia.org/w/index.php?title=Reductio_ad_abs urdum&oldid=661479163.

---. 2010. "Corpus Coranicum." Wikipedia, The Free Encyclopedia. Accessed January 8, 2019. https://en.wikipedia.org/w/index.php?title=Corpus_Coranicum&oldid=843236975.

---. 2011. "Arab Spring." Wikipedia, The Free Encyclopedia. Accessed August 10, 2015. https://en.wikipedia.org/w/index.php?title=Arab_Spring&oldid=674848388.

---. 2014a. "Children of Muhammad." Wikipedia, The Free Encyclopedia. Accessed January 12 2023. https://en.wikipedia.org/w/index.php?title=Children_of_Muhammad&oldid=1132160905.

---. 2014b. "Slavery in the Byzantine Empire: Sources of slaves." Wikipedia, The Free Encyclopedia. Accessed February 12, 2016. https://en.wikipedia.org/w/index.php?title=Slavery_in_the_Byzantine_Empire&oldid=679134386.

Worldometers.info. 2017. "How many Countries are there in the World?". Worldometers. Accessed April 1, 2017. https://www.worldometers.info/geography/how-many-countries-are-there-in-the-world/, archived at the Wayback Machine https://web.archive.org/web/20170401185603/https://www.worldometers.info/geography/how-many-countries-are-there-in-the-world/.

Yahaghi, Mohammad Jafar. 2002. "An Introduction to Early Persian Qur'anic Translations." *Journal of Qur'anic Studies* 4 (2): 105–109. https://www.jstor.org/stable/25728079.

Zantvoort, Bart. 2015. "On inertia: Resistance to change in individuals, institutions and the development of knowledge." *Cosmos and History: The Journal of Natural and Social Philosophy* 11 (1): 342–360.

Zayd, Nasr Hamid Abu. 1990. *Mafhum al-Nass: Dirasa fi 'Ulum al-Qur'an*. First ed. Cairo: al-Hay'a al-Misriyya al-'Amma li-l-Kitab.

Ziadeh, Farhat J. 1995. Law: Sunni Schools of Law. In *The Oxford Encyclopedia of the Modern Islamic World*, edited by John L. Esposito. New York: Oxford University Press.

BOOKS IN THIS SERIES

In this part of the book, I provide an overview of the first three volumes of the series "The Qur'anic Revelation: A Reformed Understanding"—published concurrently.

For the latest updates and to discover additional volumes in this series, please visit my website. For direct access, you can find the link and QR code at the end of this section.

The first three volumes of the series argue that the religion of Islam or rather the numerous interpretations of Islam are unacceptable representations of the Qur'anic revelation. The proposed interpretation of the Qur'anic revelation challenges the standpoints of Traditional Islam on three key issues: inclusiveness, the sources of religious knowledge, and the composition of any acceptable Qur'anic-based interpretation of religion. Each of the first three volumes of this series is dedicated to one of these topics, respectively.

Here are the titles of the volumes along with a brief description of each:

Volume 1: The Qur'an and Its Message Versus the Three Major Monotheistic Religions

In the first volume of "The Qur'anic Revelation: A Reformed Understanding," the author argues that the religion of Islam is an unacceptable representation of the Qur'anic revelation. Furthermore, that the religions based on God's revealed scriptures, as we know them today, including but not limited to the religion of Islam, deviate from the essence of God's revelations—mainly bringing Judaism and Christianity into the discussion. The author puts forward his own interpretation of the Qur'anic revelation and, in this volume, primarily addresses its inclusiveness aspect by exploring how the Qur'an understands both inclusiveness and religion.

What Islam is the book talking about? Is it one Islam that around one-fourth of the world's population follows? Are all of the commands in the Qur'an of eternal applicability? Did the Qur'an come with a new religion and how did the Qur'an define membership in the religion? What impact did the Qur'an have on the beliefs and practices of those who accepted the revelation from the peoples of previous scriptures in the space-time of the Prophet, yet as argued, who at the same time maintained their religious identities? These questions and a multitude of others are addressed in this volume of the series.

This book is self-contained. It does not require the reader to have previous knowledge in any of the topics discussed. The book discusses topics you do not find in your typical book about the Qur'an or Islam. It would interest those who want to learn about the Qur'an and its message. Among this group would be those searching for a reformed understanding of the Qur'an and how it applies today; those curious to learn how the Qur'anic message affects followers of the previous revealed scriptures; and those interested in monotheistic religions in general.

Volume 2: The *Sunna* and the *Hadith* Through the Lens of the Qur'an

In this book the stance of the proposed interpretation of the Qur'anic revelation in regard to the *Sunna* (teachings of Prophet Muhammad) and the *Hadith* (reports on the *Sunna*) is addressed. The proposed interpretation of the Qur'anic revelation recognizes—in reference to the followers of the Qur'an—the Qur'an to be the sole source of religious knowledge. It does not consider the *Sunna* to represent an independent or complementary source of religious knowledge. Furthermore, it does not consider the *Hadith* to represent the *Sunna*, nor does it consider the *Hadith* a source of religious knowledge.

Is the *Sunna* a source of religious knowledge? Does the *Hadith* actually report on the *Sunna*? What of the *Hadith* is certain in its attribution to Prophet Muhammad? These questions and a multitude of others are addressed in this volume of the series.

This book is self-contained. It can be read as part of the series or independently. It does not require the reader to have previous knowledge in any of the topics discussed. The book discusses topics you do not find in your typical book about the Qur'an or Islam. It would interest those who want to learn about the Qur'an, its message, the *Sunna* and the *Hadith*. Among this group would be those searching for a reformed understanding of the Qur'an and how it applies today; those interested to learn about the *Sunna* and the *Hadith*—what they are and what they are not; and those interested in monotheistic religions in general.

Volume 3: The Illusion of Eternal Religious Law

In this book the stance of the proposed interpretation of the Qur'anic revelation on law is addressed. This position will prove to be of special significance particularly in the context of modernity—and the modern state. Furthermore, Islamic law and its relationship to the religion of Islam is explored. The proposed interpretation of the Qur'anic revelation does not see religion to be the source of law, but rather it sees religion to be a source of ethics. It sees that any acceptable interpretation of religion that is based on revealed scripture should have no law component. It rejects religious law altogether and calls for the implementation of secular law. In consequence, the proposed interpretation of the Qur'anic revelation would be redefining the role of religion and its domain of operation.

Are all of the commands in the Qur'an of eternal applicability? What is Islamic law (commonly referred to as *Shari'a*)? Why study Islamic law and why is it important to study it? Is there only one Islamic law? How does Islamic law relate to Islam? Why does this book call for comprehensive religious reform and not religious law reform? These questions and a multitude of others are addressed in this volume of the series.

This book is self-contained. It can be read as part of the series or independently. It does not require the reader to have previous knowledge in any of the topics discussed. The book discusses topics you do not find in your typical book about the Qur'an or Islam. It would interest those who want to learn about the Qur'an, its message, and Islamic law. Among this group would be those searching for a reformed understanding of the Qur'an and how it applies today; those interested to learn about Islamic law—what it is and what it is not; and those interested in monotheistic religions in general. This book will prove to be particularly useful to those seeking to understand the problems in the contemporary interpretations of Islam, and consequently how such problems reflect on the Muslim individual and societies in general.

Thank you for your interest in "The Qur'anic Revelation: A Reformed Understanding." I invite you to stay connected and explore more about this series and future works.

Visit the Author's Website:

www.josephthemonotheist.com

Printed in the USA
CPSIA information can be obtained
at www.ICGtesting.com
CBHW070756071224
18205CB00011B/100